89-10-26

FRANK LLOYD WRIGHT'S LARKIN BUILDING

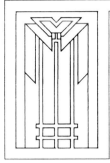
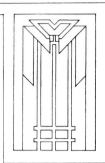

JACK QUINAN

Frank Lloyd Wright's
LARKIN
BUILDING

MYTH AND FACT

THE ARCHITECTURAL HISTORY FOUNDATION
New York, New York

THE MIT PRESS Cambridge, Massachusetts, and London, England

Library of Congress Cataloging-in-Publication Data

Quinan, Jack.
    Frank Lloyd Wright's Larkin building.

    (Architectural History Foundation books ; 11)
    Bibliography
    Includes index.
    1. Larkin Building (Buffalo, N.Y.) 2. Wright, Frank
Lloyd, 1867–1959 — Criticism and interpretation. 3. Office
buildings — New York (State) — Buffalo. 4. Buffalo (N.Y.)
— Buildings, structures, etc. I. Title. II. Series.
NA6233.B84L376   1987   725'.23   85-23687
ISBN 0-262-17004-3

Jack Quinan is Associate Professor of Art History at the
State University of New York at Buffalo.

All photographs not credited are from the author's collection.

FRONTISPIECE: Frank Lloyd Wright, Larkin Administration
Building, Buffalo, New York, 1902–6. (Courtesy Buffalo
and Erie County Historical Society)

Designed by William Rueter
Published with the assistance of the J. Paul Getty Trust.

For my mother, Dorothy Cheney Quinan

ARCHITECTURAL HISTORY
FOUNDATION BOOKS

AMERICAN MONOGRAPH
SERIES

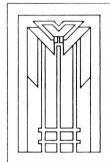

Contents

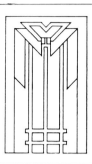

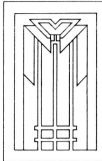

Acknowledgments

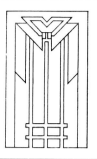

One of the particular pleasures of researching and writing this book has been my acquaintance with the descendants of John D. Larkin, the founder and President of the Larkin Company. My understanding of the company's history and of the Larkin Administration Building's place within the business is based in part on interviews with Evelyn (Heath) Jacobsen, Rev. Thomas Heath, Dr. Clark W. Heath, Harold Esty, Harry Larkin, Jr., and Elizabeth (Robb) Duane. I owe special gratitude to Daniel I. Larkin for sharing innumerable family documents, photographs, and recollections with me, for reading the manuscript and giving me a balanced view of the question of patronage raised in the book, and for providing unwavering encouragement and patience over the past five years.

Many others have contributed to the book in various ways. My thanks to Dorothy Glass, William Jordy, and Paul Sprague for reading portions of the manuscript and offering suggestions. Jim Cahill deserves particular thanks for the drawings he has supplied for the book, and Bruce Brooks Pfeiffer has been exceptionally helpful in making the Archives of the Frank Lloyd Wright Memorial Foundation avail-

able to me. For numerous kinds of information I am indebted to Reyner Banham, Carolyn M. Brackett, Earl Booth, Shonnie Finnegan, Donald Hoffmann, Theresa Hilgenberg, Jennifer Huitfeldt, Donald Kalec, Nancy Knechtel, Jonathan Lipman, Robert Mates, Colleen Mullaney, Jerome Puma, Louise Svendson, Lenore Swoiskin, Edgar Tafel, and David Van Zanten. My thanks to William Clarkson for contributing so many fine photographs, and to Guy Chase, Judith Halliday, David A. Hanks, Clyde Eller, Margaret Olin, Tom Martinson, and John O'Hern for additional photographic material. Karen Banks and Jo Ellen Ackerman of the Architectural History Foundation have performed their editorial and production tasks with exceptional skill and insight.

I have reserved special notes of gratitude for Edgar Kaufmann, jr., for his editorial suggestions and his encouragement, and for Victoria Newhouse, who first expressed interest in the project in 1979, when it was little more than a twenty-minute lecture.

Finally, my thanks to John Quinan, my son, just for being himself.

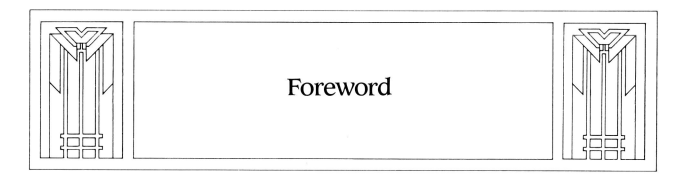

Foreword

Frank Lloyd Wright's Larkin Building of 1904 in Buffalo, New York, has become an iconic landmark of modern architecture. I remember eagerly going to see it 1946 or 1947 and finding a ruined shell. The demolition of the Larkin Building in 1950 stands deplored and, indeed, its international reputation has stood firm. But until now there has not been a rounded study of the building. Wright himself understood its exceptional quality and wrote eloquently about it in *An Autobiography* which he composed in the late 1920s to please his young new wife. At the nadir, then, of his career he was evoking the years of searching and success; factual data did not belong in his story — they were embodied in the building.

Now Jack Quinan has written this profound study of the Larkin Building in its context. After more than ten years living and teaching in Buffalo he knows the city and its people as well as he knows the way modern architecture was taking shape in the United States at the turn to the twentieth century. This provides a solid background for his text; moreover, it seems to me that Quinan raises Wright studies to a new level here. Architecture appears intertwined with economic and personal relationships yet the emergent image is not generalized or impressionistic, it is confirmed by detailed evidence from sources hitherto untapped. Quinan is able to do this thanks largely to a collection of original documents that survived in the possession of the Martin family. It was Darwin D. Martin (1865–1935), a top-level executive in the Larkin Company, who was the leader in proposing and

fostering the Wright commission. A diligent study of his papers has divulged how Wright's famous design was molded by the abilities and limitations of a set of remarkable individuals. Their requirements led Wright to create a peerless masterwork, one that ensured the architect's fame in Europe and the Far East, and that, today — demolished, known only through images and words — remains a capital achievement by the American architect.

Quinan's text is devoted to the building and the men and women involved with its inception and use; he does not recount the discovery and preservation of the crucial Martin documents. Hence I was encouraged to write this note about the struggle to control the archive. Quinan provided an essential chronology and, *viva voce*, some trenchant comments. It should be said at once that Jack Quinan recognized and protected these papers in the face of strong competition. Dealers intent on parceling out the elements for maximum yield would have obscured currents of ideas and emotions traceable only when the documents could be investigated as a sequential whole.

In 1975 Quinan initiated a course on Frank Lloyd Wright at the State University of New York, Buffalo. A year later he learned from a casual remark of Darwin R. Martin, son of Darwin D. Martin, that a substantial body of letters exchanged between Wright and Martin's father was stored in the son's San Francisco home. It was not possible then for Quinan to follow this lead across the continent. In 1979 Martin died. Unsure of Mrs. Martin's plans for the hoard of letters, Quinan asked if he might come out to see them. Early in the next year Mrs. Martin wrote to say that she had decided to sell the letters, which were thus closed to researchers for the nonce. After another year Quinan, who had begun work on the present book, again wrote to know if the situation had changed, but the estate still was not settled. Late in 1981 it appeared sure that the material would be auctioned in California the following January. A few people were allowed to examine the archive in haste, and rumors whirled through the world of Wright scholars and Americanists.

The auctioneers to whom the material had been consigned estimated its value at $30,000. Quinan, with the blessing of his university, began an intensive campaign to raise money to buy the lot. A number of important institutions and individuals, some outside the United States, were sympathetic, but time was very short. Then two donors were found who contributed substantially and further sums were committed by Buffalo agencies. Quinan could offer $50,000, but it was known that shrewd and adept traders were intent on securing the documents. It was anybody's guess how high they would be able to bid. Meanwhile, Stanford University had been alerted through Professor Emeritus Paul R. Hanna, who had built a famous house by Frank Lloyd Wright on Stanford's grounds.

At the end of January 1982, the Martin papers were auctioned off to a dealer for $75,000. To earn a profit he would have to sell the most desirable bits at very high prices, and it was not felt that any single patron would offer to save the archive as a whole. It was a black moment, especially for one who, through research, had grasped the potential of the material.

By dint of considerable effort Quinan persuaded Hanna to enlist Stanford as a partner in purchasing from the dealer, and at last they were able to offer $100,000 jointly. The documents, it was agreed, would be divided according to date, Buffalo to receive all material from 1902 to 1914. Each institution would keep photocopies of the other's holdings, strictly controlled to avoid accidental misuse. When it seemed that the dealer would agree to this joint approach there were prudent hesitations about just what was being bought, and how to be sure that the documents were restricted to use by qualified researchers. Archivists from both universities went through the papers carefully. The dealer allowed that he had photostatted some items, and turned over his copies to the new owners as part of the deal. Skeptics at the time wondered if choice copies were not held back, but of course there was no alternative to accepting the dealer's word. He did extract about thirty drawings from the written material with which they were closely related. All in all, these events constituted a fundamental defense of scholarly research in the field of American architecture, and an impressive success for a young campaigner like Quinan.

One may ask, are such struggles really worthwhile? For instance, hardly anything is known about Iktinos, Severus, or Anthemios apart from their remaining buildings and fragments, yet their qualities are vivid in our minds. On the other hand, occasionally documentary facts have been used carelessly or willfully, twisting the historical presentation. But, after reading this book, can one deny that good scholarship profits immensely from the support of broad and full records of events? Especially in the field of Wright studies this approach is welcome, and Jack Quinan deserves very special applause.

EDGAR KAUFMANN, JR.

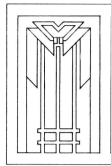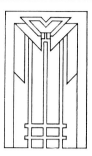

Introduction

On the evening of November 17, 1902, Frank Lloyd Wright boarded a train in Chicago that would take him to Buffalo, New York, some five hundred miles to the east. There he was met by Darwin D. Martin, a successful businessman who had come to admire Wright's work and who hoped to engage him to do a house — perhaps two — and to explore the possibility that Wright might design an office building for Martin's employer, John D. Larkin. Wright stayed two and a half days discussing the commissions. Back at his office in Chicago, Wright began drawings for the Larkin Administration Building, one of his greatest achievements. He was then thirty-five years old, young for an architect, and this was his opportunity to break into the lucrative field of commercial structures.

The new building was meant to serve as headquarters of Larkin's prospering soap manufactory and premium-based mail-order business located in a group of factory and warehouse buildings a mile east of downtown Buffalo in a semi-industrial neighborhood. Wright was to provide facilities for executives and department heads and for the 1,800 clerical employees who dealt with the thousands of pieces of customer mail that arrived each day. John D. Larkin, President of the company, was Wright's principal client but he was guided by Darwin Martin, the Secretary of the company and the man who had been principally responsible for the development of its mail-order enterprise. Martin eventually became one of Wright's most active patrons and supporters.

Plans for the new building were completed in the spring of 1904 and the finished building — air-conditioned, fireproof, and light-filled — was ready for occupancy in August 1906. The Larkin executives got something more than they bargained for. Although the Larkin Company itself did not survive the Depression, Wright's Administration Building, despite its unfortunate demolition in 1950, holds an enduring place in the history of modern architecture.

In 1975 when I came to Buffalo and was asked to teach a course on Frank Lloyd Wright, I found it difficult to believe that a work as important as the Larkin Administration Building had been demolished. I drove around the industrial neighborhoods on the east side of the city in the hope that I might discover some part of the building, perhaps sheathed in Permastone or hidden beneath a mansard roof. But Nelson Reimann, the wrecker who demolished it, assured me that its bricks and mortar had been trucked to the Buffalo waterfront for landfill and that its steel beams now shored up the shafts of a coal mine in Pennsylvania. A single pier from the north wall is all that remains on the site of the Wright building.

Two years after I arrived in Buffalo a local bookstore displayed a set of photographs of the Larkin Administration Building showing areas that had never before been seen by scholars. These photographs, many of which are included in this book, suggested new and interesting aspects of the Larkin Company's attitudes toward its employees. In an effort to identify these spaces within the building, and to understand their functions, I began—at the suggestion of Reyner Banham who was then examining the entire complex of Larkin buildings—to interview members of the Larkin family and former employees of the company. I also began to scrutinize the critical and scholarly literature on the Larkin Administration Building, which, to my surprise, rarely ventured beyond summary appreciations of its bold forms and progressive mechanical equipment.

One discovery led to another, and gradually the design and functioning of Wright's building and its relationship to the scope and history of the business began to come into focus. My enthusiasm was sustained by feelings (stimulated by the course I taught about Wright) that the more I would study the building the more I would discover. Results have confirmed this.

My aims in this book are threefold. First, I have tried to gather the many illustrations and documentary sources that can serve to bring Wright's Larkin Administration Building back to life as nearly as possible and in a form useful to anyone studying Wright's work. Second, I have attempted to recreate the context of the building in both a historical and an architectural sense—the history of the Larkin Company and its attitude toward customers and employees, the program outlined by the clients, the site conditions, and the evolution of the design—all of which should help to rescue the building from its isolated status as an icon of the Modern Movement in architecture. Third, I have reviewed and commented on the critical evaluations of the building over the years. I hope this book will lead to a fresh and more accurate understanding of Wright's early masterpiece.

FRANK LLOYD WRIGHT'S LARKIN BUILDING

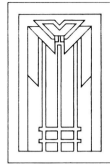

CHAPTER ONE
The Commission

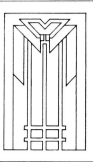

In 1902, when the Larkin Company decided to add an administration building to its expanding soap-manu-facturing and mail-order complex in Buffalo, Frank Lloyd Wright was an unlikely choice for the commission. At that time, Wright's work as an independent architect, which began in 1893 when he left the office of the well-known Chicago architects Adler & Sulli-van, was almost entirely confined to the Chicago area, with a few commissions scattered across southern Wisconsin, central Illinois, and Michigan. Moreover, with some exceptions, including unexecuted projects, his work was residential in nature.[1] The Prairie house that Wright developed between 1893 and 1900 is uni-versally recognized today as a turning point in the evolution of modern architecture, but it is unlikely that this work would have been known to more than a few people in Buffalo in late 1902. One may well wonder how a young domestic specialist from Chi-cago was asked to design this major office building.[2]

The limitations of Wright's experience and reputation in 1902 notwithstanding, there were cir-cumstances that favored his receiving the Larkin commission. In a curious reversal of the familiar American adage, "Go West, young man," most of the Larkin executives—including John D. Larkin, the founder of the company; Elbert Hubbard, the com-pany's first salesman and a founding partner; William R. Heath, Larkin's partner for fifteen years; George Barton, who worked in the Secretary's department; and Walter V. Davidson, an accountant with the

company—had come east to Buffalo from Chicago. Darwin D. Martin came from Iowa but maintained close relations with his brothers in Chicago. Chicago was the Larkin executives' principal city of refer-ence,[3] the home of the renowned "Chicago School" whose leading members—William LeBaron Jenney, Adler & Sullivan, Burnham & Root, Holabird & Roche—had given form to the modern tall office building. In view of this, a predisposition toward a Chicago architect is not surprising.

No doubt the Larkin executives were impressed by the over five years that Frank Lloyd Wright had spent in the office of Dankmar Adler and Louis Sullivan, the most progressive designers of tall office buildings during the 1880s and early 1890s. Little is known of Wright's experiences during this period; Wright's own account in his autobiography of 1932 combines anecdote (such as a bloody fight with a draftsman) and glimpses of his relationship with "lieber Meister," Louis Sullivan, as well as a concise impression of Adler.[4] Wright relates, "I had a small room next to the Master and a squad of thirty draughtsmen or more under me to supervise planning and detail-ing."[5] He adds: "Upon leaving Adler and Sullivan Cecil Corwin joined me (not as a partner) and we opened offices on this tower-floor in the Schiller Building—a building that, owing to Sullivan's love for his new home in the South, had been more largely left to me than any other."[6] In his book there is no mention of involvement with foundations, steel framing, cladding, fenestration, roofing, heating, ventilation, lighting, plumbing, and other matters that a bright young designer with some background in engineering (acquired at the University of Wisconsin) must have encountered in the more than twenty large commercial buildings that Adler & Sullivan produced during those years. Wright may have realized that this was not the stuff of interesting autobiography, yet it is apparent that he experienced the best apprenticeship available in America for the creation of an office building. The question remains, how did he actually obtain the Larkin Building commission?

According to Grant C. Manson's account in *Frank Lloyd Wright to 1910: The First Golden Age*,[7] Darwin Martin visited his brother William at the latter's new Wright-designed home in Oak Park, Illinois, late in 1902 and found himself captivated by Wright's ideas. He subsequently invited Wright to Buffalo to inspect the property where the Barton and Martin houses were to be built. Manson writes: "The commission for a new administration building for the Larkin Company came shortly on the heels of the Darwin Martin commissions."[8] Manson's account, probably transmitted to him by Wright some thirty-five years after the fact, and therefore dependent on the architect's sometimes "creative" recollections,[9] contains at least three inaccuracies and, furthermore, does not pretend to explain how Wright managed to obtain the commission.

Letters and diaries recently discovered among the Darwin D. Martin Papers in the Archives of the State University of New York at Buffalo offer the possibility of a closer examination of these events.[10] Unlike the previous accounts, the Martin documents provide a detailed chronology from the point of view of the clients. This perspective is of particular interest because it affords insight into Wright's manner of dealing with a difficult multiple-client situation that repeatedly threatened the outcome of the commission during the first year of planning and design.

On September 11, 1902, Darwin Martin did, in fact, visit his brother William in Chicago, and together they toured suburban Oak Park where William intended to build a new home. Frank Lloyd Wright's distinctive houses caught their attention and led them to seek out his Oak Park studio.[11] Darwin and William Martin did not meet Wright on that occasion,[12] but they were quite taken with his work. In a letter to Elbert Hubbard, dated September 19, 1902, Darwin Martin described his reaction:

To my uncultivated mind Mr. Wright's houses, of which there are many examples in Oak Park and vicinity, seemed very fancy, but after I had a talk with Mr. Wright's Red One [probably red-headed Walter Burley Griffin] I was convinced that the style is simplicity itself, and the startling thing about his architecture is that notwithstanding he charges 7½% instead of the conventional 5%, he makes $8,000 look like $15,000 in a house. His man said that only half a dozen builders can figure within gun shot of the proper cost of one of Wright's houses—they are so radically different that all the others bid about 300%. They do not understand them.

You need an example of Wright's architecture on the Roycroft grounds. The Wright studio—it would be a shame to call it an office—is very Roycroftie.[13]

In his reply Hubbard acknowledged knowing of "brother Wright," but he did not pursue the possibility of a collaboration.

William Martin met Wright a month later and immediately wrote to his brother Darwin. The letter is reproduced nearly in full here; it embodies an enduring enthusiasm that would eventually bring the Larkin commission to Wright:

Dear Dar

I have been—seen—talked to, admired, one of nature's noblemen _____ Frank Lloyd Wright. He is an athletic looking young man of medium build—black hair—(bushy, not long) about 32 yrs. old.—A splendid type of manhood. He is not a fraud—nor a "crank" = highly educated & polished, but no dude = a straight-forward business like man—with high ideals—I met his mother a beautiful type of woman.

He says that the way labor and materials are now, that he would not care to try for anything in his line under 5000.⁰⁰ — but thinks a design that would please me could be made.

I told him of your lot = he says it would be a <u>pity</u> — for you to build on 75 feet front — unless the houses on each side of you — stood well to one side — (which is unlikely?) For instance if the situation was like this this would give you the benefit of the sweep of the other fellows lot — to your house.

He would be <u>pleased</u> indeed to design <u>your</u> house — & further he is the man to build <u>your office</u> = he has had <u>large</u> experience in large office buildings with Adler and Sullivan was educated as a Civil Engineer was head man in A & S and stood next to Mr. S[ullivan] = he says it is strange that he is only known as a residence architect — when his best and largest experience was in large buildings — I suppose that if you discover this man — that Mr. L[arkin] would never consent to his drawing the plans — yet I am sure he is the man you want, and if some way could be devised so that Mr. L would first discover him that he would be tickled to death with his find = Mr. Wright says he doesn't want any man to accept his ideas first because they are <u>his</u> — he proposes to furnish a <u>reason</u> for his ideas & wants judgments made solely on <u>the merits</u>.

You <u>will fall in love</u> with him — in 10 min. conversation = he will build you the finest most sensible house in Buffalo = you will be the envy of every rich man in Buffalo it will be published in all the Buffalo papers it will be talked about all over the east. You will never grow tired of his work = & what more can you ask? — When will you come to see him?

Can you not manage to have him first <u>discovered</u> by Mr. L = an office such as Wright can build — will be talked about all over this country = it will be an ad. that money spent in any other way cannot buy. I am not too enthusiastic about this — he is <u>pure gold</u>.¹⁴

William Martin's opinion carried a special weight with his younger brother, even though the two had been separated when Darwin was just twelve years old.¹⁵ Darwin wrote back to him on October 29:

I herewith enclose a letter for Mr. Wright asking him to pay us a visit at Buffalo at our expense for his journey. This that we may have a look without any obligations to employ him. Mr. Larkin is quite willing to consider him as the architect for our office building.¹⁶

Wright appeared in Buffalo for the two-day visit on November 18, 1902, the first of innumerable visits that would extend over thirty years.¹⁷ As a result of this first visit, Darwin Martin commissioned a small house for his sister and her husband, George Barton. Furthermore, William Heath commissioned a house on Bird Avenue in Buffalo, and Wright was invited to make tentative sketches for a new administration building for the Larkin Company based on a list of requirements that Darwin Martin must have formulated at about this time.¹⁸ These drawings, providing a main block and a lesser annex, arrived at the Larkin Company on January 15, 1903. Martin acknowledged receipt of them with a wire stating: "As such excellent. Pls mail your estimates." ¹⁹

Problems arose once Wright's sketches arrived at the Larkin Company. William Coss, the supervisor of soap products, presented a revised plan to Mr. Larkin who in turn presented it to Darwin Martin saying, "Here is a sketch I had drawn." ²⁰ The Coss plan placed Mr. Larkin with his sons, Charles and John, Jr., in adjoining offices in the annex. Martin objected strenuously (according to his diary entry of January 16, 1903) on the grounds that "anyone, no matter who, seriously engaged in a dep[artment] in [a] factory w[oul]d not find it economical or practical to have an office across [the] street, especially as there are good offices in H [building] on Seneca Street," and he composed a letter refuting the Coss plan (Appendix B). Wright objected, too, by letter, stating that "Mr. Larkin's plan for his offices in [the] annex of [the] new office [building] would spoil it." ²¹ A compromise was reached whereby Mr. Larkin and his sons were located in adjoining offices at the south end of the main block. The incident indicates the extent of Darwin Martin's power within the Larkin Company and suggests that the responsibility for the new administration building and its architect was largely his.

If Frank Lloyd Wright's position was tentative in January, by February several Larkin executives seemed to be warming up to him — with certain reservations. Mr. Larkin announced on February 2 that he wanted R.J. Reidpath, the architectural engineer who had built many of the Larkin factory buildings, to figure the steel for Wright's building.[22] He won his point (perhaps because Darwin Martin concurred — Reidpath was Mrs. Martin's cousin), but the decision caused substantial delays.

By March the Larkin executives agreed that Darwin Martin should spend a week in Chicago and Oak Park getting to know Wright better and clearing up some of the numerous questions about the design that troubled them. In preparation for this trip Martin asked Mr. Larkin if "we (Messrs. Larkin, Heath, and Martin) could agree on a general plan, on [a] fee we are willing to pay, and let me propose it to W[right] and tell him to get up another sketch, after which we could get him here to get exact details." [23] With characteristic efficiency, Martin followed his verbal request to Mr. Larkin with an extensive written proposal:

Perhaps it will be satisfactory to you for me to discuss the office building with Mr. Wright like this:

"While the proposed office bldg. is very important, it has been allowed to simmer along for several reasons, one is probably the same as your reason for delaying Mr. Heath's sketch — we have been very busy with other matters, with our regular routine. The office bldg. is outside of it. It is an entirely new proposition to us; it has taken a great deal of thinking. It involves putting responsibility on to an untried force — yourself. We have not had time to get well acquainted with you, and Mr. Larkin always wishes to feel pretty well acquainted with those on whom he is going to depend. It will probably take another visit on your part to Buffalo, or of Mr. Larkin to Oak Park, to bring about that degree of acquaintanceship with your past experience and personality to make a definite arrangement possible.

"I infer from a conversation you had with Mr. Larkin that it would be satisfactory to you for us to depend upon our Mr. Reidpath for the calculations concerning the steel which enters into the building; that you would just as soon that we have him do this as for you to depend upon someone else. It would be much more satisfactory for us for we would not know your man. We have thoroughly tested Mr. Reidpath's ability, his knowledge and judgment and we would all much rather separate the work so far as is practical, putting the steel in his charge. We would like to show this much deference to Mr. Reidpath too.

"If you are willing to recognize the fairness of our considering the steel cost of the building no part of your responsibilities, and are willing that it shall be deducted from the cost on which we pay you commission, I feel satisfied — though no formal contract with you can be made until after we see another sketch — that we will all want you to do the work."

I would then, or perhaps as a preliminary to the whole talk, sound him more in detail than we have yet on his experience in large buildings; just what part of the architectural work in connection therewith he had in charge; what his experience has been in ventilating; his reasons for believing he has adequately provided for the ventilation of our building. Finally I would ask him to prepare another sketch, saying I believe that you will approve a plan which preserves the entrance part of the Annex about as in the first sketch with the President's office in the main block, asking him to suggest the arrangement thereof in the pleasantest part of the bldg.; providing for the wardrobes and closets in the annex also.

I would tell him that after we received this sketch and discussed it here it would then be in order for him to come to Buffalo for one or two days which we would give up to the discussion of details which would enable him to then prepare the sure-enough plan, we of course reserving the right to make still further changes.[24]

Darwin Martin's visit to Chicago and Oak Park, which lasted from March 12 to March 19, enabled him to discuss each of the problems cited above, and more. The visit is extensively documented in a five-page report of March 20, 1903, from Martin to Mr. Larkin (Appendix C), a document rich in insights into Wright's methods and into the relationships that were developing between the architect and his clients. In addition to its factual content, the report contains a powerful statement of advocacy on Darwin Martin's part. He begins on a note of highly charged enthusiasm:

At the risk of appearing to have been made intoxicated[25] by my contact with Frank Lloyd Wright, I do not hesitate to say at the outset of this, my report of my interview with him, which lasted all day on Mar. 18th, and of my visit to his houses on Mar. 14th, 15th and 18th, that I believe we have all greatly underestimated our man. This because of his youth, the newness of our acquaintanceship and its limitations and also because of the adverse things we have heard about Wright, which are due to his radical departure from conventional lines.

Darwin Martin then goes to considerable effort to dissuade Mr. Larkin from an apparent interest in having Adler & Sullivan design the new administration building, and in so doing he reveals some of the almost ruthless tactics that Wright used to obtain the commission:

The glory of the firm of Adler & Sullivan has forever departed. They failed at the end of the panic and Mr. Adler died three years ago. Mr. Sullivan is a true artist, who now, not having the companionship of a business man, does not cut as large a figure as formerly. When this house was in their palmy days however Mr. Wright was the right-hand man. I saw a copy of the Engineering Record of June 7, 1890, with plan of Adler & Sullivan offices, in the Auditorium Building. Visitors who entered their general offices could reach Mr. Adler through one door; beyond that was a large consultation room, and beyond that, Mr. Sullivan and Mr. Wright's offices side by side. In these two rooms all their work was created, and during much of the time Mr. Sullivan was away because of poor health.

Mr. Adler was a structural engineer and a business man. The $500,000 Wainwright Building and the Union Trust Building of St. Louis; the Schiller Theatre and the Stock Exchange in Chicago; the Seattle and Pueblo Opera Houses, all Adler & Sullivan's work, were, I inferred from Mr. Wright, largely his creations. He also had as much to do

with the Auditorium as a young man, just past twenty could be expected to have.

It has been a joke in Mr. Wright's office that the large building questions, with which he was in Adler & Sullivan's office almost exclusively engaged, now seldom come his way and his time is devoted to residences, with which he formerly had nothing to do.[26]

These remarks indicate that Wright, who had no practical experience with large office buildings during his first nine years as an independent architect, was determined to maximize his earlier experience with Adler & Sullivan, even to the point of making what appear to be very extravagant claims regarding his responsibilities for many of their best-known commissions. Possibly these claims were justified — Wright was, after all, an architectural genius, though a very young one when he was with Adler & Sullivan. However, his assertion that while at that firm he "had nothing to do" with residences is contradicted by the following statement from his autobiography: "With Silsbee I had gained considerable light on the practical needs of the American dwelling. Adler & Sullivan refused to build residences during all the time I was with them. The few that were imperative, owing to social obligations to important clients, fell to my lot out of office hours."[27] This contradiction, and the remark about Sullivan's "poor health,"[28] suggest that Wright was willing to set aside old loyalties and to bend the truth in pursuit of this commission.

Once he had disposed of the question of Adler & Sullivan, Darwin Martin's report followed two interwoven threads. One was a running discussion of Wright's Oak Park houses, for which Martin had a special enthusiasm and commitment; the other, a series of businesslike reports on the steel framing, the lighting, the ventilation, the magnesite trim, the control of drafts in the light court, and other factors that would contribute to the overall distinction of the Larkin Administration Building. In this part of Martin's report is a paragraph that reveals how eager Wright was for the commission and what he was willing to do to obtain it:

After I had realized somewhat of the extent of Mr. Wright's plans for this building beyond anything we had conceived of, I told him that the time elapsed since Jan. 15th, when the sketch was submitted and our uncertainty about it was all his fault because a sketch drawn to the scale of 32′ to the inch was utterly inadequate to convey to us any proper sense of his meaning, for which I did not think we were in any way responsible, and he replied that this was so and that he would never do it again. He said that he should have made a much larger sketch and brought it to us himself, and I think this is what he will immediately proceed to do. As he reiterated when he was here, he has not had tentative work to do and he didn't know how to do it.[29]

On the strength of Darwin Martin's detailed report Wright was invited back to Buffalo on April 13, 1903, to spend two and a half days discussing the office building with the Larkin executives.[30] But just when the commission seemed to be within his grasp, William Heath, the Office Manager of the Larkin Company, submitted a plan of his own for the new office —a one-story-and-basement scheme that would have covered the whole lot, with a trussed roof that eliminated posts.[31] In his business diary, Martin expressed the fear that this plan would delay the construction "a very long time." He consequently composed an argument (Appendix D) with comparative figures that indicated the wisdom of adhering to Wright's plan. This statement was well received by Heath and apparently so by the ever-taciturn Mr. Larkin, but the incident provoked Martin to write to Wright, "urging expedition, reduction of width of annex, confining stairs to court, putting elevators in outside shaft and outlining terms of payment for his services."[32] The importance of this statement will be elucidated in Chapter Three.

Wright returned to Buffalo on May 25, at which time Darwin Martin gave him a letter, signed by Mr. Larkin, accepting the plan of the new building.[33] Wright returned again on June 30 with modifications to his design which were "duly ok'd by Messrs. Larkin, Heath and Martin,"[34] but progress then ceased for a period of four months because Wright and R.J.

Reidpath were unable to come to an agreement about the structural steel frame. Reidpath specifically objected to Wright's unusually long spans, 32 feet from the posts surrounding the light court to the outer walls.[35] Finally, in November, Darwin Martin asked Mr. Larkin to intervene, and Wright's spans were retained.[36] Later in November Wright was given a contract for superintending the construction of his design — the commission was secured at last, a year after Wright's initial visit to Buffalo.[37]

Clearly the full realization of the Larkin Administration Building involved considerably more than good design on Wright's part. The Larkin clients — John Larkin, Darwin Martin, William Heath, William and Daniel Coss, and Mr. Larkin's two oldest sons, Charles and John, Jr. — represented a many-headed hydra of motives and opinions, stemming, in part, from a sharp division in the company between the soap-manufacturing and the mail-order businesses.[38] Mr. Larkin, his sons, and the Coss brothers tended to identify themselves with the basic production of soap and related products, whereas Darwin Martin appears to have been principally responsible for the growing success of the accessory mail-order business. William Coss was openly hostile to Martin on many issues, and John Larkin, Jr., who would eventually assume control of the Larkin Company and force Martin to resign, was also antagonistic.[39] The feelings of the senior Larkin remain characteristically opaque. The extraordinary financial success of the mail-order business undoubtedly pleased him and he had accordingly rewarded Martin with a very large salary, but at the same time he had taken measures to limit Martin's power. Rumors persist among the Larkin descendants that William Heath, who was Mrs. John D. Larkin's brother-in-law, was brought into the business in 1898 to counteract the possibility of Martin taking over the company. That Heath, too, was taken by Wright's brilliance and charm added weight to Martin's position on the new administration building but had no real impact upon John Larkin's intention to pass control of the business on to his sons. In view of these tensions the design of the administration building assumed a special significance within the Larkin Company: Would it be a symbol of the Larkin Company as a whole or would it be a monument to Darwin Martin's role in the business? What would be the impact of physically isolating the mail-order offices from the factory space where they had been located from the beginning? Would the building's design, which was radically different from that of the other factory buildings, accentuate the division between the two functions of the Larkin Company? While it is impossible to gauge to what extent such considerations affected the Larkin executives' thoughts, it is safe to assume that the building was of very special significance to Darwin Martin. Through years of tireless hard work he had helped to make John Larkin a rich man. Although he was amply rewarded for his efforts, Martin was increasingly surrounded by younger members of the Larkin family — John's sons, Charles, John, and Harry; his sons-in-law, Harold Esty and Walter Robb; his grandsons and nephews — who would eventually inherit the business. That Martin found this situation threatening is evident in his wish to place Charles and John, Jr., in offices in the factories rather than in the new office building, where, of course, they would have to be in order to observe the way their father ran the business. Martin was apparently unable to admit, even to himself, the inevitability of their taking over the business. To whatever extent he saw the success of the mail-order business as his own doing, the creation of a unique office building to suit a system of operation he had developed, and moreover a building designed by an architect he had chosen, must have been an exhilarating prospect.

In view of the tangled aspirations and emotions present within the Larkin Company directorship, it is remarkable that the building was built at all, but even more so that it was built much as Frank Lloyd Wright wanted it to be. This was a result of John Larkin's willingness to trust Darwin Martin's judgment, and of Wright's shrewd assessment of the interrelationship of the Larkin executives. On the slender promise of Mr. Larkin's interest in Louis Sullivan and the encouraging enthusiasms of Darwin Martin and William Heath, Wright went after the Larkin commission with all of his capabilities. He maximized his role in the Adler & Sullivan office so as to impress Mr. Larkin and convince the executives of his ability to handle the Larkin commission. Furthermore, he rushed ahead with the design in all of its complexities and detail without authorization from the Larkin Company in order to demonstrate his talents and, at the same time, to make it increasingly difficult for them to rescind their "tentative" offer.

Wright's motivation for pursuing the Larkin commission with such tenacity is understandable, even if some of his claims appear to be exaggerated. This was his opportunity to break out of residential work and enter the realm of the large building commissions upon which national and international reputations usually are based. Moreover, his six years with Adler & Sullivan inspired him to develop some ideas of his own about commercial buildings. These ideas would take form eventually in projects like the San Francisco Press building, the National Life Insurance Company building, the St. Mark's-in-the-Bouwerie tower, the Guggenheim Museum, and others which in their variety and inventiveness make Adler & Sullivan's work look conservative and formulated.

The zeal with which Wright approached the Larkin commission at the outset never waned. As the design passed through successive phases of development, Wright gathered a kind of inspired momentum that enabled him to make the design richer and more complex. Indeed, the process of designing a commission of this magnitude was so all-consuming for Wright that he would later write of the final form as having "come from me," as if it had been born after months of internal nurturing.[40]

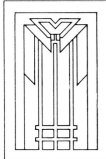

CHAPTER TWO
The History of
The Larkin Company

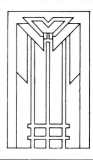

During the past forty-five years historians have tended to isolate the Larkin Administration Building from its context within the company. The company consisted of both a soap manufactory and a premium-based mail-order business, housed by 1902 in a 2-million-square-foot complex in Buffalo, with branch offices in Pittsburgh, Boston, Philadelphia, and Peoria, as well as subsidiary manufactories throughout the eastern United States. The Larkin Company produced a variety of soaps, perfumes, powders, and other household products, and purchased, warehoused, and dispensed a perpetually growing number of premium items; it was a business of considerable complexity. Wright's building was expected to accommodate the specific needs of the Larkin Company, needs that included places for executives and department heads, for systematic mail-handling and filing, and for a variety of support activities, all closely joined and expressive of the company's progressive attitudes toward the nature of work and the character of the workplace. All this played an important and hitherto overlooked part in the formulation of Frank Lloyd Wright's design for the administration building.

From its establishment in 1875 the growth of the Larkin Company was fostered by social and economic changes taking place in America following the Civil War. Large-scale population shifts from the Northeast and mid-Atlantic states to the Midwest ensured that, until about 1890, two-thirds of the American population lived in rural areas often distant from urban mercantile centers. The westward expansion of the railroads and the concurrent development of the U.S. postal system enabled many rural dwellers to maintain contact with cities.[1] Mail-order shopping became a popular means of obtaining new "city goods."[2] Although the Larkin Company began as a soap manufacturer in 1875, it had expanded into mail-order business by the mid-1880s.

Soap-making had been a cottage industry in America until the mid-nineteenth century when new manufacturing techniques made it possible to mass-produce soap so cheaply and effectively that salesmen could profitably peddle the product door-to-door. John D. Larkin (Fig. 1), the founder of the Larkin Company, became involved in soap-manufacturing quite by chance. In 1861, his older sister married Justus Weller, operator of a small soapworks in Buffalo. John Larkin was hired as a clerk in Weller's firm in 1862 and became a partial partner in 1865. In 1870, when Weller decided to relocate the business in Chicago, Larkin was invited to join him and was made a full partner.[3] The five years Larkin spent in Chicago proved significant in several respects. He was exposed to business practices in the brisk, wide-open atmosphere of America's fastest-growing city. He later remarked: "I think I know something of the energy required to succeed in Chicago."[4] Although the great Chicago fire of 1871 spared the Larkin & Weller soapworks, it made an impression upon Larkin that would influence the construction of all Larkin buildings in the future. Most important, however, were some of

1 John D. Larkin, ca. 1895. (Courtesy Daniel I. Larkin)

2 Elbert G. Hubbard, 1875. (Courtesy Daniel I. Larkin)

the personal relationships Larkin formed. Sometime in 1871 Justus Weller invited his young partner to Bloomington, Illinois, to meet the family of Dr. Silas Hubbard, Weller's uncle, who had moved from Buffalo to central Illinois in the 1850s. As a result of this and subsequent visits, Dr. Hubbard's teenage son, Elbert, was persuaded to join the Larkin & Weller firm as a soap salesman, and two years later John Larkin married Elbert's older sister, Frances.[5] The unfortunate dissolution of Weller's marriage to Mary Larkin caused John to return eastward in 1875 to establish a soapworks of his own. He traveled as far as Boston in search of a location but finally settled in his birthplace, Buffalo, which was second only to Chicago

as a transshipping and meatpacking center where the animal fats necessary for soap-making were readily available.[6] Larkin took on Elbert Hubbard as his first salesman and one-third partner (Fig. 2). In 1878 the firm became "J.D. Larkin & Co."[7]

The subsequent growth of J.D. Larkin & Co. from its modest initial capitalization (its net worth was estimated around $30 million in 1920)[8] was the result of hard work, some clever marketing innovations, and shrewd leadership on the part of John Larkin—particularly in the selection and management of executives. By all accounts, Larkin was a reticent individual, wholly devoted to his business, who allowed his principal executives to run its day-to-day operations with little or no interference.[9] Elbert Hubbard, Larkin's second in command from 1875 to 1893, played a vital role in the early development of the Larkin Company, although his biographers have glossed over those years in favor of his bohemian, post-Larkin Company existence as author, homespun philosopher, and leader of the Roycroft settlement in East Aurora, New York.[10] To an extent he led through sheer force of personality. His nephew, Horton Heath, described him in 1931:

He laughed easily and loudly. He attacked the day's work with a gusto and excess of animal spirit that had never been subjected to the sedative of alcohol or tobacco. He occasionally relieved his sensibilities of boredom by uttering an Indian war-hoop. He was a free spirit. . .[11]

In the first few years Hubbard worked on the road as a soap salesman, while John Larkin tended to soap production. Gradually Hubbard spent more time supervising the Buffalo office and writing advertising circulars, and Larkin eventually turned the supervision of soap production over to William and Daniel Coss, who had been hired as salesmen in 1875.[12] Darwin D. Martin began as a salesman, too, but was brought to Buffalo in 1879 to work as a bookkeeper under Elbert Hubbard's supervision (Fig. 3). He was then just thirteen years old.

During its first decade J.D. Larkin & Co. produced laundry and toilet soaps which were sold door-to-door and "to the trade" (that is, to storekeepers) by traveling salesmen. According to Darwin Martin, a break with conventional selling practices occurred in 1881, when the company first experimented with soliciting storekeepers by mail.[13] It was not until the cumbersome standard twelve-cake package of soap was replaced by a more manageable and handy three-cake box for ten cents (an idea variously attributed to Elbert Hubbard and to Frank Martin, Darwin's older brother) that mail orders from storekeepers began to arrive in substantial quantities.[14] This unexpected response prompted the realization that salesmen might be eliminated altogether in favor of a mail-order approach. The reduction of postal rates from three to two cents per half-ounce in 1883 provided additional impetus for direct-mail solicitation.

Additional developments changed the nature of the business during its first decade.[15] In the early 1880s someone in the Larkin Company proposed adding a modest premium item—a small chromolithograph or a handkerchief—to each box of soap. While the idea of using a premium as a sales incentive was not original to the Larkin Company, it had a profound effect on the business. The combination of direct-mail solicitation of customers rather than storekeepers and the enticement provided by the premiums made it possible for J.D. Larkin & Co. to eliminate all middlemen from its dealings with consumers by 1885.[16] The following year Elbert Hubbard conceived of the "Combination Box," a six-dollar assortment of laundry and toilet soaps shipped on thirty days' approval. This was augmented during the early 1890s by a ten-dollar Combination Box containing one hundred bars of the company's popular Sweet Home Soap,[17] nine small boxes of fine toilet soaps and creams, and a premium valued at ten dollars retail— altogether a twenty-dollar value at half the cost.[18] The first of the ten-dollar premiums, the "Chautauqua Lamp" offered in 1892, was followed by the popular "Chautauqua Desk" in 1893 and an oil stove in 1895.[19] Such substantial premiums were made possible through bulk purchasing, but they were chosen for their high quality. The "Larkin Idea" embodying the company's unique approach to business was, in effect, an investment pact between the customer and the company: If the customer was willing to commit ten dollars—roughly a week's pay for the average American family of 1900—to a direct purchase of a year's supply of soap, thereby eliminating middlemen, then the Larkin Company agreed to share the advantage in the form of an attractive premium item. The concept was clearly set forth in the Larkin Company motto: "Factory to Family; Save All Cost Which Adds No Value." Inherent in this unusual business arrange-

3 The Larkin Company executives, ca. 1920. Left to right: William R. Heath, John D. Larkin, Jr., John D. Larkin, Darwin D. Martin, Harold Esty, Walter Robb. (Courtesy Buffalo and Erie County Historical Society)

ment was a quasi-familial intimacy which the Larkin Company promoted in its advertising by calling customers "Larkinites" and by occasionally issuing such statements as, "Larkin Co. has always regarded its relations with its customer-friends as amounting to a great deal more than any ordinary exchange for money. We have abundant daily proof that the cordial feeling of the Company is heartily reciprocated by its customers." [20] This notion of customers as members of an extended Larkin family was enhanced during the 1890s by another marketing innovation (credited to an anonymous Pennsylvania housewife) known as the "Larkin Club of Ten." [21] "Clubs of Ten" consisted of groups of ten families who pooled their financial resources in order to purchase one ten-dollar Combination Box a month for each of ten con-

secutive months. Straws were drawn to see who would receive the premium each time; by the tenth month all club members had obtained the premium of their choice. In some instances a resourceful person would purchase the Combination Box and sell the excess soaps to neighbors. In either case, customers functioned as salespeople for the Larkin Company. The company acknowledged their services by designating them "Larkin Secretaries" and by inviting them, expenses paid, to visit the Buffalo headquarters in groups. Eventually the secretaries were rewarded with premium certificates. [22]

These marketing techniques had a strong impact upon Darwin Martin's role in the Larkin Company. From the time of his introduction as a boy in 1879 into the bookkeeping department, Martin had worked long hours (usually from 7 AM to 6 PM or later, as well as Saturdays and portions of most Sundays) maintaining customer accounts in ponderous ledger books and equally large index volumes.[23] As the company expanded in the 1880s, Martin's diminutive size (he was 5 feet 4½ inches in 1882) made him acutely aware of the cumbersomeness of the ledger system—each customer account had to be looked up in the index, found in the appropriate ledger volume, and entered by hand. It happened that Martin was driven by an extraordinary intellectual curiosity and spent his spare time reading, attending lectures, and taking correspondence courses in an effort to compensate for having left school at the age of eleven. Elbert Hubbard gave Martin constant encouragement, including access to the considerable library at his home in East Aurora where Martin frequently spent evenings and weekends. In 1885 Hubbard suggested that Martin catalogue the library for him. After making inquiries into the nature of the new card-indexing system at the Buffalo Young Men's Association library, Martin realized that this system could be adapted to the indexing of his ledgers. Shortly thereafter he realized that the entire ledger system would be more accessible and flexible if transferred to card files. Martin's account of the invention of the Cardex system, published in 1932 as a pamphlet entitled "The First to Make a Card Ledger," provides insight into the spirited atmosphere within the Larkin Company in the 1880s and into his relationship with Elbert Hubbard:

By that time the flexibility of index-cards was so apparent that I could see that we might make the card-index our card-ledger. I proposed that the accounts be posted directly to cards, and "when they were paid," I said, "we will simply destroy the cards." Quicker witted, Mr. Hubbard instantly responded, with a playful poke in my ribs, evidently well-pleased with this step onward in card-indexing, "No you won't, you'll keep those cards for a mailing list!" And, of course, from the start we did.[24]

The value of the new card index was proven during the swell of business following the introduction of the six-dollar Combination Box and premiums in the mid-1880s, but its full significance did not become apparent until the runaway success of the Chautauqua lamps and desks following the panic of 1893.

The partnership between John D. Larkin and Elbert Hubbard was dissolved in 1892 so that J.D. Larkin & Co. could be incorporated as the Larkin Soap Manufacturing Company with Larkin as President and Elbert Hubbard as Secretary and Treasurer.[25] Hubbard and Larkin each received salaries of $5,000; the Board of Directors consisted of Messrs. Larkin, Hubbard, Martin, and the Coss brothers. Incorporation necessitated double-entry bookkeeping and, in characteristic fashion, Darwin Martin amazed and delighted his employers by announcing that he had mastered this aspect of accounting in his spare time.[26]

In 1893 (the same year that Frank Lloyd Wright left Adler & Sullivan to establish his own practice), Elbert Hubbard surprised his colleagues in the Larkin Company by retiring to enter Harvard College where he planned to begin a career as a writer. Upon leaving the business Hubbard demanded his share of it. Although he had been an important contributor to the success of the company, his departure was clouded by the demands he made for his share of the business. He eventually received about $65,000 in cash and notes, but the experience so shook Mr. Larkin that upon reorganizing the Board of Directors he made himself Treasurer as well as President and never thereafter relinquished his tight control over the firm's finances.[27] At that time Darwin Martin was made Secretary with no raise in pay, and Charles H. Larkin, Mr. Larkin's oldest son, was added to the Board of Directors.[28] Relations between Elbert Hubbard and John Larkin remained strained during Hubbard's Roycroft years, but Martin continued his friendship with his former supervisor.[29] Nevertheless, Martin benefited from Hubbard's departure from the company; as business expanded his salary rose from $1,500 to $5,000 in 1896 to $10,000 in 1898 to $25,000 in 1899.[30] But even as Mr. Larkin rewarded Martin's service to the company, he took measures to provide for eventual transfer of control to his own sons. A second corporation was formed in 1899 with John D. Larkin as President and Treasurer, Charles H. Larkin as Vice President, Darwin D. Martin as Secretary, and John D. Larkin, Jr., as Assistant Treasurer. The Board of Directors included each of these men, the Coss brothers, and a newly hired department head, William R. Heath (see Fig. 3), a Chicago attorney whose wife, Mary, was the younger sister of Mrs. John D. Larkin and of Elbert Hubbard.[31]

In an effort to persuade William Heath to leave his law practice in Chicago and join the Larkin Company in Buffalo, John Larkin had visited him at his office early in 1899 and then had written him eight letters over a period of weeks.[32] The letters are entirely businesslike (although the uniting of Mrs. Heath with her sister and brother are mentioned), but they provide a rare glimpse into this reticent gentleman's view of his business:

By way of explanation I will say that it has been our aim to build up and strengthen our business by organizing departments and placing at the head of each, live, energetic, resourceful men capable of developing and extending their departments, and all operating together work out results that could not be obtained in any other way. We depend upon the principle of the "ounce of prevention" therefore almost entirely avoid litigation, so thus far our expenses for lawyers fees have not amounted to many hundred dollars, but as business enlarges, contracts increase in number as well as in value and importance, our collection department requires more skill to handle the delinquents, and there are many ways in which the right man could make himself useful and beneficial to the Company. Our position is an unique one in that we are pioneers in this co-operative plan to bringing manufacturers and consumers together, we have no guide to go by or compare with, and depend upon practical common sense and good judgment to make our efforts successful and give permanency to the business.[33]

Larkin's persistence with William Heath was motivated by the fact that Darwin Martin was gravely overworked. Martin had collapsed from "nervous prostration" early in 1897, missing nine weeks of work,[34] while the business had continued its inexorable acceleration. An almost exponential growth had resulted from the replacement of the fixed-premium offerings of 1892–95 with a ten-dollar premium certificate redeemable for any one of a growing number of items in the Larkin premium catalogue. Buyers for the Larkin Company were everywhere purchasing bulk quantities of bicycles, silverware, baby carriages, clothing, shotguns, and other items from manufacturers who were, for the most part, pleased to receive such large orders. Shortly after Heath arrived, the Larkin Company began to buy existing manufacturers or to establish its own manufacturing subsidiaries for such goods as pottery and china, glass, furniture, and leather goods. There were, indeed, "many ways in which the right man could make himself useful and beneficial to the Company," as Larkin had written to Heath.[35]

William Heath was hired to establish a legal department within the Larkin Company, but he soon immersed himself in the day-to-day operations of the business and was made Office Manager in 1903, a position that enabled him to share much of the burden of the company's expansion with Darwin Martin. (Although a Vice President, Charles Larkin was relatively uninterested in the business and eventually retired to pursue scholarly interests.) Heath proved to be an ideal counterpart to Martin in many respects. He was tall and slender, formally educated, philosophical in nature, and a dedicated member of the Presbyterian church. Martin was short and stocky, robust and aggressive in character, wholly self-educated, and a Christian Scientist. Martin's entire work experience was limited to the Larkin Company, whereas Heath, a former schoolteacher and school principal with ten years of experience as a lawyer in Chicago to his credit, brought a certain urbanity and a fresh perspective to the company.[36]

Martin and Heath worked well together, held each other in high esteem, and shared equally in the running of the business under Mr. Larkin's watchful eye. As Office Manager Heath was charged with maintaining the procedural rules for the operation of the

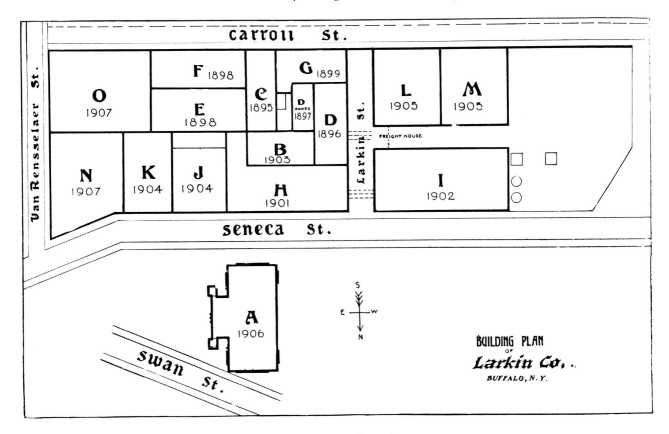

4 Larkin Company site plan, 1906. (*Ourselves,* 3, November 1, 1906, p. 2)

mail-order business, as well as overseeing personnel matters and handling legal issues (including claims); as a member of the Board of Directors, he participated in the making of policy. Martin, as Secretary, handled all premium selections and related problems, correspondence, bookkeeping, and customer accounts, and also had a voice in policy. Many of these categories overlapped, however, and the two men had other responsibilities in common. Both wrote frequently for *Ourselves,* the office publication that appeared six times a month, and traveled frequently to oversee manufacturing subsidiaries and branch offices. Both men were involved in the planning of new

construction—a constant preoccupation between 1895 and 1912. The fact that they each commissioned houses from Frank Lloyd Wright immediately prior to the commissioning of the administration building suggests that they may have joined forces in persuading Mr. Larkin to employ Wright.[37]

In contrast to Martin and Heath, John D. Larkin deliberately kept in the background of the Larkin Company and asserted himself only at the highest levels of decision-making.[38] His rare contributions to the company publications, *Ourselves* and *The Larkin Idea,* were used to announce major new company policies. For many years he refused to allow his picture to

5 Larkin factory shipping office, E and F buildings, 1901. (*The Larkin Idea,* May–November 1901, p. 40)

6 Larkin factory In-Mail Department, E and F buildings, 1901. (*The Larkin Idea,* May–November 1901, p. 37)

be used in connection with the business, and when he submitted to rare newspaper interviews he was extremely circumspect, especially regarding financial and personal matters. As he grew older and the business prospered under the motto "Factory to Family," he stepped quite easily into a patriarchal role — indeed, with his full beard and striking white hair he even looked the part. By placing his three sons, two sons-in-law, and his wife's brother-in-law in top executive positions, he made the Larkin Company into a family-core organization to which customers became "related" by way of their commitment to large orders of soap and the company's reciprocal commitment to sharing profits in the form of valuable premiums. Mr. Larkin's reticence concerning the considerable wealth that he was amassing was important in a business dedicated to assuring its customers that they were deriving wonderful benefits from the company's prudent policies.

The one indulgence that John Larkin did allow himself was a passion for construction.[39] The expansion of the Larkin building complex between 1875 and 1912 (most of which survives today) records the growth of the business itself (Fig. 4).[40] Frank Lloyd Wright's Administration Building was preceded by the construction of twelve new factory buildings ranging from eight to ten stories in height, commencing in 1895. Seven additional structures followed Wright's building in the years after 1905. Most of the factory buildings were used for the various processes involved in soap- and perfume-manufacturing — the storing of oils, fats, and other raw materials; boiling and distilling; cutting, milling, stamping, and wrapping soap; bottling perfume; and packing, storing, and shipping. In addition, there was a machine shop, a power plant, a chemistry laboratory, photography and engraving departments, and spaces for furniture receiving and premium storage. The office force was housed on several floors of the E and F buildings (Figs. 5, 6) until Wright's Administration Building was completed in 1906.[41] These steel-framed, brick-clad buildings were well designed for industrial purposes by the R.J. Reidpath Company of Buffalo, but they were less

than ideal for office work. The lighting was uneven and the spaces, some of which previously had been occupied by soap vats, tended to be dirty and noisy, and they were hot in the summer. Furthermore, the existing buildings were becoming inadequate in terms of size: There was a constant demand for space to accommodate new personnel and ever-increasing files. The Larkin Company was receiving about five thousand customer letters a day in 1903, and office staff members were hired weekly to handle the additional work. By the fall of 1902 it had become apparent that the mail-order business was no longer secondary to the soap manufacturing business. A separate office building had become a necessity.[42]

If the inadequacies of the E and F buildings provided much of the impetus for a new office building, the external environment surrounding the Larkin complex had a significant impact on the eventual design of that building. The site of the Larkin complex (Figs. 7, 8) — a predominantly industrial neighborhood along Seneca Street — had been selected because of its proximity to major railroad lines. A few hundred yards away is a point where eastbound New York Central & Hudson River lines diverged from Lake Shore & Michigan Southern lines heading south and west. The New York Central lines passed within 200 feet of the Larkin I building to the north and the Erie Railroad passed 300 feet south of E, F, and O blocks. The Larkin complex was surrounded on three sides by railroad lines and by related industries such as forges, foundries, freight houses, coal yards, and various dependent heavy industries. While the railroad lines brought raw materials and carried off manufactured goods (the Larkin Company had a New York Central spur line of its own), the smoke-laden atmosphere was not sympathetic to a busy mail-order office — particularly one representing a soap-manufacturing firm.

Thus, the Larkin Company needed an office building that would effectively bar the external environment so as to ensure spotless outgoing mail and to attract and hold the best office workers, chiefly female, in the city. No doubt these were among the

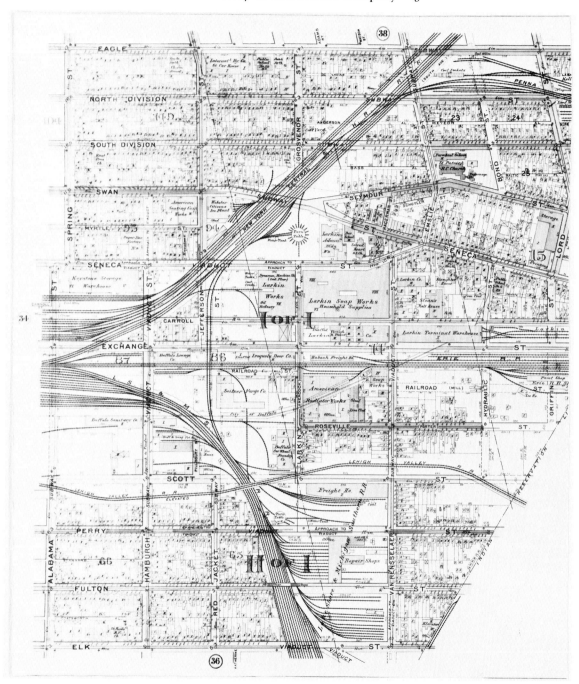

7 Larkin Company site, atlas view, 1915. (*The New Century Atlas of Greater Buffalo*, Philadelphia, 1915, pl. 37)

8 Larkin Company site, aerial view, ca. 1928. (Courtesy William Clarkson)

principal design considerations presented to Frank Lloyd Wright in 1902. Furthermore, it is probably safe to assume that the building's role as a figurehead for the business must have become apparent as well. Wright moved ahead quickly with the design, but it was to undergo substantial revisions between January 15, 1903, and April 1, 1904, a process amply documented in Wright's drawings.

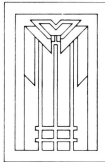

CHAPTER THREE

The Evolution and
Sources of the Design

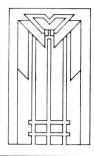

The Larkin Administration Building design was substantially altered in the course of the eighteen months immediately preceding construction (Figs. 9, 10, 11). The early drawings show an obvious debt to Wright's mentor, Louis Sullivan, but the arched, foliated entry to the annex (reminiscent of the Golden Door of Sullivan's Transportation Building at the World's Columbian Exposition of 1893) was eliminated from the final Larkin building design in favor of a more abstract geometric form.[1] Yet Wright already had eliminated Sullivanesque decoration from his residential architecture in 1900, three years prior to the Larkin commission. Why did he return to it here?[2] It is possible that Wright deliberately began with a design that would appeal to John D. Larkin's apparent interest in Louis Sullivan's work and then, once the commission was secured, modified the design to suit his own artistic vision. It is also possible that after a decade of almost exclusively residential work Wright returned to the Sullivan manner because it gave him a familiar point of departure.[3] Wright's motives can only be surmised, but it is clear that here he did not have the experience of twenty-five to thirty commissions over a period of seven years, as with his Prairie houses. The Larkin Administration Building had only one rather remote precedent in Wright's work, the design of the Abraham Lincoln Center, which Wright began in 1897 and worked on for five years before abandoning the commission.[4] The first complete rendering of the Lincoln Center (Fig. 12) was much indebted to Sulli-

van's 1890 Wainwright Building in St. Louis for its tripartite vertical organization, its pier and recessed spandrel elevations, and its emphatic corners and cornices (Fig. 13). Nevertheless, Wright's decoration was more restrained than Sullivan's, indicating that Wright was beginning to break the confines of the block — prophetic of outstanding innovations in the mature Larkin building design. The broad corners of the Wainwright block were replaced by Wright's angled buttresses and the regular rhythm of Sullivan's piers was interrupted in Wright's design by two six-story windowless slots — one marking a stairway, the other an elevator shaft — showing Wright's desire to express such functions on the exterior of a building. At street level the building wall protruded to form twin plinths with fountains and reliefs — predecessors to the Larkin entrance fountains (see Figs. 96, 97). The interior of the Lincoln Center was to include a high, balconied hall for religious purposes occupying an entire floor of the building (Fig. 14). Other floors were devoted to classrooms, gymnasiums, assembly rooms, kitchens, and living quarters for the client (Wright's uncle, Jenkin Lloyd-Jones). Wright's first façade designs failed to differentiate these varied spaces. In a second version he reorganized fenestration to reflect internal differences and lowered the rise of the building so that width was equal to height (Fig. 15). Both alterations indicate that Wright had begun to abandon Sullivan's tall-building formula as inappropriate to the commission. Thus, the Abraham

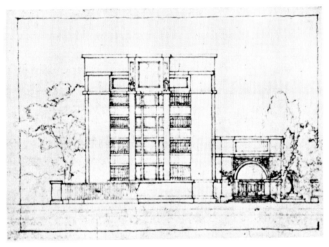

9 Larkin Administration Building, Seneca Street eleva-
tion, first set of preliminary drawings, early 1903. (Grant
C. Manson, *Frank Lloyd Wright to 1910: The First Golden
Age*, New York, 1958, Fig. 96B)

10 Seneca Street elevation, second set of preliminary
drawings, early 1903. (© The Frank Lloyd Wright
Foundation, 1987. Courtesy the Frank Lloyd Wright
Memorial Foundation)

11 Seneca Street elevation. (Courtesy The Frank Lloyd Wright Memorial Foundation)

12 Frank Lloyd Wright, Abraham Lincoln Center, Chicago, Illinois, first elevation, ca. 1899. (*Architectural Review* [Boston], 7, June 1900, p. 72)

13 Louis Sullivan, Wainwright Building, Saint Louis, Missouri, 1890–91. (Historic American Buildings Survey)

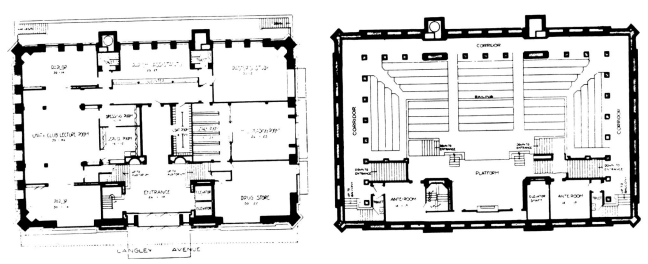

14 Abraham Lincoln Center, first- and upper floor plans, ca. 1899. (*Architectural Review* [Boston], 7, June 1900, p. 71)

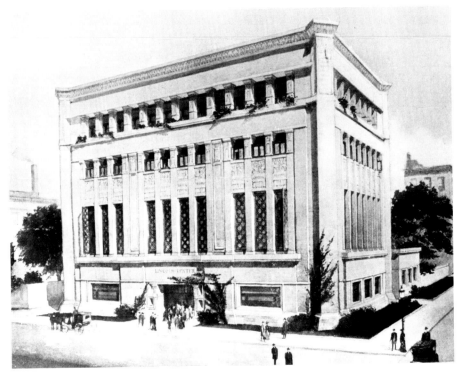

15 Abraham Lincoln Center, revised elevation, ca. 1900. (Catalogue, Chicago Architectural Exhibition, 1902. Courtesy Chicago Historical Society)

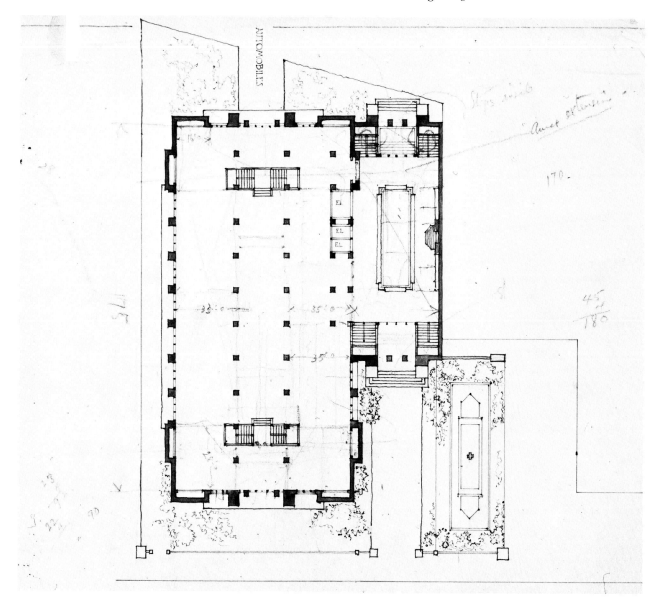

16 Larkin Administration Building, first-floor plan, first set of preliminary drawings, early 1903. (© The Frank Lloyd Wright Foundation, 1987. Courtesy The Frank Lloyd Wright Memorial Foundation)

Lincoln Center, though not completed by Wright, represents an important step toward the Larkin building's early design.

The Larkin building design evolved from Wright's tentative, somewhat derivative designs of January 1903 to a fully realized masterwork, completed by the summer of 1906. Little information survives from this long period of creative effort for Wright, but with the help of drawings and specifications in the archives of the Frank Lloyd Wright Memorial Foundation and the brief accounts Wright himself left it is possible to trace the evolution of the design and to gain insight into his methods of work and relations with clients.

The 161 drawings of the Larkin Administration Building in the archives of the Frank Lloyd Wright Memorial Foundation include two nearly matching sets of small, preliminary drawings. A third, larger set showing six floor plans apparently is preliminary to the master working drawings. Also included are thirty-four master working drawings, assorted detail sketches and presentation drawings, and approximately sixty sheets pertaining to steel framing, lighting, and furnishings.[5] Some drawings appear to have been made after the completion of the building.

The drawings are for the most part undated, but fall between January 15, 1903, and April 1, 1904, a date affixed to many master working drawings from which the Larkin Administration Building was constructed. A development toward the completed building is readily discerned among the drawings.

Darwin Martin's report to John Larkin of March 20, 1903, claims that Wright's preliminary sketch of January 15 was "utterly inadequate to convey to us any proper sense of his meaning."[6] The two similar sets of small, undated preliminary presentation drawings now in the Wright archives might include Wright's "inadequate" sketch. Both sets are scaled at 32 feet to the inch. The internal stairways and an annex light court (all eventually deleted; Figs. 16, 17) confirm that these drawings belong to a very early stage in the development of the design. The set designated here as the "first set of preliminary drawings" (partially published by Grant C. Manson in *Frank Lloyd Wright*

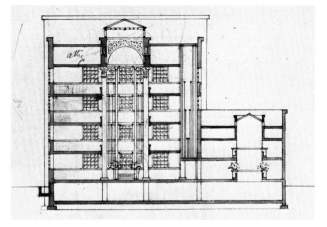

17 Transverse section through main block and annex, first set of preliminary drawings, early 1903. (© The Frank Lloyd Wright Foundation, 1987. Courtesy The Frank Lloyd Wright Memorial Foundation)

to 1910) is comprised of ten drawings—six floor plans, three elevations, and a transverse section (see Figs. 9, 16, 17), all bound together into what Manson described as a "little booklet of preliminary sketches"; these are accompanied by twenty-four pages of "skeleton specifications."[7] The set of drawings designated as the "second set of preliminary drawings" (not mentioned by Manson) consists of twelve sheets, of which ten correspond to the sheets of the first set with minor variations (compare Figs. 9 and 10).[8] Why were two similar sets of drawings made? Perhaps one was for the client and the other retained in the studio. Are either of these groups the first sketches sent to Wright's client? It seems unlikely that Darwin Martin would refer to a booklet of varied drawings as "a sketch," but it is also unlikely that Wright would produce drawings of the building at a scale of 32 feet to the inch after he and Martin agreed that a larger format was needed.[9] These two sets of drawings can be regarded as very early in date, but none can be identified exactly as the "inadequate" sketch of January 15.

These early drawings show that Wright's *parti* was remarkably mature at the outset, as Grant Manson

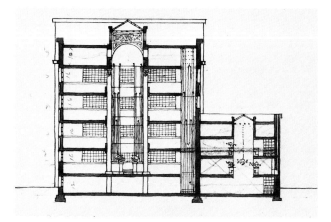

18 Transverse section through main block and annex, second set of preliminary drawings, early 1903. (© The Frank Lloyd Wright Foundation, 1987. Courtesy The Frank Lloyd Wright Memorial Foundation)

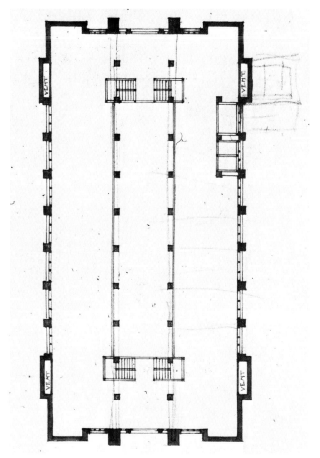

19 Third- and fourth-floor plan, second set of preliminary drawings, early 1903. (© The Frank Lloyd Wright Foundation, 1987. Courtesy The Frank Lloyd Wright Memorial Foundation)

noted.[10] Given a program that must have called for a building to accommodate 1,800 office workers who would process five thousand or more customer letters a day in clean, well-lit, fireproof, air-conditioned surroundings, Wright created a six-story, light-courted main block as the principal work space and a lesser appended annex for the entrance lobby and many personnel-support spaces. Wright's description of the main light court in the "skeleton specifications" indicates that even early on he was aware of its potential aesthetic importance: "These stories are thrown together by omitting the central portion of the floors between columns, thus making a high open, central aisle lighted from above by a continuous skylight which becomes a prominent feature in the design."[11] Moreover, ventilation ducts (which were assigned an important role in the final monumental design) were already in position—as yet without adjacent stairways—at the outer corners of the main block (see Fig. 16).

Despite the promise of the early designs, Wright decided to move the enclosed stairs from the light court, placing them at the four corners of the building. In his account of the creation of the Larkin Ad-

ministration Building in *An Autobiography* (1932), Wright related this process which greatly transformed the design with maximum dramatic effect:

And I worked to get that something into the Larkin Building, interested now also in the principle of *articulation* as related to that Order. But not until the contract had been let to Paul Mueller and the plaster-model of the building stood completed on the big detail board at the center of the

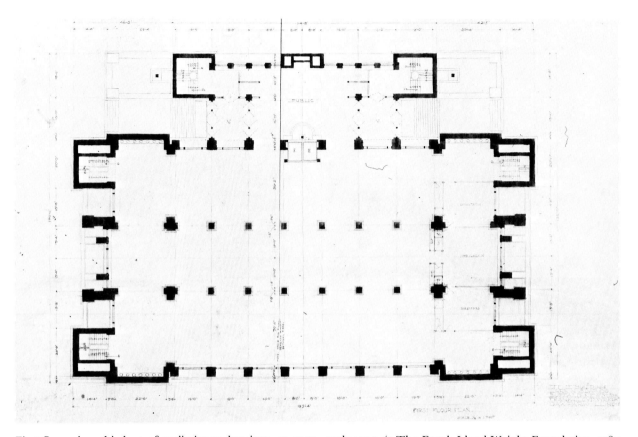

20 First-floor plan, third set of preliminary drawings, ca. 1903–early 1904. (© The Frank Lloyd Wright Foundation, 1987. Courtesy The Frank Lloyd Wright Memorial Foundation)

Oak Park draughting room did I get the articulation I finally wanted. The solution that had hung fire came in a flash. I took the next train to Buffalo to try and get the Larkin Company to see that it was worth thirty thousand dollars more to build the stair towers free of the central block, not only as independent stair towers for communication and escape but also as air intakes for the ventilating system. It would require this sum to individualize and properly articulate these features as I saw them.[12]

Wright's "flash" of inspiration makes a stirring account, but the drawings in the archives of the Frank Lloyd Wright Memorial Foundation suggest that the final form of the building actually took shape in a less dramatic fashion, and there are entries in Darwin Martin's diaries that support such a contention. Let us return to the first and second sets of preliminary sketches. Despite their close similarities, the drawings of the second set can be distinguished by a number of firm pencil overstrikes (Fig. 18; see Fig. 10) that foreshadow the closing in of the annex light court and the relocation of the stairways.[13] The exploratory nature of these overstrikes is indicated by the eccentric placement of a stair tower against the air-intake unit of the main block on the side of the building where it did not appear in the final design (Fig. 19).

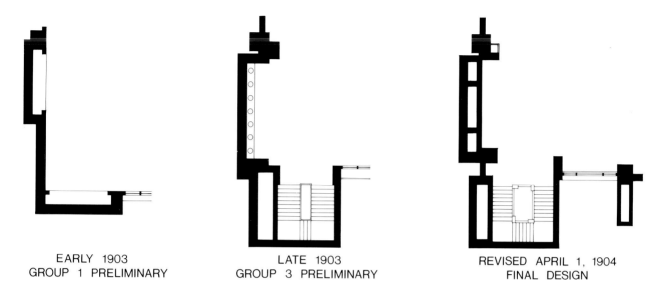

EARLY 1903
GROUP 1 PRELIMINARY

LATE 1903
GROUP 3 PRELIMINARY

REVISED APRIL 1, 1904
FINAL DESIGN

21 Evolution of corners of the Larkin Building from early 1903 to April 1, 1904. (Drawn by James Cahill)

In addition to these two sets of preliminary drawings there is the undated set of six floor plans that appears to be preliminary to the master working drawings (Fig. 20). Not only do they show stair towers at the outer corners of the building, but their dimensions are nearly equal to those of the master working drawings. The six floor plans measure 36″ × 25″; the master working drawings measure 37″ × 25″. An important difference separates the early plans from the final form of the building: Figure 21, a comparison of one corner of the Larkin building at each stage of its development, reveals that Wright did not immediately turn the stair towers into fully individualized freestanding forms as *An Autobiography* states. At some point between the drawing of the third preliminaries and the completion of the master working drawings Wright inserted a narrow recessed strip of vertical windows between the exhaust trunk and the stair and intake towers. The deep shadow that resulted effectively set the stair tower free of the main building (see Fig. 11).

Further evidence of Wright's struggle to achieve the articulation he wanted is suggested by the uncertainty as to just when his "flash" of inspiration actually took place. Darwin Martin's business and personal diaries show no record of such an event. His report to John D. Larkin of March 20, 1903, indicates that he had just then asked Wright to prepare drawings larger than the "utterly inadequate" sketch of January 15.[14] Wright subsequently spent April 13 through 15 in Buffalo discussing the building with Larkin executives, after which Darwin Martin wrote him (on May 14) urging that he "reduce the width of the annex, confine stairs to the court, and place elevators in outside shaft";[15] this is the earliest indication that Wright wished to remove the stairs from the light court. Wright returned the following month with plans and modifications that were "duly ok'd by the Larkin executives."[16] The *idea* of removing the stairways seems to have occurred in May or June 1903; indeed, Wright completed the excavation plan, with externalized stairs, on September 10, 1903. Yet his autobiographical statement ("But not until the contract had been let to Paul Mueller . . . did I get the articulation I finally wanted")[17] places the moment of inspiration early in 1904 when, according to a letter from Darwin Martin to his brother William, Wright carried a contract to Chicago for signing by the contractor (Paul Mueller).[18] How can Wright's apparent interest in moving the stairs from the light court in May 1903 be reconciled with his autobiographical account that the inspiration occurred nearly a year later? Had the sequence of events faded in his memory after thirty years? Did he simplify the process for dramatic effect? These questions may never be satisfactorily answered, but they warrant consideration because the relocation of the stairs altered Wright's entire conception of his building and had a profound impact upon his subsequent architecture and on that of several generations of architects. Wright himself commented on the importance of this early innovation in his 1952 lecture, "The Destruction of the Box": "I think I first consciously began to try to beat the box in the Larkin Building — 1904. I found a natural opening to the liberation I sought when (after a great struggle) I finally pushed the stair-case towers out from the corners of the main building, made them into free-standing, individual features. Then the thing began to come through as you may see."[19]

Wright's decision to move the stairways to external towers triggered a number of revisions to the entire design, the most striking of which was the creation of the pylon-like assemblage of interlocked towers, air-exhaust units (or pseudo-towers), and oversized piers that comprised the building's two principal façades. Wright quickly recognized the expressive potential of these elements and took measures to maximize their visual impact. He broadened the stair towers by shifting the air-intake ducts from the front corners of the building, where they appear in the preliminary plans, to the sides of the towers; he eliminated rectangular panels and belt courses in order to provide a maximum of uninterrupted vertical expanses of brick for the towers (Fig. 22); and the penciled overstrikes visible in Figure 10 indicate that Wright adjusted the height of the air-exhaust towers at about this time.

Moving the stairways precipitated revisions to the design and placement of the annex as well. In the preliminary plans (see Fig. 16), Wright placed the annex on the east side of the main block away from the dirt and smoke of the New York Central trains operating near the building's west side. The annex was also pushed to the north edge of the lot, against Swan Street, in order to open a deep entrance forecourt on the Seneca Street side of the building. This arrangement would have produced an inferior elevation on Swan Street where the façades of the main block and annex would have been co-planar. Wright must have realized almost at once that the creation of prominent stair towers for the main block necessitated stair towers for the annex as well as a means of harmonizing the two units. But considering that there was no room for an annex stair tower on the northeast corner of the lot, Wright was forced to move the annex to a symmetrical position along the east side of the main block, thus siting the whole building more comfortably on its lot (Fig. 23).

While most of Wright's revisions appear to have been determined by aesthetic considerations, two alterations — the narrowing of the annex and the elimination of its light court — may have been prompted by financial considerations. Mr. Larkin may well have asked Wright to defray the $30,000 that was necessary to relocate the stairways in external towers by cutting back on other aspects of the design. The evidence for this, however slim, is worth considering: Penciled overstrikes on Figure 10 (one of the preliminary elevations from early 1903), Figure 18 (an early section), and Figure 19 (plan of the third and fourth floors) suggest that Wright began to consider closing in the annex light court at the same time that he contemplated moving the stairs to external towers. Moreover, Darwin Martin had asked Wright to reduce the width of the annex as early as May 14, 1905.[20] Whether the motivation was economic or aesthetic, the elimination of the annex light court added three stories of useful floor surface where there had been a 37-foot light court surrounded by narrow, almost useless, balconies.

Each of Wright's adjustments contributed to a

22 Seneca Street elevation. (Courtesy Buffalo and Erie County Historical Society)

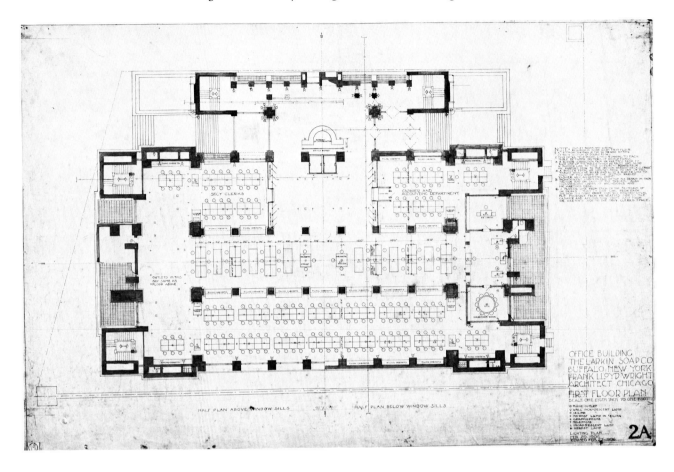

23 First-floor plan, master working drawings, "revised February 27, 1906." (© The Frank Lloyd Wright Foundation, 1987. Courtesy The Frank Lloyd Wright Memorial Foundation)

transformation of the essential character of the Larkin Administration Building. By repositioning the annex midway along the east flank of the main block Wright exchanged a stage-like conception based upon the deep forecourt and Sullivanesque arched entrance for one emphasizing the three-dimensional presence of the building's geometric masses. Toward this end, the freestanding fountain in the forecourt was incorporated into the walls of the annex. The addition of prominent stair towers to the narrowed annex had the effect of drawing it closer to the main

block, an illusion that Wright enhanced by giving the annex towers the same unadorned surfaces, copings, and general proportions of width to height as those of the main block.

The repositioning of the annex also caused a revision of the entrance sequence. In the original scheme visitors would have entered the 37-foot annex light court prior to reaching the greater light court within the main block. The lesser light court, a prelude to the larger one, would have substantially diminished the latter's impact. By narrowing the annex and adding stair towers to it, Wright converted the grandiose archway of the original scheme into a shadowed crevice between the towers of the main block and the annex, thus forcing the visitor to contemplate the whole building (in search of the obscured entrance) before proceeding inside. Wright already had explored such an arrangement in some of his Prairie houses. In the final Larkin design, visitors experienced a narrow, compressive lobby space from which the discovery of the 76-foot-high light court in the main block came as a surprise, a moving revelation.

Each of the alterations and refinements that contributed to the final form of the Larkin building represents a progression in Frank Lloyd Wright's thinking away from Sullivan's concern with surface decoration toward an architecture in which structure, mechanical functions, and space are combined in an expressive, abstract composition. Because the commission required a monumentality unlike the low, horizontal, articulated Prairie houses, it tested the universality of Wright's organic design. The early binuclear *parti* was a somewhat organic solution to the needs of the Larkin Company, but each of Wright's revisions constituted a new validation of his principles. The relocation of stairs benefited the design inside and out — it freed the light court as a pure work space and the new towers broke out of the corners of the original conventional block in dramatic fashion. Wright's decision to move the annex more symmetrically alongside the main block provided equal entrances where there had been a major entrance facing the factories. A building with a strong front and weak back became more fully developed in space, more responsive to its site. Finally, in eliminating decorative panels and belt courses, Wright made the design truer to materials and to the idea that function should be expressed openly.

The preceding discussion of Frank Lloyd Wright's eighteen-month struggle to reshape his initial conception for the Larkin Administration Building is riddled with speculations because Wright left so little information about the process. Indeed, in *An Autobiography* and throughout his writings Wright never discussed the details of the development of his designs or their historical sources. He seems to have been embarrassed by Sullivan's open reverence for the work of H.H. Richardson and he was no less so over his own youthful forays into stylistic modes like English Tudor (Nathan Moore house, 1894), Colonial Revival (George Blossom house, 1892), and Dutch Colonial (Frederick Bagley house, 1894).[21] Wright dismissed the whole notion of historical style with a single word, "sentimentality," and preferred to treat the creation of his own buildings in terms of personal struggle. "Rebellious and protestant as I was when the Larkin Building came from me," he wrote, "I was conscious also that the only way to succeed, either as rebel or as protestant, was to make architecture genuine and constructive affirmation of the new Order of this Machine Age."[22] In his autobiography and elsewhere Wright occasionally offered brief glimpses of ideas that influenced his thinking, such as his exposure to the Froebel kindergarten method and his discovery of the Japanese print.[23] Wright's approach in this is consistent with his descriptions of designing buildings — offering systems of thought rather than specific sources. Wright treats the inquiring historian much as he treats visitors to the Prairie houses — easy access is denied, the entrance is obscured, one is forced to pause and consider the subject in its entirety.

The revelation of sources is often difficult for any artist, but it posed a particular problem to Wright because of his claim to a new, uniquely American architecture: "I think our building is wholly American in its directness and freshness of treatment. It wears no badge of servitude to foreign 'styles' yet it avails itself gratefully of the treasures and the wisdom bequeathed to it by its ancestors."[24] This was in opposition to the derivative nature of the nineteenth-century academic tradition. The revelation of any source, historical or otherwise, could only diminish the force of Wright's revolutionary architectural statement, and Wright was well aware of this. Nevertheless, his work does have a certain relationship to the past and to the world around him, and if it is to be

24 Burnham & Root, The Rookery Building, Chicago, Illinois, 1885–88. (Historic American Buildings Survey)

25 D.H. Burnham & Co., Ellicott Square Building, Buffalo, New York, 1896. (Courtesy Buffalo and Erie County Historical Society)

26 Burnham & Root, Society for Savings Building, Cleveland, Ohio, 1887–90. (Courtesy of the Society National Bank)

27 George Wyman, Bradbury Building, Los Angeles, California, 1893. (Historic American Buildings Survey)

understood in any terms other than those established principally by Wright himself in his writings and lectures then those sources and influences deserve to be given consideration. The atrium, or light-courted, building type is a case in point.

The history of the light court as used in the Larkin Administration Building reaches far into the past, to Renaissance *palazzi*, to medieval Italian town houses, and ultimately to the *insulae* of ancient Rome. But this study will focus on the skylit metal-and-glass versions of the type that appeared during the nineteenth century.

Prior to the invention of the electric light and of effective methods of heating and ventilating large volumes of space, most American office buildings were either U-shaped in plan (Sullivan's Prudential Building, Buffalo, 1894–95), or narrow and slab-like (Burnham & Root's Monadnock Building, Chicago, of 1889, for example), so as to provide each office with direct access to light and fresh air. A third, less common format was the rectangularly planned building that enclosed a central skylit space, which could take several forms. In some, such as Burnham & Root's Rookery Building in Chicago (1885–88; Fig. 24) and D.H.

28 E.G. Lind, Peabody Institute Library, Baltimore, Maryland, 1875–78. (Courtesy David Eisendrath)

Burnham & Company's Ellicott Square Building in Buffalo (1896; Fig. 25), the interior light court was covered by a metal-and-glass roof just above the second-floor level so that a light-filled dry courtyard was preserved below and the shaft of space above remained open to the sky. In other instances, such as Burnham & Root's Society for Savings Building in Cleveland (1887–90; Fig. 26) and George Wyman's Bradbury Building in Los Angeles (1893; Fig. 27), the skylight was located at the top of the light shaft so as to provide a taller volume of weatherproof space and light. Regardless of the placement of the metal-and-glass shed roof, the enclosed spaces were used consistently as pedestrian traffic areas. Offices facing inward onto these light courts usually were equipped with windows and doors that opened onto balconies which in turn connected to flights of stairs (and elevators in some instances) leading down to the main floor of the light court.[25] The popularity of this building type in Chicago, Minneapolis, Buffalo, Rochester, and other North American cities stemmed from the fact that it provided indoor access to shops, restaurants, newsstands, and other establishments around the perimeter of the main floor out of the harsh winter weather. The main floor under the skylight was not used for office work because its air mass was difficult to regulate and because it was conceived as a public area in otherwise rented-space office buildings.

29 Larkin Administration Building, light court. (Courtesy Buffalo and Erie County Historical Society)

Some single-function buildings—such as retail stores, post offices, and libraries—also were designed around the light-court building type during the second half of the nineteenth century. E.G. Lind's Peabody Institute Library in Baltimore of 1875–78 is an outstanding early example (Fig. 28).[26] Conceived as a single volume of space ringed by five tiers of balconies for book stacks, and topped by a skylight beneath which the main floor served as a reading area, the Peabody Institute Library represents a compelling prototype for the Larkin Administration Building (Fig. 29). Frank Lloyd Wright may not have known this building, but he certainly knew the type. During preliminary negotiations for the Larkin Building in 1903,[27] he directed Darwin Martin to inspect D.H. Burnham & Company's Marshall Field Store in Chicago of 1902 (Fig. 30).

The earliest drawings for the Larkin Administration Building in the archives of the Frank Lloyd Wright Memorial Foundation suggest that the light-courted building type materialized early in the design process. Grant Manson believed this to be true and wrote that the design "occurred to him at once in that intuitive way which characterizes the inception of most of Wright's major successes."[28] Manson is almost certainly correct in this. Wright already had designed small, multistoried, balconied spaces for the Hillside Home School, for the principal hall of the Abraham Lincoln Center, and for his own working environment in his Oak Park Studio, but a second possibility deserves consideration: that Wright's unprecedented use of this building type for a great communal office may have originated with his clients. The Larkin executives also would have been aware of the light-courted building type from the three examples then standing in Buffalo and from similar examples in other cities.[29] By April 1, 1904, it had been determined that Darwin Martin and William Heath would occupy the very center of the main floor of the light court, a highly unorthodox arrangement that would leave them no privacy and none of the status traditionally associated with an executive office at the top of a tall building.[30] The Larkin arrangement must

30 D.H. Burnham & Co., Marshall Field Store, Chicago, Illinois, 1902. North well. (Courtesy Marshall Field & Co.)

have been worked out with the full consent of the executives, if not at their request. Similarly, the library-like interior organization of the Larkin Building may owe a lot to Martin, who already had adapted one library feature—the card catalogue—to the problem of customer account-keeping when he invented the Cardex card-indexing system in the 1880s.[31] The balconied interior of the Larkin Building was, in a sense, a library of built-in filing cabinets containing thousands of customer account records. Indeed, it could be argued that the entire configuration of the interior of the main block of the Larkin Administration Building was a reflection of Darwin Martin's role in the Larkin Company. The great balconied hall was perfectly suited to the activities involved in mail-order processing, bookkeeping, and maintaining premium catalogues, whereas the soap-

31 The Dakota grain elevator, Buffalo, New York, ca. 1910. (Courtesy Buffalo and Erie County Historical Society)

manufacturing side of the business was given no visible expression in the building. In this regard, the visibility of Martin and Heath, as opposed to the lack of visibility of Mr. Larkin and his sons (who would occupy offices underneath the west balcony), may be significant.

Wright is characteristically mute on the subject of his sources for the Larkin Administration Building —he writes of the "solution" that "came in a flash" and of getting the articulation he wanted as though the entire development of the design occurred within his mind with no input or influence from external sources. The special significance that Wright attributed to the Froebel method in his autobiography has encouraged historians to regard the Larkin Administration Building and the rest of Wright's mature works as products of his rejection of historical architectural precedent in favor of the primary geometric

"gifts" that were given to him by his mother when he was a child.[32] This clever piece of myth-creation places Wright securely in the realm of child genius, but it also tends to shield his work from other kinds of injury. The following alternative interpretation of the genesis of the exterior of the Larkin Building will be conspicuously lacking in mythic content—so much so, in fact, that it may by its very ordinariness provide a new understanding of the design and of Wright's need to shroud its creation in an aura of myth.

From November 1902 when he first met Darwin D. Martin until the summer of 1906 Frank Lloyd Wright traveled by train between Chicago and Buffalo monthly to oversee the construction of the Barton, Martin, and Heath houses and the Larkin Building.[33] On each trip his train passed through the district on the south side of Buffalo where numerous grain elevators lined the banks of the Buffalo River and Lake

32 Evans grain elevator, Buffalo, New York, ca. 1863. (Courtesy Buffalo and Erie County Historical Society)

Erie. Elevators today are made of reinforced concrete and are cylindrical, but prior to 1903 the silos were usually square in plan (Figs. 31, 32) and the elevator mechanisms were housed (as they still are) in tall oblong shafts to which the brick towers of Wright's Larkin Administration Building (see Fig. 11) bear a strong resemblance. Wright hardly could have been unaware of these unusual structures for they had the physical size of large buildings with a unique scale owing to their lack of windows and their elongated, functionally determined proportions. There is a compelling eeriness about these huge receptacles that has made them a source of fascination for artists, photographers, and architects for generations. Did the elevators actually influence Wright's design? Reyner Banham and Vincent Scully have each suggested as much,[34] and in addition to their formal similarities there is a strong parallel between the functions of the elevators and of Wright's towers—one carries grain from the holds of ships to the tops of the silos, and the other carries people and clean air to each floor of the office building. Furthermore, in keeping with Wright's lifelong concern that his buildings be indigenous, there were more than ten grain elevator groups within a mile of the Larkin complex when Wright's building was being designed and built.

Given the likelihood that Wright's building was influenced by the grain elevators, one can appreciate the importance of protecting the revolutionary character of Wright's work. America was in the throes of the Beaux-Arts classical revival during the years of the Larkin Building's design and construction. In the face of a national preoccupation with an academic style that derived its formal vocabulary and spatial organization from the Greco-Roman tradition, any indication that the design for a major office building had been inspired by utilitarian structures considered only marginally architectural was bound to be a cause for ridicule. Wright himself does not appear to have been much preoccupied with protecting his sources. His 1901 essay, "The Art and Craft of the Machine,"[35] and his references to music, nature, the Japanese print, and the Froebel method, seemed to suffice for him. European modernists who immediately followed Wright took inspiration from him but had a very different attitude about sources; they present another reason why Wright might have been served better by remaining silent about sources.

Walter Gropius, Le Corbusier, and Eric Mendelsohn each discovered and published photographs of American grain elevators during the 1910s and 1920s and described them as important in creating their modernist aesthetic.[36] Mendelsohn wrote:

Mountainous silos, incredibly space-conscious, but creating space. A random confusion amidst the chaos of loading and unloading corn ships, of railways and bridges, crane monsters with live gestures, hordes of silo cells in concrete, stone and glazed brick. Then suddenly a silo with administration buildings, closed horizontal fronts against the stupendous verticals of fifty to a hundred cylinders, and all this in the sharp evening light.[37]

Le Corbusier expressed an even greater excitement in his book, *Vers une Architecture:* "Thus we have the American grain elevators and factories, the magnificent FIRST-FRUITS of the new age. THE AMERICAN ENGINEERS OVERWHELM WITH THEIR CALCULATIONS OUR EXPIRING ARCHITECTURE."[38] The enthusiasm of the European modernists for American grain elevators leads one to believe that Wright too had been inspired by their powerful imagery. Europeans regarded Wright as an important forerunner, and they shared his formalist-functionalist view of architecture; it seems logical that they must have shared similar sources of inspiration. Wright was unwilling to acknowledge this, however. By 1932 when he had completed *An Autobiography,* it had become clear to Wright that European modernism represented a preoccupation with white cubist form in architecture that was wholly alien to his organic approach.[39] In view of his disdain for the International Style, it would have been inconsistent of Wright to lay claim—prior claim, at that—to the modernists' sources.

These speculative observations on Wright's sources are intended to complement the previous scholarship on the subject, not to negate it. To the extent that Wright's Froebelian training was a vital force in his artistic consciousness, it would have heightened his appreciation of the monumental forms of the grain elevators and conversely, the visual impact of the elevators may have reinforced his belief in the significance of the Froebel method to his own development. In any case, the Larkin Administration Building is Wright's boldest essay in geometry up to 1903, and in its defense he wrote:

I confess to a love for a clean arris; the cube I find comforting; the sphere inspiring. In the opposition of the circle and the square I find motives for architectural themes with all the sentiment of Shakespeare's "Romeo and Juliet": combining these with the octagon I find sufficient materials for

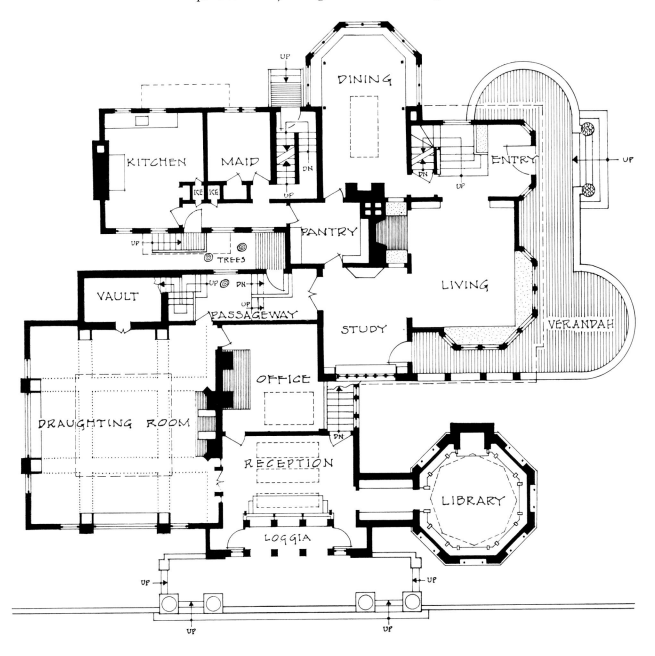

33 Plan, Studio and Home, Oak Park, Illinois, 1898–1909. (Courtesy Donald Kalec, *The Home and Studio of Frank Lloyd Wright in Oak Park, Illinois, 1889–1911*, Oak Park, 1982)

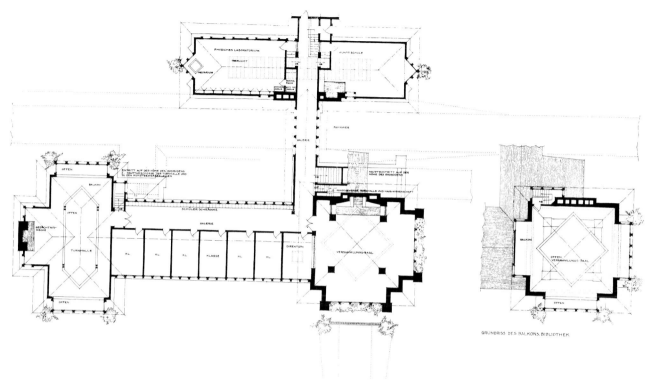

34 Plan, Hillside Home School, Spring Green, Wisconsin, 1902. (Plate x in *Ausgeführte Bauten und Entwürfe von Frank Lloyd Wright,* Berlin, 1910)

symphonic development. I can marry these forms in various ways without adulterating them, but I love them pure, strong, and undefiled.

The atrium, or light-courted, building type had been in use throughout the nineteenth century, but in eliminating stairs and elevators from the central space and applied decoration from its surfaces Wright gave the type a new clarity and, as we shall see in Chapter Five, new meaning as well.

The bi-nuclear main block and annex plan appears to have been Wright's own invention. It has no precedent among the tall buildings of Adler & Sullivan and the rest of the Chicago School, but it may be regarded as a further rationalization of Sullivan's functionally

inspired tripartite vertical division of the office building. A tendency to separate differing functions into discrete units is apparent in Wright's Oak Park Studio design of 1898–1900, where a small reception room intervenes between the drafting room and the library (Fig. 33), and even more so in the Hillside Home School of 1901 (Fig. 34), in which three building units —the assembly hall, the gymnasium, and the physics laboratory and art studio—are separated by long corridors and links of classrooms. Wright continued to employ bi-nuclear planning for major commissions throughout his career, notably in Unity Temple, the Johnson's Wax headquarters, and the Guggenheim Museum.

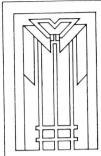

CHAPTER FOUR

Functional Aspects of the Design

Larkin Company publications from the two first decades of the twentieth century indicate that the directors held progressive views concerning the treatment of employees.[1] Picnics, weekly concerts, educational incentives, and profit-sharing schemes were some of the benefits that made the Larkin Company, in the words of a former secretary, "a class place to work in Buffalo. . . . They took *care* of you."[2] Larkin executives believed, as most business people still do, that such benefits and a clean, safe, and attractive office environment augmented productivity. Thus, two considerations—the business activity and the comfort and well-being of the office staff—dominated the planning of the Administration Building. Frank Lloyd Wright created a six-and-a-half-story light-courted structure for the principal work and a smaller annex for most of the support activities in an effort to keep the two functions as separate as possible.

The principal office activity, handling customers' mail, was performed in the first four stories and basement of the main block. (Soap production, advertising, and warehousing remained in the factory buildings.) In 1903 the company was receiving five thousand letters in six separate deliveries daily including Saturdays.[3] They included orders for premiums, inquiries, and complaints, all demanding prompt attention for the sake of good customer relations. The mail was driven through an arched opening on Swan Street (Fig. 35) to a receiving area in the above grade basement (Fig. 36) where it was loaded onto elevators and taken to the third floor. Here mail

was sorted into "state groups," a system established in the 1890s, long before Frank Lloyd Wright's involvement.[4] Ten state groups cared for Larkin customers east of the Mississippi, while mail from western states was handled in a branch office at Peoria, Illinois.[5] The state groups were distributed with programmatic precision (Figs. 37–40): Four groups were accommodated on the fourth floor, three on the third (Fig. 41), two on the second, and one on the first. This implies a close collaboration between architect and clients. Wright did not simply provide a large volume of space for the Larkin Company to fill as they pleased. The design was carefully detailed, probably by Wright working with Darwin D. Martin, whose skill in organization had been vital to the growth of the Larkin mail-order business.

While the circulation of mail through the Administration Building was an expression of Larkin organization, it was also consistent with Frank Lloyd Wright's ideal of organic architecture.[6] Once the mail

35 Larkin Administration Building, Swan Street elevation, master working drawings, "revised April 1, 1904." (© The Frank Lloyd Wright Foundation, 1987. Courtesy The Frank Lloyd Wright Memorial Foundation)

36 Basement floor plan, master working drawings, "revised April 1, 1904." (© The Frank Lloyd Wright Foundation, 1987. Courtesy The Frank Lloyd Wright Memorial Foundation)

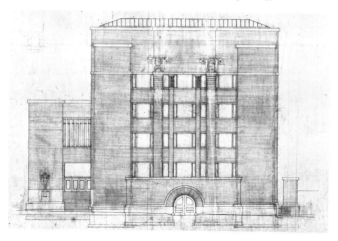

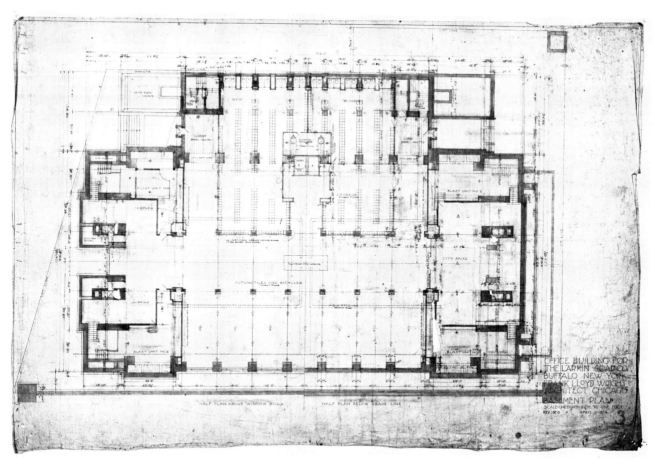

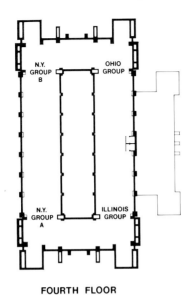

FOURTH FLOOR

37 Fourth-floor schematic plan of mail room setting arranged by States. (Drawn by James Cahill)

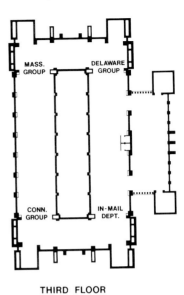

THIRD FLOOR

38 Third-floor schematic plan showing location of In-Mail Department and mail-order state groups. (Drawn by James Cahill)

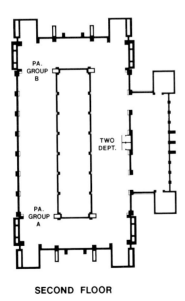

SECOND FLOOR

39 Second-floor schematic plan showing Typewriter Operators' Department and mail-order state groups. (Drawn by James Cahill)

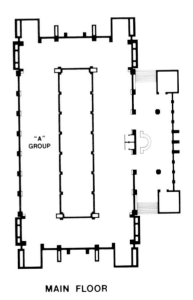

MAIN FLOOR

40 Main floor schematic plan of mail-order group A. (Drawn by James Cahill)

41 The In-Mail Department, third floor. (Courtesy The Frank Lloyd Wright Memorial Foundation)

42 "A" mail-order group, west side of main floor. (Courtesy William Clarkson)

43 Built-in file cabinets, southwest end of third floor. (Courtesy Buffalo and Erie County Historical Society)

left the third floor its flow was primarily downward, or gravitational, except for some mail that went to the fourth floor. This vertical pattern appears again in Wright's Solomon R. Guggenheim Museum, where visitors are carried by elevator to a point one turn short of the top of the museum. From there they have the option of walking to the top of the ramp or of immediately commencing the downward spiral, in gravitational circulation.[7]

Most incoming Larkin mail consisted of orders systematically processed within the Administration Building. Customer account filing was facilitated by Darwin Martin's card-index system for which Wright designed built-in metal file cabinets located throughout the building (Figs. 42, 43). Letters of inquiry or complaint were referred to correspondents who dictated responses into graphophones (Fig. 44). The cylindrical recordings were taken by messengers to the

44 Correspondent using graphophone. (Courtesy Buffalo and Erie County Historical Society)

45 Typewriter Operators' Department, east side of second floor. Visitors' balcony is at right. (Courtesy William Clarkson)

46 Main floor light court. View from Darwin Martin's desk facing south.

47 Office of John D. Larkin, south end of main floor. (*The Larkin Idea*, 9, March 1913, p. 5)

48 Office of Charles, John, Jr., and Harry Larkin, south end of main floor. (Courtesy William Clarkson)

49 Directors' meeting room, south end of main floor. (Courtesy William Clarkson)

50 Cashier's and Accounting Office, southeast corner of main floor. (Courtesy Buffalo and Erie County Historical Society)

"Typewriter Operators' Department" on the second floor (Fig. 45) and transcribed, after which they were reviewed and sent to the basement for delivery to the Buffalo Post Office.

The main floor of the Administration Building (Fig. 46) was the seat of executive authority in the Larkin Company. Darwin Martin, the Larkin Company Secretary, and William Heath, the Office Manager, and their respective departments occupied the entire floor beneath the skylight and also the northeast corner of the floor under the balcony. John D. Larkin's office (Fig. 47), his sons' offices (Fig. 48), and the directors' meeting room (Fig. 49) were located along the south end of the main floor, nearest Seneca Street and the factories. These were semiprivate offices. The Cashier's and Accounting Office (Fig. 50) adjoined Mr. Larkin's office to the southeast. At the opposite end of the floor were the Secretary's (Mr. Martin's) Department, the advertising executives' offices (Fig. 51), the Office Manager's (or Personnel) Department, and the Claims Department (both under Mr. Heath's supervision). Although a group of mail clerks filled the west side of the floor beneath the balcony, most of the personnel on the main floor were concerned with selecting the purchasing premium items and with maintaining the premium catalogue, or, more responsibly, with supervising personnel and the overall expansion of the business. Seen from the balconies, the main floor must have presented a spectacle of intense busyness (see Fig. 29).

From the start the Larkin Company grew at an almost exponential rate. New premium items were added constantly to the catalogue, additional customers wrote daily to the company, and new personnel were hired weekly to handle the increasing workload. The effective performance of the office

51 Main floor light court, ca. 1920. (Courtesy William Clarkson)

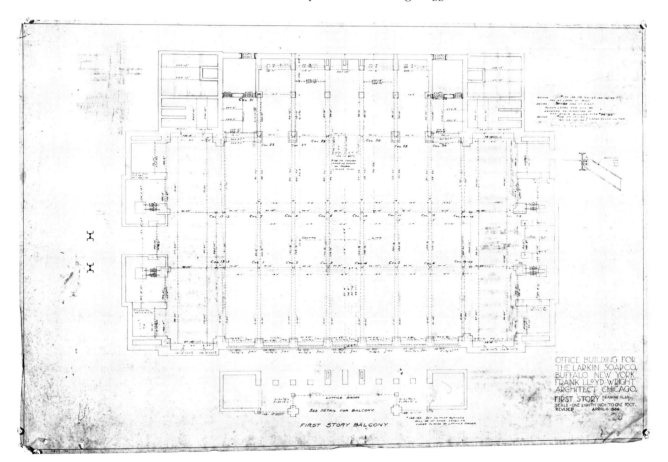

52 Steel framing plan, first floor, April 1, 1904. (© The Frank Lloyd Wright Foundation, 1987. Courtesy The Frank Lloyd Wright Memorial Foundation)

53 Construction view from factory buildings. (Courtesy The Frank Lloyd Wright Memorial Foundation)

staff in such a pressured atmosphere was dependent on the quality of the work environment, among other factors. Order and comfort were essential. Wright placed most of the support functions in the annex in order to provide a maximum of clarity and focus for the business activities in the main block. Stairs were housed in semiattached towers at the outer corners of the building and elevators were placed near the entrance and reception area. Room for food preparation and dining was provided on the fifth story, the last full floor on the main block. Vehicular traffic, blast units, and elevator machinery were housed in the basement.

The threat of fire held a special significance for John D. Larkin, an eyewitness to the vast destruction caused by the Chicago fire of 1871. He insisted that all Larkin buildings be constructed in the best available fireproof manner.[8] In the administration building the loss of customer records quickly would have closed down the business. With this incentive Wright created a building steel-framed and clad in brick, inside and out (Figs. 52–55). Exterior details were executed in red sandstone; the entrance doors, windows, and skylights were of glass. Floors, desk-tops, and cabinet-tops and sides were covered with magnesite for sound absorption. This was a chalky gray substance, mined in Greece, containing magnesium carbonate; it was mixed, poured, and troweled like cement.[9] For the floors magnesite was mixed with excelsior and poured over a layer of felt to impart resiliency.[10] Magnesite also was used for the sculptural decoration of the piers surrounding the light court and for panels and beams around the executive offices at the south end of the main floor (Figs. 56–60). The magnesite was handsome in its smooth, pale gray surfaces, but under the great weight of Wright's metal office furniture it chipped and cracked.[11]

All office furniture in the main block was designed

54 Construction view. (Courtesy The Frank Lloyd Wright Memorial Foundation)

55 Construction view, Swan Street side. Masons at work near arched entrance to basement. (Courtesy The Frank Lloyd Wright Memorial Foundation)

56 Interior construction. Magnesite molders at work on interior trim. (Courtesy The Frank Lloyd Wright Memorial Foundation)

57 Interior construction. Magnesite trim slabs being hoisted into position on second-floor balcony front. (Courtesy The Frank Lloyd Wright Memorial Foundation)

58 Interior construction. Unfinished pier at fifth-floor level. (Courtesy The Frank Lloyd Wright Memorial Foundation)

59 Interior construction. Laborers on fifth floor preparing to pour magnesite floor. (Courtesy The Frank Lloyd Wright Memorial Foundation)

60 Metal desk with magnesite panels. (Courtesy The Frank Lloyd Wright Memorial Foundation)

61 Metal desk with attached chair in open position.

62 Metal desk with attached chair folded.

in metal, an additional fireproofing measure. Three different types of desks and four different types of chairs, as well as filing cabinets and lighting fixtures, were fabricated to Wright's designs by the Van Dorn Iron Works of Cleveland, Ohio.[12] The rectangular chairs and desks were made of folded and punched sheet steel riveted somewhat like the framing of a building. The freestanding office chairs with cast-iron bases (see Fig. 49) were exceptionally heavy.[13] Wright was proud of the easy cleaning made possible by his design for folding chairs that cantilevered from most metal desks (Figs. 61, 62), but in use these chairs allowed only a limited arc of movement and may have been uncomfortable over the course of a full work-day. Wright's three-legged office chair was so unstable that it became known as the "suicide chair" among office personnel. These problems led to a minor insurrection in 1913 when some department heads threatened to import more comfortable wooden chairs on their own.[14] The Larkin executives were able to quell this uprising, but it indicates that Wright considered appearance before comfort in his furniture design.

Wright promised Darwin Martin that the new ad-

63 New York A and B mail-order groups, east side of fourth floor. (Courtesy Buffalo and Erie County Historical Society)

ministration building would be "as light as out-doors,"[15] but the dense exterior massing—stairs, ventilation towers, and piers—seemed to preclude the possibility. Wright's fulfillment of the promise is one of the least understood aspects of the Larkin Administration Building. All sides of the main block had tripartite windows located high above built-in filing cabinets, generously diffusing daylight across the balconies (see Fig. 43). A great skylight above the court provided more powerful illumination, flooding the main floor and blending with the side light (Fig. 63). Wright carefully eradicated darkness throughout the building. The basement, being above grade, received natural illumination from windows in the foundation wall and from skylights. Although the annex seems to interfere with the passage of light into the main building (Fig. 64), the narrow canyon Wright opened between the two (Fig. 65) brought light into the upper

64 Annex, Seneca Street elevation. (Courtesy William Clarkson)

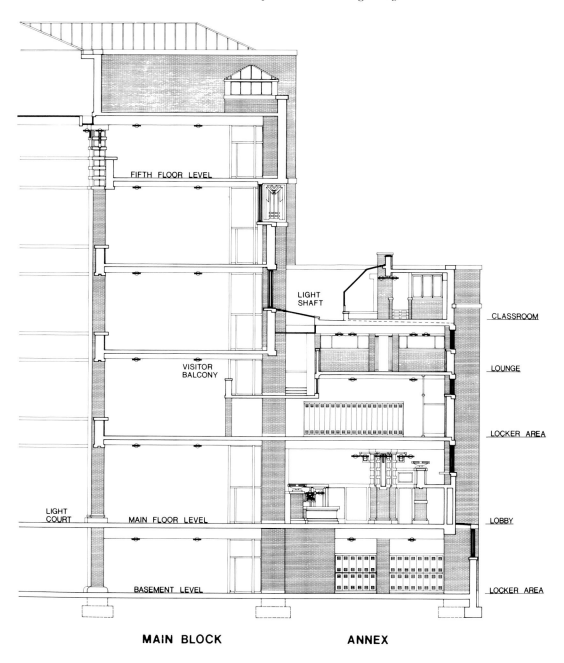

65 Section through annex and main block. (Drawn by James Cahill)

three floors of the annex and the third and fourth floors of the main block. Wright also placed deep-reaching skylights next to the landings leading into the annex in an effort to illuminate the basement at this junction. In spite of these measures the entrance lobby was only partially illuminated by windows high on its east wall, above the visitors' balcony. To solve the problem Wright introduced large, undivided sheets of clear glass, framed as entrance doors (Fig. 66), an innovation that has become commonplace in commercial architecture. The seemingly solid stair towers were lit by skylights and by narrow vertical windows set back between stair towers and air-intake units. The Dutch architect Jan Wils[16] described how these windows were placed to obviate glare for users. The Typewriter Operators' Department on the second floor of the main block (see Fig. 45), despite Wright's ingenuity, required artificial illumination, which was supplied by 150-candlepower Nernst Glowers (the latest improvement) attached to the ceiling. Buffalo's short winter days necessitated clusters of Nernst Glowers on the balconies, and the floor of the light court had freestanding bronze stanchions each supporting four 100-candlepower Nernst lights.[17] Nevertheless, the natural light was impressive, for the Larkin Company took special note of it in a brochure addressed to prospective employees:

Visitors from everywhere express greatest enthusiasm over the Administration Building's striking and appropriate architecture, and the sunlight which floods the building through its generous windows and skylight.[18]

Heating and ventilation in the Larkin Building was as vital to its success as illumination. The whole complex of Larkin buildings was surrounded on three sides by trains whose coal-burning engines poured out clouds of pollution (Fig. 67). Without an effective air-cleaning apparatus the daily accumulation of soot, especially on desk-tops, was bound to result in soiled correspondence — hardly appropriate for a soap company. Besides, the Larkin Company needed clean, comfortable offices to attract highly qualified typists and clerks to an industrial neighborhood outside the city center.

The heating and ventilation system of the Larkin Administration Building was misunderstood from the beginning, when the dean of American architectural critics, Russell Sturgis, failed to recognize that the heating plant was located in a separate building.[19] Wright himself added to the confusion by referring to the system as "Heating and Ventilation" in preliminary specifications and in early writings on the building.[20] But subsequently, in the second edition of his autobiography (1943), he wrote: "The Larkin Administration Building was a simple cliff of brick hermetically sealed (one of the first 'air-conditioned' buildings in the country)."[21] Was the Larkin Building air-conditioned or not? Reyner Banham, in his pioneering study, *The Architecture of the Well-Tempered Environment*, says not, on the grounds that the cleaned air was not cooled until 1909 when a Kroeschell refrigeration unit was installed and that the air was never humidity-controlled.[22] New evidence indicates that the Larkin Building was in fact air-conditioned and at a date significantly earlier than 1909.

The final, Wright-approved, master specifications for the Larkin Building, dated 1903,[23] required a mechanical blast system of heating and ventilation described in Item 91, "Scope of the Work," as follows:

The apparatus is to be divided into four units, both on the blast and exhaust systems. There are also to be four separate air purifying and cooling devices, one for each blast heating apparatus. The fresh air is to be taken from the top of the building through fresh air shafts to the basement where it is exhausted over the tempering coils, passed through water sprays, thence through the eliminator fans, discharged through the re-heating coils into plenum chambers and expanded through the ducts to the different floors.

The foul air is exhausted in the winter time from the floor line; in the summer time from the ceiling, thence through the vertical vent flues and trenches to the exhausters in the basement and discharged through foul air shaft to the atmosphere.[24]

66 Annex entrance viewed from inside lobby. (Courtesy William Clarkson)

67 Swan Street elevation. Turntable of New York Central Railroad is visible in lower right corner of photograph. (Courtesy William Clarkson)

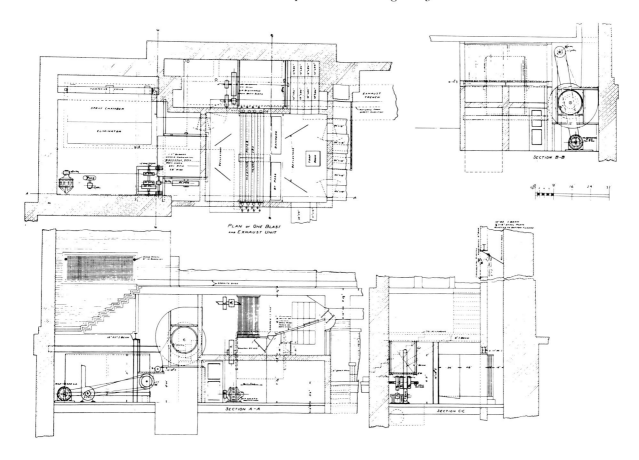

68 Engineering documents of heating and ventilating apparatus, "September 10, 1903, revised April 1, 1904." (Courtesy Daniel I. Larkin)

Item 92, "Guarantees," established the tolerances allowable in heating, air cleaning, air cooling, and humidity control:

The contractor will guarantee to thoroughly heat the building uniformly to 70 degrees in −10° Fahr. weather, and that each of the blast fans will move 28,000 cu. ft. of air per minute . . .

He will also guarantee that the air delivered into the building through the air purifying system shall be freed of 98% of all dust and dirt or foreign matter afloat in the air, and that the average humidity in the building will be 70% with a variation of 3 degrees either way in extreme cases. The apparatus is to be capable of reducing the temperature of the air passing through it to within four (4) degrees of the water temperature, when natural or city water is used.[25]

Item 102 specified that an "Acme Air Purifying and Cooling Apparatus, manufactured by Thomas and Smith of Chicago" would be used and would be "divided into four units and placed in connection with the blast heating and ventilation apparatus, occupying in each case a position between the tempering coils and the fans or heating stacks, as indicated on

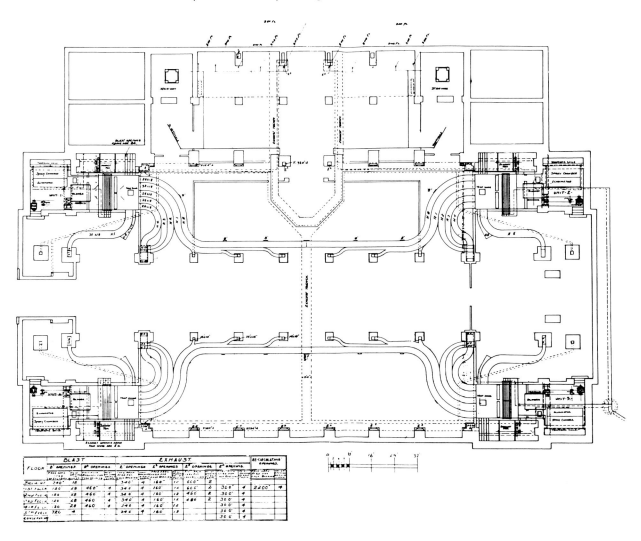

69 Engineering documents of ventilation duct system in basement, "September 10, 1903, revised April 1, 1904." (Courtesy Daniel I. Larkin)

70 Basement view, looking from main block to annex. (Courtesy William Clarkson)

plans'' [26] (Figs. 68, 69). Item 103 described a final component, the refrigeration system:

There is to be furnished and erected, as included in work of "Refrigeration System" a Carbonic Anhydride [CO_2] Refrigerating Machine of sufficient capacity, with an electric motor for driving same. This refrigerating apparatus is to include all circulating pipes, condensers, evaporators, regulating valves, etc. required in connection with Air Pumping and Cooling Apparatus, and is to be installed under direction of manufacturer of this latter, complete and guaranteed to reduce the temperature of the water for air cooling to 50°, if it is required.

The compressor is to set at Blast Unit No. 1, under plenum chamber and a system of circulating pipes, properly insulated, will be run to each unit of the air purifying and Cooling System.[27]

The combination of an air-purifying and -cooling apparatus and a refrigeration machine enabled Wright to guarantee that air in the building would be cleaned and cooled, with an average humidity of 70 percent regardless of external temperature. This is air conditioning as Willis Carrier, the acknowledged father of that art, defined it.[28] The humidity control may be less sophisticated than Carrier's for the Huguet Silk Mills in 1907,[29] but the mechanisms for saturating the air with water, for cooling it to lower its dew point, and for reheating it to diminish its relative humidity were unquestionably present in Wright's specifications of 1903. The date, 1909, for the installation of a Kroeschell refrigeration system in the Larkin Administration Building was derived by Banham from Margaret Ingels's *Willis Carrier, Father of Air Conditioning,* which erroneously implies that Wright's system was originated several years after the period (1902–7) when Carrier and others developed modern air conditioning.[30] The Larkin air-conditioning system was conceived by 1903, soon after Willis Carrier installed the "world's first scientific air-conditioning system" in the Sackett-Wilhelms Lithographing and Printing Company, late in 1902.[31] It is not clear precisely when the Larkin system was installed, but it was

in place by April 1907, when George Twitmyer, a Larkin chemist, wrote "A Model Administration Building" for *The Business Man's Magazine.* Twitmyer described the Larkin "Fresh Air System" this way:

. . . In cold weather the warm air is admitted near the floors and exhausted from near the ceiling. In hot weather the order is reversed. For use in hot weather there is provided with each blast apparatus a mechanical cooling device. The temperature of the fresh air coming in contact with these pipes is lowered sufficiently to make the building comfortable during the hottest weather.[32]

Frank Lloyd Wright's Larkin Building air-conditioning system does not rival Willis Carrier's pioneering work, which involved theoretical studies and the practical application of his findings, nor does it modify Reyner Banham's assessment of the Larkin building as "a watershed . . . a bridge between the history of modern architecture as commonly written — the progress of structure and external form — and a history of modern architecture understood as the progress of creating human environments."[33] But Wright was well informed earlier than has been recognized, and his 1903 Larkin system of air conditioning should be regarded as equally progressive as the other technological innovations in the Larkin design.[34]

Despite the advantages of fireproofing, good lighting, and a clean, cool environment, some 1,800 people worked together in the Larkin Administration Building under considerable pressure, with virtually no privacy. To balance this, Wright built a small annex on the east flank of the main block, echoing the forms of the larger building and containing five levels, each measuring approximately 2,200 square feet (see Fig. 65). The basement (Fig. 70) and the first and second floors of the annex were continuous with those of the main block, but the third and fourth stories were lowered. Wright made good use of these spaces to add variety to the work experience.

The first floor of the annex formed the entrance lobby to the entire building. Twin glazed vestibules

71 Annex foyer. (Courtesy The Frank Lloyd Wright Memorial Foundation)

72 Reception desk, annex lobby, ca. 1925. (Courtesy Daniel I. Larkin)

73 Reception desk and elevator shaft in annex lobby as seen from visitors' balcony. (Courtesy Buffalo and Erie County Historical Society)

74 Visitors' balcony, east wall of annex lobby. (Courtesy William Clarkson)

75 Wall-hung toilets, second floor of annex. (Courtesy William Clarkson)

(Fig. 71) inside the north and south entrance doors led to an ample semicircular reception desk that directed callers toward the high main hall (Fig. 72). Open elevator housings backed the reception desk (Fig. 73), while opposite it (a domestic note) there was a fireplace surmounted by a small balcony where visitors could write postcards describing their tour of the Larkin complex (Fig. 74). The fireplace was flanked by relief sculptures (see Figs. 99–102). The lobby was not large but Wright was able to impart monumentality to it by a bold use of pier, lintel, glass, and judicious ornament.

The second story of the annex, not well documented in photographs, contained metal lockers, wash basins, showers, and wall-hung toilets in separate sections for men and women (Figs. 75, 76). Wright introduced an elevator landing that protruded somewhat into the locker room, and from the landing visitors could observe the typewriter operators working in the main block. To enter the locker room workers could use small doorways under the visitors' balcony (visible in Fig. 45) or the annex stairs.

The third floor of the annex had a 10-foot ceiling, compared to 16 feet on the working balconies. On

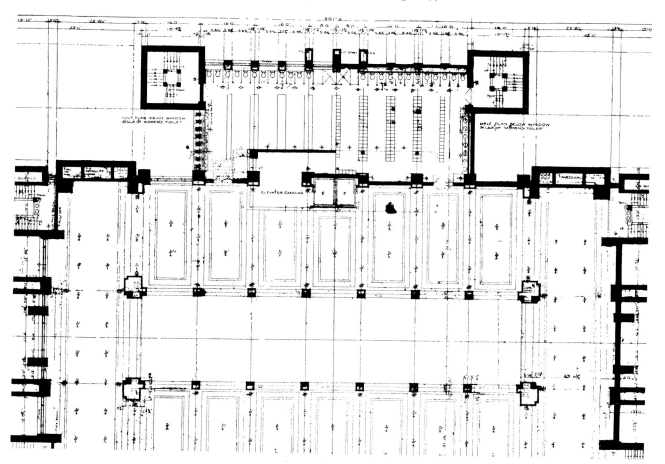

76 Plan of annex second floor. (H. Th. Wijdeveld, ed., *The Life Work of the American Architect Frank Lloyd Wright,* Saantport, Holland, 1925, p. 5)

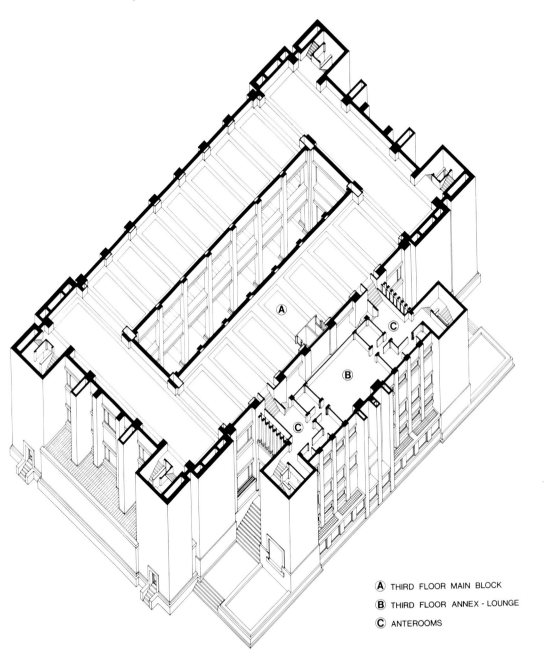

A   THIRD FLOOR MAIN BLOCK

B   THIRD FLOOR ANNEX - LOUNGE

C   ANTEROOMS

77 Axonometric view showing the differing levels of third floors in the annex and main building. (Drawn by James Cahill)

78 Lounge, third floor of annex. The skylight above the piano receives light from the light shaft between the annex and the main building. (Courtesy William Clarkson)

either side of a lounge space (Figs. 77–79) there was a set of emergency rooms with cots, an anteroom, and a small toilet room. The lounge, a refuge from the tensions of the workplace, was equipped with a fireplace, remarkably comfortable-looking wood and leather easy chairs, and some small tables, all designed by Wright. Drapes and flowers made this space warm and personal.

A fourth floor of the annex, shown in preliminary designs, was expanded in the master working drawings dated April 1, 1904. The floor, with 8-foot ceilings, was divided into three spaces: a classroom where office personnel were to be taught various aspects of English grammar and writing (Fig. 80); a small branch of the Buffalo Public Library (Fig. 81); and a YWCA room. Here were opportunities for self-improvement

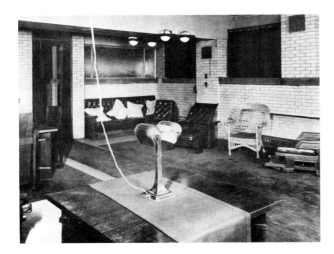

79 Lounge, third floor of annex. A fireplace is visible
behind the lounge chair at the right.

80 Classroom, fourth floor of annex. Behind the students
is the light shaft and the main building.

81 Library, fourth floor of annex.

82 Annex library as seen from third floor of main building. (Courtesy Buffalo and Erie County Historical Society)

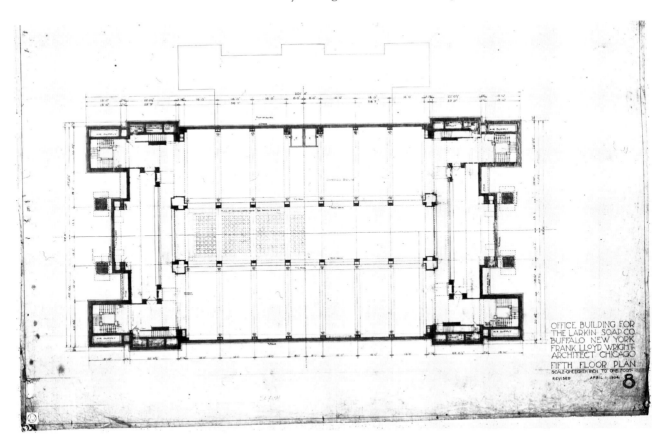

83 Fifth-floor plan. (© The Frank Lloyd Wright Foundation, 1987. Courtesy The Frank Lloyd Wright Memorial Foundation)

84 Kitchen, fifth floor.

85 Restaurant, fifth floor.

that benefited both the Larkin Company and the individual. The outside wall of the annex had no windows at the fourth-floor level; to illuminate the classroom Wright set a glazed shed on its west side facing the main block (see Fig. 80); the library and YWCA room had large rectangular skylights that also lit the access stairways.

The annex could accommodate many personal needs of the office worker, but Wright made access to it slightly difficult, as though to discourage overuse of the facilities. For example, anyone wishing to enter the second-floor locker rooms from the main block had to pass between groups of typists working beneath the low balcony used by visitors. It was something of a gauntlet.

Because of the low ceilings in the annex, the third floor of the main block stood midway between the third and fourth floors of the annex (see Fig. 76). Access from the main block to the annex was by way of twin sets of stairs that led upward to the YWCA and library and downward to the lounge (Fig. 82). Wright had separated the upper floors of the annex from the main block to create a light shaft which was bridged by these stairs. One flight passed tall windows (visible above the main entrance door in Fig. 97). These windows illuminated both the stair and the wash basins below. The stairs provided access to the annex but, like the low doorways beneath the visitors' balcony, they discouraged too-easy access.

The size of the annex indicates that only a fraction of the office workers were expected to use it at any one time. This was not true of the dining facilities, which served as many as two thousand people in shifts of up to six hundred during lunch hours. The dining area occupied two long sides of the fifth floor (Fig. 83); the ends housed the kitchen and bakery (Fig. 84). The dining area had low ceilings and blank outer walls like the fourth floor of the annex (Fig. 85). Light shone from the large skylight over the court and from small diamond-shaped skylights or from Nernst Glowers. Wright designed eight-person dining tables[35] with swivel tops that converted into benches for meetings; more than a thousand people could be seated. The dining spaces opened into the main hall and seem to have shared the spirit of familial unity. Messrs. Larkin, Martin, Heath, and the other executives dined here with the office staff and some of the factory force as well. Public visitors also were encouraged to dine here as part of their tour of the Larkin Company— good publicity for the idea of the Larkin extended family.

Frank Lloyd Wright's Larkin Administration Building is remarkable for the thoroughness with which it accommodated the Larkin working system and the working staff. Yet, beyond its problem-solving accommodations, Wright's design conveyed the humane ideals of the Larkin Company to the people who worked within it as well as to the public.

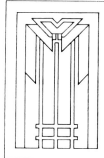
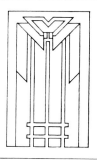
The idea that commercial buildings might convey some indication of corporate identity emerged during the Industrial Revolution and was realized most clearly in two building types: the industrial complex and the tall urban building. Both types had some bearing on the design of Frank Lloyd Wright's Larkin Administration Building. Manufacturing complexes often were depicted for advertising purposes in bird's-eye views; the panoramic sweep suggested years of solid growth and experience, and—by implication—high-quality products.[1] Tall buildings, on the other hand, often achieved distinction in the urban environments by way of great height (as in the Singer and Woolworth buildings), or unusual shape (as in the Fuller "Flatiron" Building), or by other features. In Larkin Company postcards (Fig. 86), letterheads, and general advertising one sees that John D. Larkin preferred panoramic views of the factory complex—not surprising in the light of his passion for building. Yet his original interest in having Louis Sullivan design a new administration building also suggests that he wanted a structure of uncommon distinction, perhaps similar to the Prudential Building Sullivan completed in downtown Buffalo in 1896. Wright's design for the Larkin Administration Building mediates between these two nineteenth-century commercial building types. At six and a half stories, it was lower than most of the Larkin factory and warehouse buildings, yet its powerful geometric forms made it distinctive. A glance at the administration building for Sears, Roebuck and Company (Fig. 87),

completed like the Larkin in 1906, reveals the extent to which Wright's design departed from the prevalent Beaux-Arts mode. Wright rejected the associative values of academic classicism to favor a more abstract architecture that does not immediately appear to refer to anything beyond itself. How, it might well be asked, could such a building convey meaning?

In fact, several levels of meaning were directed at observers inside and outside the Larkin Building. The present fame of the building rests principally upon its forthright exterior massing. Stair towers were echoed in towers for air exhaust; sculpture-bearing piers contained ducts carrying fresh air to internal balconies, while smaller piers were purely load-bearing. No portion of the design appears arbitrarily conceived.[2] While the Larkin Building's expression of function is generally considered to be its main contribution to the development of the Modern Movement in architecture, the expressive power of its sheer abstractness should not be underestimated. Thanks to an utter confidence in geometry and a fine sense of proportion, Wright was able to transform mundane mechanical devices into heroic features worthy of comparison with the pylons of Luxor or the westworks of the Romanesque churches. In Buffalo, what passer-by, ignorant of the internal functions, would not be impressed by the overwhelming order and authority of Wright's massing?

Despite Russell Sturgis's denunciation of the plainness of the Larkin Administration Building,[3] it included a thematically conceived program of sculpture

86 The Larkin complex, postcard view, ca. 1915.

87 Nimmins & Fellowes, Sears, Roebuck and Company Administration Building, Chicago, Illinois, 1906. (Courtesy Sears, Roebuck and Company)

88 Richard C. Bock and Frank Lloyd Wright, pier sculptures on main façades of Larkin Administration Building. (Courtesy Buffalo and Erie County Historical Society)

89 Bock and Wright, pier sculpture for main façades. (Courtesy Richard C. Bock Collection, Greenville College, Greenville, Illinois)

90 Bock sketch for pier sculpture. (Courtesy Richard C. Bock Collection, Greenville College, Greenville, Illinois)

developed by Wright in collaboration with Richard Bock, an artist of modest talent who was willing to follow Wright's lead.[4] The sculpture program was essential to the full realization of the Larkin Building. Exterior sculpture consisted of two sets of freestanding putti and globes atop the large piers of the north and south façades (Figs. 88–92); capitals on structural piers along the flanks of the building (Figs. 93, 94); and intaglio reliefs with fountains alongside the two main entrances (Figs. 95–98). The sculpture program continued inside with twin bas-reliefs on either side of the fireplace in the entrance lobby (Figs. 99–103), and with capitals for the piers defining the light court (Figs. 104, 105). Sculpture was used sparingly, but it

91 Bock and Wright, sculpture for piers of main façades. (Courtesy Richard C. Bock Collection, Greenville College, Greenville, Illinois)

served important functions: together with a plenitude of related inscriptions it accented the design at crucial points; it provided continuity between exterior and interior; it conveyed elevating messages to the Larkin office force about the nature of work; and it declared the aspirations and identity of the Larkin Company.[5]

The most conspicuous sculptures were the 6-foot globes supported by teams of putti atop four over-sized piers on the front and back of the building at fifth-floor level (see Fig. 88);[6] these were the only free-standing sculptures used. Each pair of putti held aloft a scroll bearing the word "Larkin" at right angles to the façade (see Fig. 89). There were eight such scrolls approximately 18 inches high; their placement high on the building in often shaded areas made them difficult to read from the street.[7] Wright appears more concerned with the formal value of the pier sculptures than with their message. Other spherical motifs visible in preliminary sketches would seem to support this contention. Among Richard Bock's papers there is a

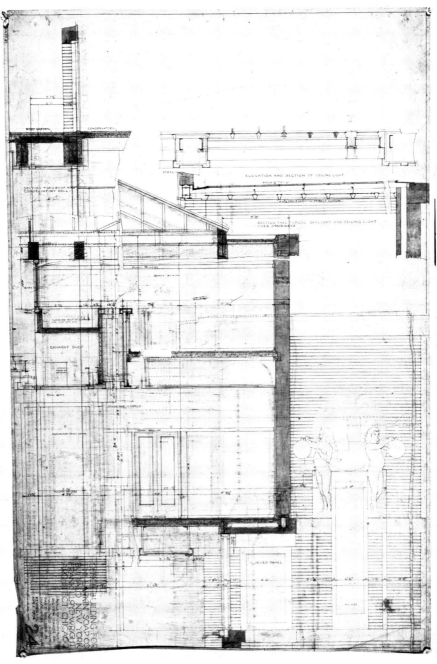

92 Fifth- and sixth-floor section (master working drawing) with sketch of pier sculpture. (© The Frank Lloyd Wright Foundation, 1987. Courtesy The Frank Lloyd Wright Memorial Foundation)

93 Bock and Wright, pier capitals at fourth-floor level of east and west façades. (Courtesy Richard C. Bock Collection, Greenville College, Greenville, Illinois)

sketch of a globe supported on the backs of four kneeling female figures (see Fig. 90), and among the Larkin drawings in the archives of the Frank Lloyd Wright Memorial Foundation is a façade sketch with a putto blowing an enormous soap bubble (see Fig. 92); both sketches are thematically weak (if not downright silly), but they suggest that Wright's principal concern was a spherical motif. The sculptures, as finally realized, were not distinguished works of art, but were well suited to Wright's larger aesthetic considerations. The architectonic stiffness of the putti's crossed arms relates them to the planes and crisp edges of piers and towers, while the smooth spherical globes provide counterpoint to the unrelenting rectilinearity of the building.

The sculptural configuration on the façades was also essential to connecting the exterior and the interior of the building—a particularly important consideration in a building that was designed to shut out its environment and that provided little indication on its exterior of the bright airiness within. The position of the oversized, sculpture-bearing piers on the north and south façades aligned exactly with the piers that frame the great light court inside. Furthermore, the vertical development of the exterior piers rising from simple rectangular brick shafts to striated tops, and then to putti and globes, foreshadowed a similar but more significant vertical development within the light court itself—the culmination of the entire design.

The capital of each pier along the exterior flanks of

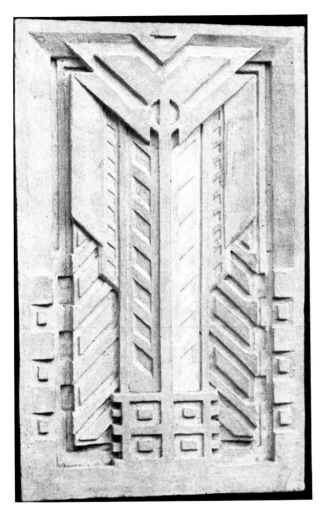

94 Bock and Wright, model for pier capitals. (Courtesy Richard C. Bock Collection, Greenville College, Greenville, Illinois)

95 Bock and Wright, intaglio relief and fountain on Swan Street façade of annex. (Courtesy Buffalo and Erie County Historical Society)

the main block of the Larkin Building consisted of three matching terra-cotta plates, molded with bases supporting vertical shafts from which chevrons branched upward at a 45-degree angle, easing the transition from vertical pier to the broad horizontal wall of the fifth story (see Figs. 93, 94).[8] The similarity between these chevrons and the vee created by the crossed arms of the globe-supporting putti must have

been intended by Wright. The upward thrust of these patterns worked against the rectangular forms of the building and moreover caused the fifth-floor wall to appear to sit lightly in place.

The fountain reliefs at the bases of the annex stair towers continued the theme of global enterprise established in the pier sculptures but with the inclusion of inscriptions devised by William R. Heath, Larkin's Office Manager; they carried a message for the office force as well as for the public (see Figs. 95, 96).[9] The fountains were formed by 8-foot-square intaglio panels placed above a thin sheet of water falling into a long rectangular basin. Each relief included two heraldic figures facing each other across an inscribed panel above which rested a small globe backed by crossed keys. The figures, personifications of virtues,

96 Bock and Wright, intaglio relief and fountain on Seneca Street façade of annex. (Courtesy The Frank Lloyd Wright Memorial Foundation)

97 Annex, Seneca Street entrance. (Courtesy Buffalo and Erie County Historical Society)

98 Elevated view of Seneca Street entrance. (Courtesy Daniel I. Larkin)

wear quasi-classical drapery subjected to Wright's geometrizing.[10] Similar abstract, architectonic figures became commonplaces of the 1930s style in American buildings.

On the Swan Street fountain relief a helmeted male figure held a torch, symbolizing truth, in one hand and what appears to have been a scroll, suggesting the importance of knowledge, in the other (see Fig. 95). His female counterpart carried a caduceus, representing commerce, and a sprig, for peace. The appearance of a globe in this relief in conjunction with an inscription, "FREEDOM TO EVERY MAN AND COMMERCE WITH ALL THE WORLD," reaffirmed the Larkin Company's desire to be recognized as a worldwide business enterprise. It also iterated the promise of the Larkin Company motto — "Factory to Family; Save All Cost Which Adds No Value" — that everyone, both customers and employees, would gain a measure of economic freedom (and spiritual freedom as well, as we shall see) through the success of the company principles.

The fountain relief on the Seneca Street side was nearly identical to the one just described (see Fig. 96).[11] It bore the inscription, "HONEST LABOR NEEDS NO MASTER SIMPLE JUSTICE NEEDS NO SLAVES," addressed more directly to the Larkin employees, most of whom entered the building on this side because of its proximity to the factories. With this inscription William Heath established the theme of the virtue of work that he elaborated on the interior of the Larkin building.

Surviving photographs do not indicate how Frank Lloyd Wright used the two fountains to draw people into the experience of his building. Because the fountains were located a full story above ground level, persons standing on the street would perceive the intaglio relief and the falling water in two dimensions (see Fig. 97), but as they mounted the first set of steps along the path of entry (see Fig. 98), it would become apparent that the thin sheet of water met the long rectangle of water in the catch basin in a neat 90-degree juxtaposition of planes. The visitor then walked on the same level, immediately next to the surface of water in the catch basin. Moreover, Wright's fountain configurations stood immediately beside and parallel to landings, stairways, and glazed entries, thus comprising the full approach sequence to the building. Wright's fountain involved the visitor in graduated increments: first, the symbolic reliefs, then the more explicit inscriptions, and finally, the subliminal effects of water heard and even felt as well as seen. The water carried connotations of cleanliness and freshness that were wholly appropriate to a soap-manufacturing company, but it is tempting to imagine in Wright's refined water planes a subtle reference to the cool interior of the building and the air-washing apparatus that produced it.[12]

The lobby reliefs continued themes established on the exterior — the virtues of work and the global aspirations of the Larkin Company. The lobby sculptures were conditioned also by the functions and configuration of the lobby space, a small semipublic area through which most of the 1,800 Larkin office workers passed each day, and into which groups of visitors were gathered for tours of the building and the rest of the factory complex.[13] Wright planned three relief panels to frame the fireplace on the east wall of the lobby (see Fig. 100), but a long panel meant to surmount the fireplace was never realized. No photograph of the east wall survives, but line drawings of the flanking panels (see Fig. 101), a lone photograph of the "Aurora" panel in situ (see Fig. 102), and three sketches and working drawings (see Figs. 99, 100, 103) provide intimations of iconographic intentions.[14] Figure 99 indicates that Wright considered mosaic panels and art glass windows for the east wall of the lobby, but these were changed to sculpture after April 1904. Aurora and her counterpart were winged figures in geometrized drapery, standing in cruciform postures with attributes in extended hands.[15] They functioned, in part, as directors of traffic: To one entering the building their barrier-like attitudes suggested a turn toward the light court, while to one leaving the light court their arms pointed to the exits. Inscriptions on vertical panels beneath their arms carried inspirational messages intended primarily for the Larkin office force. Beneath Aurora's right arm supporting a

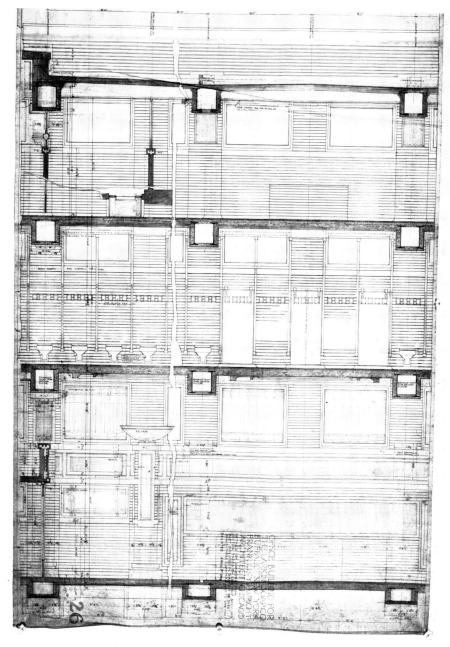

99 Elevation (master working drawing), east wall of annex. Lobby portion shows long rectangular mosaic over fireplace, visitors' balcony, and art glass windows. Relief panel to the left of the fireplace is reduced in the drawing. (© The Frank Lloyd Wright Foundation, 1987. Courtesy The Frank Lloyd Wright Memorial Foundation)

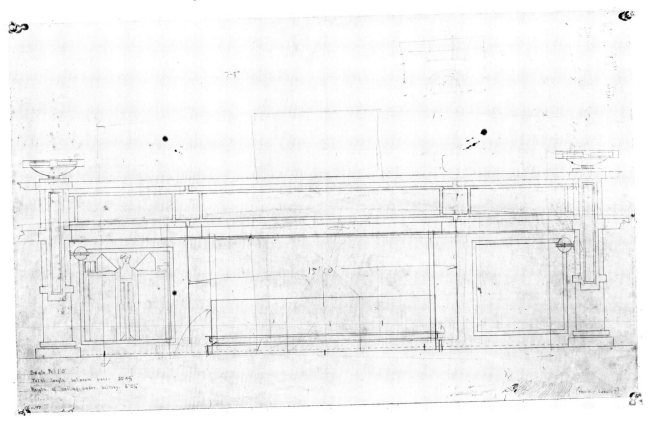

100 Sketch of east wall of annex lobby showing location of relief panel. (© The Frank Lloyd Wright Foundation, 1987. Courtesy The Frank Lloyd Wright Memorial Foundation)

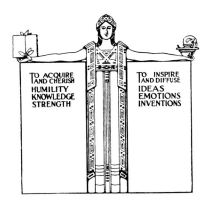

101 Drawings based on relief sculptures on east wall of annex lobby. (From a Larkin restaurant menu)

102 Bock and Wright. "Aurora" panel, east wall of annex lobby. (*Buffalo Arts Journal*, 2, October 1925, p. 54)

laurel wreath (a symbol of achievement) appeared the following: "To Encourage and Reward PURPOSE EFFORT ACHIEVEMENT"; her other hand held a globe, a symbol of authority (and, given its appearance elsewhere in the Larkin sculpture program, a symbol of the company's ambitions, as well), which is associated with the inscription, "To Establish and Maintain ORDER HARMONY EXCELLENCE." The other maiden held a book and a lamp representing learning and enlightenment; the inscription read, "To Acquire and Cherish HUMILITY KNOWLEDGE STRENGTH" and "To Inspire and Diffuse IDEAS EMOTIONS INVENTIONS" (see Figs. 101, 102). The close correspondence between the inscriptions and the attributes in these reliefs is indicative of collaboration between Wright, Richard Bock, and William Heath, the author of the inscriptions.

103 Bock, sketch for annex lobby relief. (Courtesy Richard C. Bock Collection, Greenville College, Greenville, Illinois)

The image of power and authority conveyed by the brick towers of the Larkin Administration Building gave way to a lighter more skeletal interior for which no figurative sculpture was designed. The simplicity of the Larkin reticulated interior as seen in the standard photographs is somewhat deceptive (see Fig. 29); Wright, in collaboration with his clients, was able to manifest the ideals of the Larkin Company inside in a highly affecting manner.[16]

104 View from fifth-floor balcony of main building toward kitchen and conservatory above. (Courtesy Buffalo and Erie County Historical Society)

By 1903, when Wright was designing its building, the Larkin Company had established itself as a progressive organization fully committed to the idea of industrial betterment intended to enhance the workers' morale and commitment to the business.[17] The dominant theme proclaimed in the light court — the virtuousness of work — gave this program a plausible unity. The Larkin Company provided noon-hour concerts and lectures, workers' clubs, annual picnics, educational incentives, low-cost loans, and other benefits in order to promote the workers' positive attitude toward the company, but work itself re-

mained, inevitably, the central function of the business. Sculptures and inscriptions directed the employees away from the common notion of work as mindless drudgery and toward the belief that work well done is inherently edifying.[18] Additional possibilities of advancement and success through hard work frequently were presented in the Larkin staff publication, *Ourselves*.

Larkin executives and their architect, Frank Lloyd Wright, sincerely believed in the virtue of work. All were men of strong, if varied, religious convictions who achieved considerable success. John D. Larkin

105 View across light court, fifth-floor level. The inscriptions have been retouched in this photograph. (Courtesy Buffalo and Erie County Historical Society)

and Darwin D. Martin began working at the ages of eleven and twelve, respectively, and are remembered by their descendants as men all but consumed by work throughout their lives.[19] According to the historian Daniel T. Rodgers, Elbert Hubbard, following his departure from the Larkin Company,[20] made the dignity of labor a consistent theme of his voluminous popular writings. And Edgar Tafel, a former associate of Frank Lloyd Wright, recalls that Wright's idea of recreation was to change from one kind of work to another for a period of time, a practice eventually institutionalized for his apprentices in the Taliesin Fellowship.[21]

Comments on work appear frequently in the correspondence of Larkin executives. John Larkin, hoping to persuade William Heath to join the Larkin Company in 1899, wrote: "We have learned that to succeed requires close attention to the business at hand and plenty of hard work." [22] Similarly, when Wright complained to Darwin Martin in 1910 that the people of Oak Park were snubbing him because of his affair with Mrs. Cheney, Martin wrote to him: "Abide your time. Meanwhile work. Mow away little things already at hand. . . . Take care of the puttering things DDM has asked you to do. Take care of every darned little thing that confronts you. You never in your life have tried this before." [23] Wright's reply reveals that he, too, was immersed in the work ethic: "Remember, I started to work, too, when I was eleven—educated myself and paid my board from that time on and if you think the stand I have taken in Architecture is not the fruit of sweat and concentration and grind you must go and guess again." [24]

In the Larkin light court, work was exalted almost to a religious level. This atmosphere was attained by careful orchestration of staff, structure, sculpture, light, and explicit inscriptions. At fifth-floor level across the short ends of the light court were two quotations from the Sermon on the Mount: "All Things Whatsoever Ye Would that Men Should Do to You, Do Ye Even So to Them," and "Ask and It Shall Be Given You. Seek and Ye Shall Find. Knock and It Shall Be Opened unto You" (see Fig. 104). Between

piers on the sides of the court (see Fig. 105) there appeared fourteen sets of three inspirational words each, such as:

GENEROSITY	INTEGRITY	IMAGINATION
ALTRUISM	LOYALTY	JUDGMENT
SACRIFICE	FIDELITY	INITIATIVE[25]

These word groups are explained in an unsigned article in *The Larkin Idea* of May 1907 (Appendix E), probably written by William Heath, the author of most of the inscriptions:

On each of the panels at the side of the court are three words, sequential in meaning. Simple words were inscribed rather than great quotations because they permit independence of thought and individuality of interpretation. A great thought once in words, however aptly put, is like a carved image; it is accepted as complete by all but the closest reasoners. A simple word is suggestive; it is a text for the exercise of reason or imagination. And so these simple words, the great words of the English language, rather than quotation . . .[26]

When the inscriptions in the interior of the Larkin Administration Building are considered, it becomes apparent that Wright and his clients aimed at a transcendental atmosphere; indeed they were fairly steeped in transcendentalism. Quotations from Ralph Waldo Emerson appear with some frequency in the Larkin staff publication, *Ourselves.*[27] William Heath and his wife held weekly readings and discussions of Emerson with other Larkin executive families,[28] and Elbert Hubbard, who remained on close terms with the Martins and the Heaths after he left the Larkin Company in 1893 (Mrs. Heath was his sister), published an edition of Emerson's *Nature* in 1905 when the Larkin Administration Building was still under construction.[29] In the letter to Wright, of October 1910, Darwin Martin admonishes him: "Do not forget Emerson. He gave it to us straight." [30] The historian Raymond H. Geselbracht identified Wright's part in a transcendental renaissance of the arts between 1890

106 View of light court, looking north from second-floor balcony. (Courtesy Daniel I. Larkin)

107 Capitals of piers surrounding the light court at fifth-floor level. (Courtesy William Clarkson)

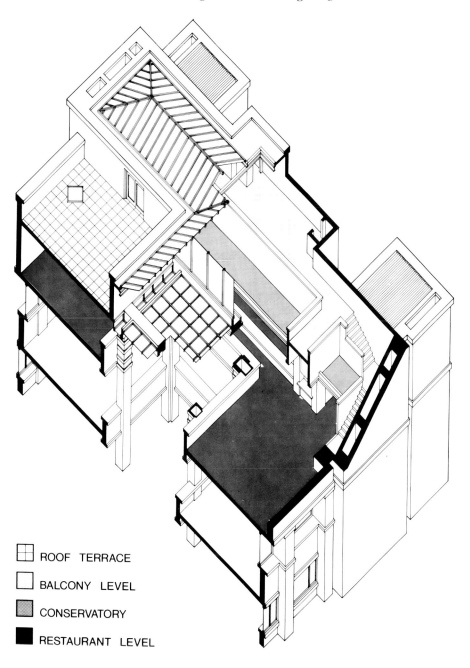

ROOF TERRACE

BALCONY LEVEL

CONSERVATORY

RESTAURANT LEVEL

108 Axonometric view of fifth-floor (restaurant and kitchen level), conservatory, and balcony levels. (Drawn by James Cahill)

109 Fifth floor, conservatory, and balcony under construction. (Courtesy The Frank Lloyd Wright Memorial Foundation)

110 Conservatory, sixth-floor level. (*The Larkin Idea,* 7, July 1907, p. 3)

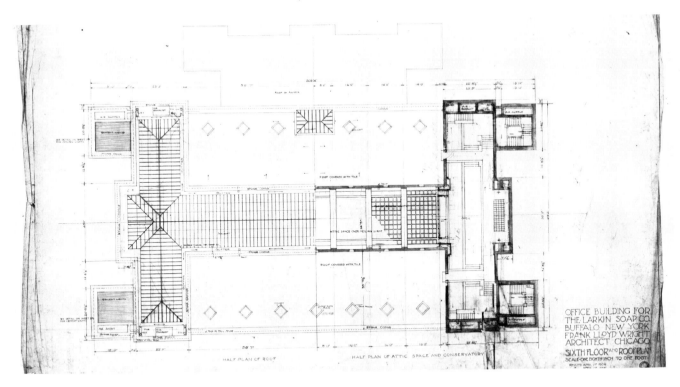

111 Sixth-floor plan. (© The Frank Lloyd Wright Foundation, 1987. Courtesy The Frank Lloyd Wright Memorial Foundation)

and 1920 in the *New England Quarterly*, 1975,[31] and Wright acknowledged his indebtedness to Emerson in *An Autobiography*.[32]

The Larkin light court thus can be seen to exemplify Emerson's belief in the unity of all things in nature and in the aspiration of all matter to a spiritual ideal. The brick piers surrounding the light court rose 76 feet from the main floor to a double-glazed skylight through which diffused light — Wright's medium of transcendence — flooded into the space (Fig. 106). The sculptured pier capitals dissolved into scintillating fragments with the play of light (Fig. 107). Gilded inscriptions on the balcony fronts shone brightly, while nearby, at the ends of the sixth floor, palms, ferns, and vines glistened in the brighter light of single-glazed conservatories (Figs. 108–111).[33] The Larkin executives' awareness of the impact of these factors is apparent in *The Larkin Idea* of May 1907:

The letters of these words are wonderfully decorative. In form, they are in harmony with the design of the building. They are done in gold. Viewed from the floors below they and the accompanying decorative arrangements of rectangles catch and reflect the gleam from the skylight, giving against the montone of the magnesite work a novel, though strikingly beautiful effect.[34]

The hierarchy — from plain, solid piers to elaborate capitals to living plants (from dead to living matter), and then, with light accenting gilded inscriptions, to the realm of ideas — is wholly Emersonian. In accord with Emerson's belief that man is the highest organization in nature, the system was completed by the presence of Darwin Martin and William Heath

112 A noon-time event in the light court: evangelist Billy Sunday addresses the Larkin employees, ca. 1915.

at the center of the main floor beneath the skylight.[35] These two men, who actually ran the company for John Larkin, embodied the ideal of virtuous work.

Did Wright's interior design succeed? There are no surviving records on which to base a factual assessment. Judging from recollections by former Larkin employees and visitors, however, no one had negative memories. Carolyn Prather, secretary for several years beginning in 1911, recalled the interior of the administration building as "beautiful . . . beautiful,"[36] and John Mueller, a Larkin commercial artist in the 1920s, described the building as "a work of art."[37] More informative comments can be cited. Mrs. Milton Davidson (her son Walter was an accountant for the Larkin Company after 1906 and commissioned a house from Wright in 1908) visited the Administration Building in 1907 and wrote to her other children describing a noon-time concert: "Their three numbers were not only a great pleasure to listen to, but it was also a joy to see the tier upon tier of young faces and applauding hands [Fig. 112]. You have both seen the office. . . . After lunch father saw some of the details of the great office and you know that the nobility underlying the mere structure and the successful accomplishment of the betterment of working conditions there carried out must impress anyone, but more so a nature such as father's."[38]

The eminent German modernist architect, Eric Mendelsohn, wrote to his wife from the floor of the light court in 1924, marveling at the hum of work activity that enveloped the thousand employees within the great space.[39] Others have corroborated his impressions. Evelyn Jacobsen (daughter of William Heath) worked in the Administration Building in the early 1920s, shortly after her graduation from Vassar College. Mrs. Jacobsen recalls Frank Lloyd Wright with considerable antipathy; his numerous and demanding visits to the Heaths, especially when he was plagued by personal notoriety, were a source of some embarrassment to this highly principled and religious family. Nevertheless, in two separate interviews Mrs. Jacobsen recalled an almost magical aura of calmness and order within the Larkin light court, despite the activity of so many office workers. She felt Wright "must have been a genius to design that building,"[40] and remembered being unhappy when her own office was moved out of the Administration Building to a converted church building next door.

The consideration given by Wright and his clients to the exaltation of work in the Larkin Building was pursued with the same zeal and thoroughness that went into the design of air conditioning, fireproofing, acoustics, and planning. If these features contributed to the uniqueness of the building, they also contained the seeds of its doom. The central placement of Darwin Martin and William Heath on the main floor of the light court may have suited their temperaments and beliefs about work, but it ignored the possibility that they might be replaced by other executives with different, even conflicting, ideas and beliefs. When this happened, in the 1920s, the future of the Larkin Administration Building was thrown into uncertainty.

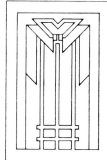

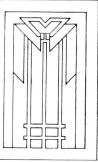

From the moment the Larkin Administration Building was completed in the fall of 1906 Frank Lloyd Wright and his clients in the Larkin Company attempted to justify its unique design and obvious costliness in a series of published statements that continued over five decades. Eleven of the first fifteen articles written about the building (from 1906 to 1913) were published by the Larkin Company, and Wright wrote about the building eleven times between 1906 and 1957 (see Appendix F). Wright, in fact, did more than anyone to shape the critical estimate of the Larkin Building that prevails today.

This unusual phenomenon in the history of architecture raises a number of questions: In what way did Wright's writings and the company's articles affect present-day views of the building? What can be learned about it from these texts? An inquiry into criticism of the Larkin Building reveals that these writings, though often undistinguished, are useful in trying to re-create a fair and comprehensive image of the building. It also becomes apparent that facts were used selectively by Wright, by the Larkin Company writers, and by modern historians to form a positive, simplified view of the building. This chapter will present a critical history of the building, assembling resources for a deeper and more truly balanced criticism of the Larkin Administration Building.

Frank Lloyd Wright was asked in 1906 by his patrons, the Larkin executives, to write an article for *The Larkin Idea* (Appendix G),[1] a monthly magazine addressed to consumers, justifying the new office building. Cost was of particular concern to a company

whose motto was "Factory to Family; Save All Cost Which Adds No Value." Wright's article, the first published on the building, remains the most informative one written on the subject despite writings on the building by virtually every historian of modern architecture since the 1920s. Wright's major premise is that fireproofing, clean air, sanitary conditions, and a quiet, peaceful environment are worth extra cost because they promote worker productivity and efficiency. He explains how numerous design innovations implement the functional requirements of the commission. Citing the unhealthy, noisy site, he writes: "The design of the building derives its outward character from this circumstance perhaps more than from any other."[2] Wright explains that stair towers and ventilation ducts were set at the outer corners of the building to maximize natural light for the balconies and the court, and to provide ample fire escape routes and easy communication between floors, as well as ready access to enclosed mechanical systems. Innovative office furniture and plumbing fixtures are said to save time and money, and the use of imported materials (magnesite imported from Greece, iron fencing from Chicago, capstones quarried on Lake Superior) is justified on the grounds of durability and quality. Wright addresses the functional determination of every part of the design and the careful interaction of part to part, function to function. Style was so inevitable a product of such design that he discusses it only briefly: "Simplicity, straightforwardness, good materials and dignified proportion of the various parts are all that give it architectural effect . . ."[3] And in conclusion he writes:

Finally—it seems to me—that the American flag is the only flag that would look well on or in this building; the only flag with its simple stars and bars that wouldn't look incongruous and out of place with the simple rectangular masses of the exterior and the straightforward rectilinear treatment of the interior. I think our building is wholly American in its directness and freshness of treatment. It wears no badge of servitude to foreign 'styles' yet it avails itself gratefully of the treasures and the wisdom bequeathed to it by its ancestors.[4]

This direct assertion of an American architecture was more fully articulated in Wright's "In the Cause of Architecture" in the *Architectural Record* of March 1908.

The Larkin Company published five additional articles on the office building during the six years following its completion. William R. Heath's "The Office Building and What It Will Bring to the Office Force" (Appendix H)[5] and the anonymous "Inscriptions on the Court of the Administration Building" (Appendix E)[6] are of minor interest here since they do not deal specifically with Wright's design; Rogers Dickinson's "A Great American Success," from *The Larkin Idea,* February 1907, likewise has only two paragraphs pertaining to the "great office building."[7]

Two major articles are George E. Twitmyer's "A Model Administration Building," published in the *Business Man's Magazine* of April 1907 (Appendix I) and abridged for *The Larkin Idea* of August 1907,[8] and Marion Harland's *My Trip Thru the Larkin Factories* (Appendix J),[9] a ninety-four-page booklet commissioned by the Larkin Company in 1913. Both authors are primarily concerned with literal descriptions of the building and quantitative data; neither is particularly sensitive to architectural qualities. Twitmyer's few aesthetic observations derive from Wright's article in *The Larkin Idea,* November 1906. Compare his statement, "In general form and all prominent points the building is rectangular, massive cliff-like walls, relieved by splendid deep reveals . . . ,"[10] to

Wright's, "Outside the building is an enormous pile of impervious brick with splendid deep reveals."[11] Marion Harland quotes the eminent Dutch architect H.P. Berlage, who visited the Larkin Building in 1911 and published his evaluation of it in an article in 1912 (quoted below).[12] Their shortcomings notwithstanding, the Twitmyer and Harland texts are essential for an understanding of the total functioning of the Larkin Building. Twitmyer, a Larkin chemist, describes the major dimensions of the building, the materials, the fresh-air system, the electrical lighting, the furniture, and the principal uses of space. Twitmyer's article complements Wright's overview.[13]

Marion Harland's *My Trip Thru the Larkin Factories* is uniquely valuable because she treats the Administration Building as part of the whole Larkin factory complex—something no recent historian has done. Moreover, her concern with women's activities is indeed pertinent. Hundreds of thousands of Larkin customers were housewives, and the Administration Building was occupied chiefly by women office workers. Ms. Harland, an accomplished author, devoted nine pages and five illustrations to the Administration Building, emphasizing restaurant and kitchen, support spaces in the annex, and daily tasks of transcribers and stenographers.[14] Her sensitivity to the human activities within the building complements Wright's and Twitmyer's texts, and, writing in 1913, she had the advantage of observing the building after several years of operation.

None of these authors is infallible. For instance, Twitmyer says that the Larkin Building has seven floors while Harland states emphatically that it has five;[15] and some of Wright's claims for his furniture innovations recently have been disputed.[16] Yet, considered together, the Wright, Twitmyer, and Harland writings provide a substantial body of information from which the now-demolished Larkin Administration Building can, with the aid of plans, drawings, photographs, and interviews, be reconstituted in near entirety.

The first article from outside the Wright-Larkin ambit, Charles Illsley's "The Larkin Administration Building, Buffalo," appeared in a Chicago periodical, the *Inland Architect and News Record* of July 1907.[17] It introduced negative criticism; although Illsley was enthusiastic about some aspects of the building, he objected to the contradiction between massive outer towers and an open, light-filled inner court, claiming "a long honored canon of architecture is that a building's exterior must so match its interior as to proclaim its intended use . . . all through, outside as well as inside."[18] Illsley ignored the functional reasons for Wright's design and the unexpected delight so many visitors experienced upon entering the building and discovering the great light court.[19] He was the first of many historians and critics who used Gothic designations to describe Wright's building. Perhaps it was "cathedral-like" as Illsley said, but "nave," "aisles," "triforia," "clerestory," and "galleries" reveal his refusal to deal with the building on its own terms.[20]

Illsley's article was noticed by the current periodicals editor of *Architectural Review* (Boston) which in July 1907 published two exterior photographs of the Larkin Building along with this comment:

The most notable thing in *The Inland Architect* for July is Mr. Frank Lloyd Wright's Administration Building for the Larkin Company in Buffalo—about as fine a piece of original composition as one could expect to find. This sort of thing is absolutely in the line of creative architecture.[21]

This was followed by the significant publication of the Larkin Building in America's leading architectural publication, the *Architectural Record*.[22] The March 1908 issue contained a folio of thirty-four Wright buildings and projects illustrated in eighty-seven photographs accompanied by the first installment of his fundamental statement of principles, "In the Cause of Architecture." The Larkin Building was presented first and most extensively in eleven photographs—probably an indication of Wright's own high regard for this building. His Figures 1 and 2 are accompanied by a lengthy caption, written by the architect, in which the demands of the site, the functional organization of the building, and its principal design innovations are set forth concisely. Concerning style Wright makes only a brief comment: "Here

again most of the critic's 'architecture' has been left out. Therefore the work may have the same claim to consideration as a 'work of art' as an ocean liner, a locomotive or a battleship."[23] This caption is, in effect, a condensation of Wright's "The New Larkin Administration Building," in *The Larkin Idea* of November 1906.

Wright had little time to enjoy this lavish appreciation; the succeeding issue of the *Architectural Record* carried an unfavorable review of the Larkin Building by the dean of American critics, Russell Sturgis (Appendix K). Sturgis, a Victorian architect turned critic, achieved eminence through writings: a three-volume *Dictionary of Architecture and Building* (1901), *How to Judge Architecture* (1903), two volumes of a four-volume *History of Architecture* (1906), and other books and critical essays. Despite this background, or perhaps because of it, Sturgis was unable to understand Wright's building. He wrote about the building from photographs instead of visiting the site and he made careless factual errors. Sturgis's lifelong commitment to the great historical styles of architecture is evidenced in a Gothic descriptive vocabulary like Charles Illsley's and in such further inappropriate terms as "attic base" for the foundation walls of the building and "fan light" for the large rectangular window above each entrance door (see Fig. 66).[24]

Sturgis's article has been characterized as profoundly negative on the strength of this paragraph:

Few persons who have seen the great monuments of the past, or adequate photographs of them; who have loved them and have tried to surprise their secret of artistic charm, will fail to pronounce this monument, as seen in Fig. 1, an extremely ugly building. It is, in fact, a monster of awkwardness, if we look at its lines and masses alone.[25]

As a whole, however, the review is more equivocal than this brief condemnation suggests:

[The Larkin Building] is only capable of interesting that student who is quite aware that the architects of the modern world during fifty years of struggle have failed to make anything of the old system—the system of following the ancient styles with the avowed purpose of developing some one of them and going on to other things.[26]

Later he continues:

If, now, we seek to take up a sympathetic position, to consider the building as perhaps the architect himself considered it, there are to notice the care given to the plan and disposition of the halls and rooms, the care which has evidently resulted in a successful utilitarian building.[27]

Ever equivocal, Sturgis turns to formalist critical principles, light and shadow, mass, proportion, and color. Convinced that "all design in pure form . . . is design in light and shade," [28] Sturgis suggests, at considerable length, how the Larkin Administration Building could be improved by the addition of moldings, sculpture, and color patterns in the brick. Concluding, he passes quickly over massing and proportion (the most striking formal aspects of the design) in favor of a discussion of color—a peculiar choice for one judging (admittingly) from black-and-white photographs only.[29]

The impact of Russell Sturgis's article cannot be measured, but it is worth considering that no American critic contested this review or even wrote about the Larkin Building for almost twenty years. Thirty years passed before Wright received another administration building commission (the Johnson's Wax headquarters in Racine, Wisconsin). Throughout an extraordinarily prolific career Wright received only a handful of large-scale commercial commissions of any kind. There are various explanations for this: Wright made his reputation as a domestic architect, and, after all, many of his ideas about architecture and other things were too "experimental" for the traditionally conservative element of American business. Such people ignored the extraordinary potential of the Larkin design.

Wright composed a strong "Reply to Mr. Sturgis's Criticism" (Appendix L).[30] This apparently was submitted to the *Architectural Record* but was withheld from publication out of deference to the critic, who died on February 11, 1909 at the age of seventy-two.

The Larkin Company, nevertheless, published a thin, hardcover volume in April 1909 containing Wright's reply to Sturgis accompanied by reprints of the full text and photographic section of his "In the Cause of Architecture" from the *Architectural Record*, the Sturgis review, and a Sturgis obituary from the magazine *Outlook*. The Larkin publication must have been limited; only a single copy is known to exist today. At any rate, Wright's passionate and articulate defense of his work and his architectural principles has remained totally unknown since 1909.

Wright's principal attack is centered on the critic's desire to decorate the blank walls of the Larkin Building. Angered by Sturgis's insensitivity to the simple, functional design, Wright denounces historical eclecticism in the strongest possible language, tinged with scorn, in the opening paragraphs:

To see an eminent architectural critic picking over, bit by bit, his architectural rag-bag for architectural finery wherewith to clothe the nakedness of the young giant whose very muscularity offends as it confronts him is pathetic.

"Admitting that the chase of the Neo-Classic, of the Gothic, and of the French Romanesque has come to nothing," I submit that we are further away from a living style of architecture than ever, chiefly because of the conception rooted in the mind of the architect and the critic alike that architecture consists, or ever did consist, in manufacturing with ornamental moldings and chamfered edges a fabric flickering with light and shade, to be applied to a structure as a porous plaster might be applied to an aching back, or worn as a dickey in the time of our grandfathers—*for effect.*[31]

Wright contests Sturgis's article point by point, sometimes using the critic's own phrases (as in the preceding paragraph) to undermine his credibility. John Ruskin, one of Sturgis's heroes, is excoriated for falsifying "the nature of our aesthetic problem" (that is, for calling for an eclectic approach), and for leaving "in his wake a train of reactionaries not yet disposed of." Wright also takes exception to certain of Sturgis's descriptive terms. Whereas the critic claims that the stair towers "mask" the structure, to Wright they give it "emphasis." Wright rejects the use of the word "ugly" in relation to the Larkin Building on the grounds that it is an entirely subjective term and, in this case, unsubstantiated. Having said this, Wright reverses himself and descends momentarily to the level of the critic: "I make no plea for ugliness, nor is ugliness necessary, —although I think the buildings Mr. Sturgis, in an unguarded moment permitted himself to build, are very ugly." [32]

The pervasive ineptitude and equivocation in Sturgis's article provoked Wright to include in his reply a uniquely concise statement of his architectural principles. He had already published such a statement in March 1908, but that piece, "In the Cause of Architecture," addressed the concept of the Prairie house and suffered from being overambitious and diffuse. Sturgis's negative criticism provided Wright with the stimulus to refine his aesthetic principles.

Wright says (quoting Sturgis), " 'When the great buildings of the world were designed' they were legitimate expressions of the industrial order and social ideal underlying them." He characterizes industrial conditions in the early twentieth century as "totally different in cause and effect from anything which determined previous forms." Having established this point of departure Wright argues for a return to "first principles" — "for less heat and parasitism, and more light and pragmatic integrity; for less architecture in quotation marks and more engineering. I feel that the sceptre of his art has all but passed from the hands of the architect to the hands of the engineer, and if it is ever to be the architect's again he must take it from the engineer by force of superior virtue." [33] This is succeeded by a paean to abstract form unmatched in eloquence throughout Frank Lloyd Wright's copious writings:

Concerning the aesthetics of the bare, square forms which Mr. Sturgis finds so impossible, the designer of the Larkin Building wishes here to record in type what he has already recorded in buildings, that he prefers to think in terms of clean, pure, unadulterated forms. A clean cut, square post could not be improved for him by chamfering the edges. There is a certain aesthetic joy in letting the thing alone

which has for centuries been tortured, distorted, and dickered with in the name of Art, letting its native dignity show forth once more. I confess to a love for a clean arris; the cube I find comforting; the sphere inspiring. In the opposition of the circle and the square I find motives for architectural themes with all the sentiment of Shakespeare's "Romeo and Juliet": combining these with the octagon I find sufficient materials for symphonic development. I can marry these forms in various ways without adulterating them, but I love them pure, strong, and undefiled. The ellipse I despise; and so do I despise all perverted, equivocal versions of these pure forms. There is quite room enough within these limitations for one artist to work I am sure, and to accord well with the instinct for first principles. [34]

Wright's "Reply to Mr. Sturgis's Criticism" contains secondary fulminations directed at Sturgis personally, no doubt provoked by the critic's failure to visit the Larkin Building prior to writing. Relying on photographs, Sturgis confused the east and the west façades, [35] had no idea how the building was heated, and registered no awareness of the experiences one would have while approaching the doorway, passing through the lobby, and entering the light court. Demonstrating Sturgis's ineptitude, Wright provides a detailed insight into one of the building's refinements:

In the interior view, Fig. 3, does Mr. Sturgis fail to notice how the fourth story gallery front is dropped behind the piers, associated in like materials with the capitals, in effect freeing the shafts above the third floor, broadening the court at the crucial point, and enriching the whole as it composes with skylight, capitals, and the ceiling beams which sweep over them to the outer walls on either side? Does he not notice how this simple expedient gives rhythm to the arrangement when otherwise it would have lacked it? Is he insensible to the manner in which the forms are all held well together in scale and character with a unity rare in this day and generation? He may not like the forms, prefer repoussé to retroussé, yet intelligently acknowledge the virtue of the one while preferring the other. [36]

Wright is particularly incensed by Sturgis's use of several photographs — characterized by the architect as "wide-angle slanders" — which, having been taken from the third story of the Larkin factory across Seneca Street, flattened the façade. In reference to the position from which Sturgis's Figures 1 and 2 were taken, Wright accuses the critic of not being "on the ground," thereby imputing to Sturgis a kind of lightness that can be variously interpreted. Wright holds that Sturgis's proposed ornament would "emasculate the surfaces" of the building and that Sturgis's eclectic architecture is "perverted," something Wright "despise[s]." The architect refers to the critic as one offended by "the muscularity . . . of the young giant," and as a "man who, startled, clutches his lifeless traditions closer to his would-be-conservative breast and shrieks, 'It is ugly!' " The general intention becomes clear. Such a personal attack is indefensible, but it reveals the intensity of Wright's attitude toward the Larkin commission, and it suggests why editors of the *Architectural Record* might have been reluctant to publish the reply shortly after Sturgis's death.

The "Reply to Mr. Sturgis's Criticism" was not Wright's last word on the subject, nor was it his most influential statement. From 1910 until 1925 the Larkin Building received no significant critical attention in America, but its impact upon European architects during that period was considerable. A photograph from the *Inland Architect and News Record*, reproduced in the *Architektonische Rundschau* of 1908, is the earliest known European publication of the building.[37] But it was the publication of Wright's entire oeuvre by Ernst Wasmuth in Berlin — the double folio *Ausgeführte Bauten und Entwürfe von Frank Lloyd Wright* (1910) and the smaller photographic volume, *Frank Lloyd Wright: Ausgeführte Bauten* (1911)[38] — that brought Wright fully to the attention of the European architectural community. Most leading European modernists indicated an awareness of Wright after 1910, and for many of them the Larkin Administration Building was the cardinal work. After his 1911 visit to the United States, H.P. Berlage lectured on Wright's work in Holland, Germany, and Switzerland; his lectures were published in part, as mentioned above. Concerning the Larkin Building he wrote:

Having been told that Wright's masterpiece was the Larkin Company office building in Buffalo, New York, I went to see it and must confess that this is an understatement. The building consists of only one large room, thanks to the American concept that offices should not be divided into separate rooms. The head of the office works at the same table as his employees, and from his table his view encompasses the entire room with its various floors which, like galleries, surround the central hall. This hall has excellent light in spite of the large brick masses that form the exterior corner towers; indeed, the effect is similar to Unity Temple where the corner staircases are lighted from inside.

The building is conceived in terms of contrasting masses — and these have a very powerful effect. Whatever may be one's concept of an office, particularly here in Europe, I assure you that there is no building here with the monumental power of this American design. The exterior and interior are both of brick with floors and ceilings of concrete. Detailing is handled naturally, in accordance with Wright's originality, and clearly shows his creative genius.

I left convinced that I had seen a great modern work, and I am filled with respect for the master who created a design that is without equal in the whole of Europe.[39]

In a recorded conversation with Peter Blake in 1961, Ludwig Mies van der Rohe recalled the impact of Wright's work on his own development:

For Philip Johnson's book, [*Mies van der Rohe*, New York, 1940], I wrote about Wright and the influence he had on us in Europe. Certainly, I was very much impressed by the Robie house and by the office building in Buffalo. Who wouldn't be impressed? He was certainly a great genius — there is no question about that.[40]

A statement by Jan Wils, a younger Dutch modernist, was published in *Elsevier's Geïllustreerd Maandschrift* in 1921 (recently it was published in English for the first time by H. Allen Brooks in *Writings on Wright*):[41]

Two buildings deserve our special attention. They are Unity Temple and the office building of the Larkin Company. Except for these two structures, Wright has not yet had an opportunity to design public buildings. Nevertheless these examples prove that he can create the great monument of our time.

Again it is the function which determines the plan. In the office building the ground plan was determined by the concept of the enterprise, by the need for easy control from each part of the building, and by the requirement to have all the employees together yet at a certain distance from each other. And the church was conceived as a gathering place for a group of people, who in strict separation from the world, want to concentrate for some time on a different thought.

The forms which Wright conceived are utterly simple, but in their simplicity they give an impression of the greatest monumentality possible.

The ground plan of the Larkin Building is very simple in its arrangement. There is an inner court, around which the several stories are laid out, being held up by piers which go from the floor to the roof. Daylight enters through a skylight over the inner court, and through windows between the piers on the outer wall. Next to the main building one finds an auxiliary structure containing such services as toilets, wardrobes, etc. On the top floor of the main building there is a lunchroom along with everything needed to keep people occupied between working hours. And on top of that there is a wintergarden as well as a roofgarden.

The various parts of the building are clearly expressed on the outside. Just as in Wright's houses, each part is separate from the others. Like two strong anchors the stairwells hold the core (the stairs are lit by small skylights at a right angle with the flights, in order to avoid facing the light when mounting). Between the stairwells the big inner court extends forward, with the piers extending still further in order to support the unbroken space of the kitchen on the top floor. At the side it is the length of the inner court which is expressed. The parapets are simply strung between the piers. The stairwells close off the corners.

The entire composition is so simple and so logical that no further description or explanation is needed. One sees it, and one senses the tempo of our time; it is here that the spirit of creativity is at its highest, where system and order form the basis of the enterprise, and where, in spite of the high demands made on the employees, their material interests have not been overlooked and everything possible has been done to provide for work, as well as for rest and recreation.

And so this building radiates strength, not only because of the large size of all the planes and masses, but even more because of the monumental proportions. Just as nothing on the inside was left to whim, so on the outside there are no complicating elements; the same clarity of movement is found inside and out. The businesslike spirit, the inner strength of the building, gives it an outward appearance which places it on a level with the great architectural monuments of the past, but to us it has a higher value because it is a monument of our time.[42]

Wils's sense of the significance of the Larkin Building is matched in a letter written by Eric Mendelsohn to his wife on October 22, 1924. Mendelsohn's statement is included in full here because of his exceptional critical keenness, which ranges from the largest aspects of the building to details that no other observer has bothered to mention:

Wright's Administration Office for the Larkin Soap Co. was a great experience. The building is not excessively large, but it is the peculiarity of monumental works that their effect overtakes the actual dimensions and enlarges them to the eye.

Built eighteen years ago, it is a really great architectural achievement. Outwardly, to us today, it is still — or already — somewhat rhetorical, more suitable for a sacred purpose than an industrial institution.

But expressing the power of an age has always been the best task for art. It is the only one that compels us and leads us on.

The severe discipline of the building readily includes the ornament, which is here completely static and therefore structurally conceived. It is brutally close to the street — on the other side of which are the old factory buildings — with a wide open entrance in glass and metal. A harbor for those going into the building, who look into the heart of it at once.

No secrets, no obscurities — an immediate aura of work and reality.

I have tried to take pictures from points that show unambiguously the spatial interplay of the separate wings, the way they flow together.

The interior is of great energy and receptiveness.

I am sitting on the inner court, in the great hall which you know from my photographs. Four floors, lit on all sides give out on to this hall. There are a thousand people at work here. You hear no single sounds. The general noise from the working of a thousand individually almost silent type-writers, calculating machines and adding machines simply forms the background hum for the ordinary field of activity and portion of duty.

Amid the sharply-cut, bespectacled, worldly official types there is a sprinkling of flower-like girls, with their provincially demure but smart light summer dresses. All wear pearl necklaces, a dollar each.

On the window ledges of the great hall there are chrysanthemum plants which are changed constantly — refreshing colors for the eyes of people wearied with writing, thinking and talking. The directors are only separated from the employees by a railing.

This has a double aspect — an incentive and democracy.

There are undivided plate glass windows, about 170 square feet in area, which, with their fitted areas of light — cloud white, light blue — give points of color, points of focus, resting points to the rough verticalism of the yellowish-white screens.

The lighting is unevenly swung out as a cantilever on either side of the supporting beams, in close metallic contact with them.

Stone and steel go right down to the tables and chairs, lamps and the parapet walls.

The building conveys a spontaneous *élan* out of an early felt logic of development — too early for this intransigently rough colonial country, but early enough to arouse a whole generation, to instruct them and to drive them on further. . . .[43]

These enthusiastic European testimonials, and additional attention from J.J.P. Oud, Bruno Taut, Werner Moser, C.R. Ashbee, H. de Fries, H. Th. Wijdeveld, and others,[44] forced the American architectural establishment to recognize the importance of Wright's work to the development of European modernism. Consequently, after the mid-1920s, a dramatic change took place in the attitude of American critics and historians toward the Larkin Building. Commencing with surveys of modernism by Sheldon Cheney, Fiske Kimball, Suzanne LaFollette, and Henry-Russell Hitchcock,[45] the Larkin Building has been included in almost every study of modern architecture up to the present.[46] Most of these writings have been laudatory, influenced by the strength of the European modernist view of the building and by Wright's own commentary on its importance.

No doubt encouraged by the European enthusiasm for his work, Wright refined the story of the building in his autobiography published in 1932. Under the heading "The First Protestant," he discusses innovations much as he had done in previous writings, but his account of the decision to move the stair and ventilation towers to the outer corners of the building is given the powerful new dramatization cited here in Chapter Three. Rarely has an image of artistic inspiration been used as effectively to shape the historic record. On one hand, the phrase "came in a flash" [47] has deflected critics and historians from inquiry into Wright's ideas and sources. On the other hand, the paragraph in its entirety established the conviction, already manifest in the building itself, that the significance of the design lay in its expression of functional form — a view that has prevailed ever since 1932. Wright's mystification of his design process was so effective that some thirty years later, when Grant C. Manson attempted to deal with the evolution of the Larkin Building design in *Frank Lloyd Wright to 1910*, he could only write: "The general *parti* of the building seems to have occurred to him at once, in that intuitive way which characterizes the inception of most of Wright's major successes." [48]

Frank Lloyd Wright's design of a mythical history for his building, just as he designed the building itself, might be partly due to a need to rectify the damage done by Russell Sturgis, but it is also indicative of the extraordinary zeal and thoroughness Wright brought to his work — an intensity itself of mythic proportion. The Larkin Administration Building was considerably more complex in its structure, its spatial arrangement, its functions, its mechanical services, and its expressive intentions than all the writings about it indicate.

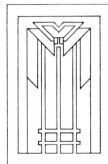

CHAPTER SEVEN

The Demolition

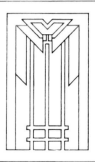

In these times of widespread architectural preservation it is astonishing to realize that the city of Buffalo authorized the demolition of the Larkin Administration Building in 1950. The building had long been recognized as a masterpiece of early modern architecture by such eminent historians as Henry-Russell Hitchcock, Nikolaus Pevsner, and Sigfried Giedion.[1] Had the building's site been on commercially desirable land, the demolition might have been justifiable on some level; but the industrial activity that once had characterized the neighborhood had largely subsided by 1950, leaving the property with relatively little real-estate value. Today, more than thirty years after the demolition, the site of the building remains a barely-used parking lot, a forlorn landscape of pitted asphalt and overgrown weeds. The circumstances that led to the destruction of Frank Lloyd Wright's Larkin Administration Building were mainly economic but they represent a part of its critical history; demolition is after all a drastic critical comment.

During the late 1920s and early 1930s the development of cross-country highways, the rise of the trucking industry, and the opening of a major shipping canal in nearby Ontario that circumvented Niagara Falls each contributed to the weakening of Buffalo's position as a vital Great Lakes port city and railroad center.[2] The conditions that had led to the popularity of the Larkin mail-order business began to change, as well.[3] Chain stores proliferated in small towns where people previously had relied upon mail-order catalogues. The increased availability of automobiles

after the 1920s made it possible for country people to shop in urban centers where stores frequently offered cut-price sales with which the fixed-price Larkin catalogue could not compete. Opportunities for women in business and industry during and after World War I seriously diminished the appeal of Larkin "Clubs of Ten" as a means of augmenting family incomes. As a result, a marked leveling off of the company's growth began around 1920. The first of several hundred "Larkin Economy Stores" was opened in 1918 in an effort to stem the tide of chain-store competition, but otherwise an era of retrenchment was under way.[4] Two subsidiary manufacturers, the Buffalo Leather Company and the Greenburg (Pennsylvania) Glass Company, were sold in 1920; the Larkin furniture-manufacturing plant in Memphis, Tennessee, was sold in 1924; and the Los Angeles branch office was closed that same year.[5]

The Larkin Company's internal problems were no less serious. Despite John D. Larkin's commitment to hard work and progressive business practices and his tight control of finances, there was one inconsistency in his approach to business: He regarded it as a family operation to be continued by his sons and sons-in-law, while at the same time he allowed Darwin D. Martin, the only nonfamily member of the Board of Directors, to become practically indispensable. Some observers actually believed that Darwin Martin ran the Larkin Company,[6] an illusion based upon John Larkin's reticence and willingness to delegate responsibility. Mr. Larkin's oldest son, Charles, had joined the

113 Seneca Street elevation, ca. 1932. The pier sculptures have been removed from the principal façades and windows have been cut into the fifth floor. (Courtesy Daniel I. Larkin)

114 Seneca Street elevation, ca. 1935. (Courtesy Buffalo and Erie County Historical Society)

115 Swan Street elevation, ca. 1935. The annex chimney has been extended above the roof line; the Larkin auditorium has been demolished for the parking lot in the foreground. (Courtesy Buffalo and Erie County Historical Society)

company in the 1890s, but he was never very enthusiastic about business and retired in 1920. Other sons and sons-in-law were made executives in the first decade of the twentieth century. As early as 1915, John D. Larkin, Jr., began to assert himself in matters of policy, a step that would lead to his eventual takeover of the company in 1926.[7] Real turmoil began within the ranks of the Larkin Company in June 1924, when William Heath, Office Manager since 1902, suddenly announced his retirement.[8] Darwin Martin followed in 1925 after a heated exchange with John Larkin, Jr., during a Directors' meeting.[9] Three key members of the Secretary's Department retired shortly after the departure of Martin,[10] and that department, cornerstone of the Larkin mail-order business, was moved from its symbolic position on the main floor of the light court to the fifth floor and was renamed the "Buying Department." The displaced restaurant was moved to a factory building across Seneca Street.[11] Thus, in short order, John D. Larkin, Jr., brought about the retirement of most of the men who had been instrumental in developing the mail-order business. Following the death of his father at the age of eighty-one on February 15, 1926, the fate of the Larkin Company rested entirely in his hands.[12] The younger John Larkin had little regard for Wright's building; despite the architect's protests at the site, he authorized the cutting of large, disfiguring windows into the walls of the fifth story (Figs. 113–115), and he moved the Engineering Department into a former small classroom at the top of the annex (see Fig. 80). Furthermore, he installed soap business offices where the In-Mail Department and some clerical activities had been located.[13]

From 1926 until 1940 the Larkin Company faced increasing indebtedness as a result of its President's determination to maintain a large, diversified premium catalogue in the face of new competition, diminishing sales, and the economic Depression.[14] Other experiments were tried in an effort to rejuvenate the Larkin business; most involved direct retail sales through outlets like Larkin Economy Stores,

Home-Craft Stores, and Household Shops.[15] One of the retail stores established in 1918 was expanded into a full-fledged department store in one of the factory buildings in 1925, and it flourished, despite its location outside the downtown shopping area, thanks to continued public confidence in the Larkin name.[16] Such ventures did not, however, offset the losses of the mail-order business.

By 1939 the Larkin Company was in such serious financial trouble that the Board of Directors was forced to act to avoid bankruptcy. New corporations were formed in order to separate Larkin Co Inc. (the company's official title at that time) from the company's real-estate holdings.[17] Wherever possible, properties were sold to pay off the Larkin debts. Harry Larkin became President of Larkin Co Inc. in 1939 in place of John D. Larkin, Jr., who soon resigned from the Board of Directors altogether.[18]

The Larkin Administration Building was sold to Larkin Co Inc. in 1939, and the Larkin department store was moved into the first three floors of the main block (Fig. 116).[19] Floors four and five were left for a much diminished mail-order business. In 1941 additional corporations were set up, helping the stockholders to salvage portions of the business. In the meantime, a creditors' committee was formed, most of Larkin Co Inc.'s assets were liquidated, and by 1943 creditors were all paid off. Larkin Co Inc. was left with no assets other than the Administration Building, on which $85,000 back taxes were owed.[20]

In 1943 a contractor from Harrisburg, Pennsylvania, purchased Larkin Co Inc. and the Administration Building in the belief that the taxes owed would help offset some large profits he was realizing from laying a transcontinental pipeline.[21] Discovering that the Federal Government would not allow this tax break, he abandoned the building, and it stood untended and unheated—harsh treatment in Buffalo's severe winters—until the city of Buffalo took it over in a $104,616 tax foreclosure proceeding in 1945.[22] The building had no in-house heating plant, its court configuration did not lend itself easily to adaptive reuse, and it was too far from downtown Buffalo to be useful as an office building. The assessed value in 1946 was $240,000.[23]

An undisclosed buyer offered the city $26,000 for the building in 1946, but the City Comptroller persuaded the Common Council that a nationwide advertising campaign would bring a more attractive offer.[24] The plan was tabled, however, while the feasibility of turning the building into a housing project was explored and then rejected by the Commissioner of Public Works.[25] The advertising campaign was launched in January 1947 in the *New York Times,* the *Wall Street Journal,* the *Chicago Journal of Commerce,* and several other publications.[26] When, by March, the advertising had produced no results, the City Comptroller contacted the State Selective Service officials in an effort to interest them in using the building to store records.[27] Nothing came of this, and the building continued to decay. According to one newspaper account, "everything removable has been stripped by vandals. Lighting fixtures, door knobs, plumbing, and even part of the copper roof have been torn away systematically by thieves."[28] Another stated, "Every double-paned window is shattered. The tall iron grate which graces the entrance has toppled from rusted hinges. The iron fence topping a low brick wall around the structure went into a wartime scrap collection."[29]

In spite of its dismal condition, the Larkin Building attracted ninety-day purchase options during 1947 and 1948 from an undisclosed client who offered $25,000,[30] from a local brewer who offered $26,000,[31] and from others.[32] These offers were refused on the grounds that the assessed value of the property was $225,000.

The last significant attempt to reuse the Larkin Administration Building was made by a councilman, Joseph F. Dudzick, on April 18, 1949.[33] Decrying the deterioration of the world-renowned building, Dudzick announced that he would submit a resolution to the Common Council recommending that the building be turned over to the Capital Expenditures Committee for inclusion in its program of city improvements. Dudzick said: "The Building could be altered to house a basketball and tennis court, gymnasium equipment, and facilities for various other types of recreation . . . we've got a community blight on our hands. But it can be transformed into a worthwhile medium to combat Juvenile Delinquency, to protect youngsters from possible death and injury by giving them a place to play off the streets and to restore a small measure, at least, of the building's beauty."[34] The resolution was defeated.

Realizing impending disaster, the *Buffalo Evening News* published the following editorial on April 15, 1949:

A SHAME OF OUR CITY

The City of Buffalo is the sole owner of the Larkin Building. The question is: What use will our municipal authorities make of the cadaver of what at its completion in 1906 was deemed the most beautiful building in this metropolis?

That some use must be made of it doesn't need to be argued, because its present condition constitutes a municipal disgrace. The title to the building legally passed to the city about two years ago, when unpaid taxes mounted to the point that the then owners had no remaining value in the property and were pleased to shift the burden of its ownership to the city.

To architects, the Larkin Building continues one of the great examples of the genius of Frank Lloyd Wright, who recently received at the Houston meeting of the American Institute of Architects the Gold Medal award for 1948. Buffalo members who attended that convocation report that he looked through a glass darkly at a professional honor he said should have been accorded two decades ago. Be that as it may, the Larkin Building and the D.D. Martin house at Summit and Jewett were among the architectural triumphs thus belatedly attested by his fellow craftsmen of line, design, form and function.

Buffalonians' continuing interest in seeing some good use made of the Larkin Building is again attested by Ralph A. Coppola's suggestion to the Common Council that the Larkin administration building be converted into a Buffalo

116 Light court converted for department-store use, ca. 1937. (Courtesy Buffalo and Erie County Historical Society)

117 View of demolition, 1950. (Courtesy Buffalo and Erie County Historical Society)

Conservatory of Music. John W. Jarnot, writing in Everybody's Column, applauded the idea as a noteworthy means of doing something useful with what he deems Buffalo's most beautiful building. The News hopes that these are but the precursors of a stream of suggestions of uses to which the Larkin Building could be constructively put.

The city allows the Larkin Building to go to pieces day by day. The area from street to site is carpeted with broken bricks, sticks, rubbish and waste, demeaning the city's signs that the structure is for sale. The parallel sides are even more cluttered with fallen plaster, masonry and rubble. Gangs of urchins have fun hurling brickbats and plaster chunks at one another and at visitors to the structure. There is no reason why this spectacle of decay cannot be

118 View of demolition, 1950. (Courtesy Buffalo and Erie County Historical Society)

amended, so that at least the Larkin Building need not look like the result of deliberate inattention on the part of the public authorities.

On August 20, 1949, the Western Trading Corporation offered the Common Council $5,000 and a promise "to raze the Larkin Building and replace it with a taxable improvement of not less than $100,000 within eighteen months." [35] The property was then valued at $128,960. Two months later this sale was approved by Mayor Bernard Dowd and the Common Council to the considerable relief of a newly elected City Comptroller, who referred to the building as a "white elephant . . . inherited" from predecessors. [36]

There was some outcry over the impending demolition in the local and national press. The *New York Times* reported the sale this way: "BUFFALO LANDMARK SOLD City Gets $5,000 for Building that Cost $4,000,000 in 1906." [37] The *New York Herald Tribune* ran an editorial deploring the destruction of famous landmarks such as the Larkin Administration Building; it included a statement by Andrew Ritchie, a former Director of the Albright Art Gallery in Buffalo.[38] Moreover, a letter to the *Herald Tribune* was reproduced as a news item in the *Buffalo Evening News:*

"As an architect," writes Mr. Sharp, "I share the concern of many others over the destruction of Frank Lloyd Wright's world-famous office building in Buffalo. It is not merely a matter of sentiment; from a practical standpoint this structure can function efficiently for centuries. Modern engineering has improved upon the lighting and ventilation systems Mr. Wright used but that is hardly excuse enough to efface the work of the man who successfully pioneered in the solving of such problems. The Larkin Building set a precedent for many an office building we admire today and should be regarded not as an outmoded utilitarian structure but as a monument, if not to Mr. Wright's creative imagination, to the inventiveness of American design." [39]

This and others' comments notwithstanding, the firm of Morris & Reimann began demolition in February 1950 (Figs. 117, 118). The work proceeded slowly because of the unusual nature of Wright's construction. Each floor consisted of 10-inch-thick concrete slabs in 17 × 34-foot sections supported by 24-inch steel girders extending from the piers surrounding the light court to the outer walls of the building.[40] Nelson Reimann recalled the whole demolition process as a "headache"; while his men attempted to cut the concrete floor slabs into smaller units, entire sections collapsed onto the floor below, seriously endangering the crew.[41] The building had to be dismantled almost by hand, and cost Morris & Reimann most of its $55,000 fee in wages paid to laborers.[42]

In May 1951 the Western Trading Corporation had plans drawn up for a truck terminal on the site of the Larkin Administration Building, but by November they petitioned the Common Council to allow them to change the location of the terminal to a larger lot.[43] The request was approved, thereby removing the ostensible reason for the demolition of the Larkin Administration Building.

When word of the demolition reached Frank Lloyd Wright he reportedly said that the building had served its purpose and deserved a decent burial.[44] He had long been aware of the unfortunate alterations to which his building had been subjected (see Figs. 114, 115).[45] He gave vent to his feelings in his autobiography where he wrote, "They [the Larkins] never realized the place their building took in the thought of the world — for they never hesitated to make senseless changes in it in after years." [46]

In 1950 Wright was eighty-three years old; he had endured more than his share of adversity and realized the impermanence of earthly matter. As a true Emersonian he could take solace in the fact that his building occupied a special place in that more enduring realm he chose to call "the thought of the world."

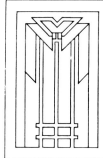

APPENDIX A
Darwin Martin's Office Building Requirements

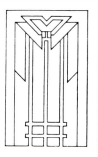

12/18/02.

OFFICE BUILDING REQUIREMENTS.

Size: 100 × 170'. Four stories and basement.

Height of Stories: Basement, 10', 1st, 2nd, 3rd and 4th, 20' to centers. Two mezzanines, hung from 2nd and 4th floors, 8' in clear.

General.

Absolutely fire-proof construction.

Exterior, brick.

Interior, glazed brick.

Tutti-colori floors.

Steam pipes laid in floors.

Open light court 30 × 90' through 2nd, 3rd, and 4th floors with 4' bridge across center.

All columns around court.

Complete mechanical ventilating system; windows all sealed; ventilator openings all concealed; pipes in walls.

Heat, steam, Light and power, electricity, from another building.

Carrying capacity of floors, 100 lbs. per sq. foot.

Windows to begin 5' above floors, continue to ceiling.

Individual desk 16 c.p. lights; chandeliers for general lighting.

Two main staircases, 8' wide.

One passenger elevator. 6 × 7', 2½ tons.

One freight elevator, 8 × 10', 2 tons.

Basement: Space for:

Bicycle room, 200 wheels.

Automobiles,

Storage for Adv. Dep., 2000 sq. ft. with freight doorway; freight elevator also with outside doorway to be in this room.

Engineering Dep.

Dining Room; kitchen.

One dozen individual lockers.

Two water closets.

Receiving Dep.

All columns around court.

Complete mechanical ventilating system; windows all concealed.

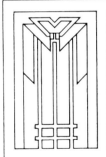

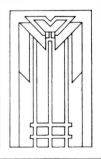

APPENDIX B

Darwin Martin Letter to John Larkin refuting the Coss plan

1/17/03

Mr. Larkin: —

OFFICE BUILDING. Two points admit of no argument.

1st. Offices in the Annex would be delightfully pleasant. They could not be improved upon in this respect in any other location in the bldg.

2nd. If there is any place in the main bldg. which may not be perfectly light and pleasant it is the south east corner of the ground floor.

However, to follow the sketch you had made would transform the Wright lobby (which is the most delightful feature of this bldg. and excels in beauty and taste any office bldg. I have ever seen) into a most commonplace corridor, admitting of little opportunity for individuality.

The space given for your office in your sketch is 1280 sq. feet. On the plan that I drew I provided just half that = 640 sq. ft. for your offices and 1350 sq. ft. for the Secy's Dep. If you would be willing, for the sake of retaining the lobby somewhat as planned by Wright, to put your offices into he main bldg. it can easily be arranged to give you 1280 ft. directly beside either the windows on the east side in front of the annex, or on the south end. I had no idea when making my tentative sketch that I would appear to be hornswoggling all the windows. In my sketch every Dep. is allotted liberal space so that the Secy's Dep. can be reduced from 1350 sq. ft. to something less, the Traffic Dep. from 1300' to something less, so that the space for the President's suite of offices could easily be increased from 640 to 1280'. Aside from the location in the annex, one beside the east windows or south windows would probably be the most pleasant.

As stated at the outset, however, offices in the annex would be more pleasant than they could possibly be anywhere else in the bldg. (unless on the top floor) and as we probably all agree that we do not want the mezzanine over the annex or the court, or whatever it is Wright has planned in the middle of the annex, it is quite possible that Wright could plan the annex, which contains 4240 sq. ft., to include your offices and not destroy the artistic effect he is planning for or sacrifice the beauty and dignity of the approach from Seneca St. to an entrance set 90' from the fence line. Your offices would be much more pleasant if located 90' from Seneca St. than if 30' therefrom as in your sketch?

Neither your plan nor Wright's necessitates sacrificing the greenhouse so far as space for it is concerned.

D.D.M.

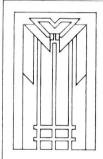

APPENDIX C
Darwin Martin Letter to John Larkin reporting on Wright

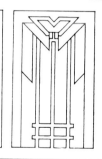

[March 20, 1903]

Mr. Larkin:

At the risk of appearing to have been made intoxicated by my contact with Frank Lloyd Wright, I do not hesitate to say at the outset of this, my report of my interview with him, which lasted all day Mar. 18th, and of my visit to his houses on Mar. 14th, 15th and 18th, that I believe we have all greatly under-estimated our man. This because of his youth, the newness of our acquaintanceship and its limitations and also because of the adverse things we have heard about Wright, which are due to his radical departure from conventional lines.

The glory of the firm of Adler & Sullivan has forever departed. They failed at the end of the panic and Mr. Adler died three years ago. Mr. Sullivan is a true artist, who now, not having the companionship of a business man, does not cut as large a figure as formerly. When this house was in its palmy days however, Mr. Wright was the right-hand man. I saw a copy of the Engineering Record of June 7, 1890, with plan of Adler & Sullivan offices, in the Auditorium Building. Visitors who entered their general offices could reach Mr. Adler through one door; beyond that was a large consultation room, and beyond that, Mr. Sullivan and Mr. Wright's offices side by side. In these two rooms all their work was created, and during much of the time Mr. Sullivan was away because of poor health.

Mr. Adler was a Structural Engineer and a business man. The $500,000 Wainwright Building and the Union Trust Building of St. Louis; the Schiller Theatre and the Stock Exchange in Chicago; the Seattle and Pueblo Opera Houses, all Adler & Sullivan's work, were, I inferred from Mr. Wright, largely his creations. He also had as much to do with the Auditorium as a young man, just past twenty, could be expected to have.

It has been a joke in Mr. Wright's office that the large building questions, with which he was in Adler & Sullivan's office almost exclusively engaged, now seldom come his way and his time is devoted to residences, with which he formerly had nothing to do.

All of his employees have come to him voluntarily seeking the opportunity of a course in his office. One, Miss Mahoney, stands the third highest in an examination of Architects in the State of Illinois, (unlike New York, Illinois Architects have to pass examination to obtain a license). Another left a position at $25.00 a week to come to his offices — deeming it a privilege. Three others are there and they came of their own volition — and Mr. Wright says, realize why they are there.

Mr. Wright's two oldest boys are doing such good drawing work in the public schools that samples of their work have circulated through the Illinois Public and Normal schools as exhibitions of what children of their age can do.* (Mrs. Martin learned this from Mrs. Wright).

One of Wright's earliest houses has changed hands twice. The last time, a few days ago, six weeks after the owner (a C.&N.W. R.R. man) was notified of the necessity of his removal from Oak Park, Ill., to Mason City, Ia. Both times

* Handwritten marginal note: D.D.M.: My chil.[dren] same kind —very smart W.R.H. [William R. Heath]

the house brought a profit tho' the land value has not increased. In the language of Mrs. Thompson, wife of the present owner: "A Wright house is like an Oriental Rug, it increases in value, is better understood and admired ten years after its erection than when new and will be worth more yet in twenty years".

We were inside of five and talked to owners of four of Wright's houses. You never witnessed such enthusiasm. Not one will admit a fault in their house. They will admit faults in other of Wright's houses but not in theirs. That, Mr. Wright says is because he studies his client and builds the house to fit him, so his different houses do not fit his clients who live in other houses.

In Mr. Wright's estimate of the cost of the office building, he allows $25,000 for steel. He says he would have to pay 3% to a Structural Engineer to take this responsibility from him, and he didn't hesitate therefore, to agree to allow us to compensate Mr. Reidpath, and deduct cost of the steel from the sum on which we are to pay him commission. He wishes Mr. Reidpath to be his Structural Engineer just as would be a Chicago man if he employed him. He is not sure that he will not still employ a Chicago man and to do so will cost him $250.00 to recheck Reidpath's figures because he says he may not feel (it will depend upon his acquaintance with Reidpath) that he can risk the reputation of his building without it. I told him I thought he would become well satisfied with Reidpath. He mentioned the point that Reidpath might over-estimate on the steel and thus unnecessarily increase the cost of the building. I told him that would be entirely contrary to our impression of Reidpath, but after all I thought we had no actual knowledge whether this was possible or not.

In answer to my question on ventilation: "How do you know your ventilation will be ample?", he said: "Because I would consult and employ the best ventilating expert in America and would have to pay him well. The fees for consultation will be no small part of my fees." He has not yet — without any definite contract — engaged this counsel but says he has, himself, had sufficient experience in ventilation to say authoritatively that he has made ample provision.

As to the question of light. He says there is absolutely no uncertainty. The whole building will be as light as out doors.

We have, at least I have — greatly under-estimated the value of the basement. It will be in every way equal to such offices as are in the basement of the Real Estate Exchange, the Board of Trade Building, the Bell Telephone Building, and it will have windows 5' above grade, and all the folding, filling and mailing of our Advertising Department can be done in the basement, thus avoiding all elevating.

He says we cannot have a freight elevator without door entrance in the northwest corner of the building as we cannot break through the buttress at the corner. We cannot consent to having the freight elevator against the wall midway on the north side where the windows are, hence Mr. Wright suggested having the freight elevator beside the passenger elevator as the most practical way as well as the most economical. And the wagon entrance midway on north side of building is o.k. for handling freight.

After I had realized somewhat of the extent of Mr. Wright's plans for this building beyond anything we had conceived of, I told him that the time elapsed since Jan. 15th, when the sketch was submitted and our uncertainty about it was all his fault because a sketch drawn to the scale of 32' to the inch was utterly inadequate to convey to us any proper sense of his meaning, for which I did not think we were in any way responsible, and he replied that this was so and that he would never do it again. He said that he should have made a much larger sketch and brought it to us himself, and I think this is what he will immediately proceed to do. As he reiterated when he was here, he has not had tentative work to do and he didn't know how to do it.

I visited on Mar. 17th, the Chicago National Bank and saw their engine room, ventilating and spraying system. It was all installed by one Chicago firm (Andrews & Johnson? Mr. Wright will furnish correct name). Mr. Harper, the Engineer at the Bank will be very glad to show anyone we send, through. I had no letter of introduction but was courteously shown everything. The air is changed at the rate of 6,500 cu. ft. per minute. The light is entirely from a skylight. The exhaust is on this skylight, which serves to keep it clear of snow and ice in the Winter so that the room is always as light as day. The water is sprayed fan-like from the upper side of pipes and the air circulates through the sprays.

By the way, I noticed that in the working departments of this Bank, with its magnificent mosaic decorations portraying the history of Chicago, that the floors are of maple.

Mr. Wright showed me samples of Monolith, — which is apparently as soft to the feet as wood, and yet, greatly resembles a mineral—as a suggestion for our fire-proof floors.

I believe Mr. Wright is correct in locating all wardrobes and closets in the annex: those for the ground floor and the basement in the basement annex; those for the second, third and fourth floors in the second story of the annex, which will be level with the second story of the main block. The area is abundant and for a long time no clerk will have to travel more than one flight. When finally the fourth floor is used for clerks a passenger elevator could be placed at their service. The ground floor workers will have only a short flight to the basement.

It is my opinion that Wright can answer satisfactorily all objections to his work in the past or offered to us. I think he is perfectly competent to defend himself.

His houses are called "freak" houses. They are all nicknamed. I declared one of them to resemble an automobile barn with a second story dancing pavilion. It is a Banker's residence, nevertheless. The owners, whom we met, were not freaks but were much above average people and they were consistently enthusiastic.

I selected a plan of Wright's for a simple, inexpensive house which he can furnish blueprints of with no work on his part—only some modifications by his draughtsmen, which therefore, should be ready for me in a few weeks and which I will proceed at once to build, probably by day's work. In a few months, therefore, we will all be able to better judge the consistency and practicability of Wright's ideas in so far as a little house can exemplify them.

I saw Mr. Heath's preliminary sketch and the office is at work upon it—but I refuse to anticipate.

Mr. Wright says his houses are not cheap. They are simple—as a tailor-made gown is simple.

Mr. Wright has just built a $40,000 house in Kankakee, Ill., for Mr. Bradley, of the Bradley Plow. He also provided every rug, hanging and piece of furniture for it.

The problem of open court is no problem at all. There is no question of draughts, of heating or of lack of heat involved. There are two open courts each about $50 \times 75'$ in Marshall Field & Co., one in an eight story and the other in a twelve story building. The departments in the court on the ground floor are the pleasantest in the buildings.

D.D.M.

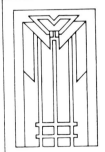
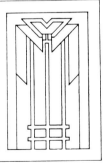
May 12/03

Mr. Larkin:

OFFICE BUILDING

Before writing a letter to Mr. Wright, which would, I feel, be very unsatisfactory to him unless it embodied—and which you did not authorize my including—a definite statement of the terms under which we suppose him to be working. I have thought it would not be out of place for me to outline my views of the matter, to which, as you know, I have given a great deal of thought.

I understand that there are three reasons for the tentative departure from the line we have until now been working on, as follows:

FIRST: The cost of the plan.

SECOND: The inadaptability of the building for other purposes.

THIRD: The advantage of a main floor for general office of 30,000 sq. ft. over the location of the general office on floors of 13,000 sq. ft. which is distributed around a central court of 3,000 sq. ft.

In taking up the first point let us consider the plan No. 2 [the Heath plan] being that of a building with a basement of 30,000 sq. ft. 12 ft. high and ground story of 30,000 sq. ft. with a 30 × 100 ft. annex 16 ft. high; a second story consisting of a 30 ft. wide quadrangle containing 17,000 sq. ft. making a total floor area of 82,000 sq. ft. contains 41,000 sq. ft. of outdoor wall area (parapets not figured) and 9,000

lineal ft. of foundations.

Plan No. 1 [Wright's preliminary plan] containing a 12 ft. basement of 16,000 sq. ft., a 16 ft. ground story of 16,000 sq. ft. with an annex of 4,000 sq. ft; a second, third and fourth story of 13,000 sq. ft. each 16 ft. high with two annex floors, say, 3,000 sq. ft. and an attic story of 13,000 sq. ft. 10 ft. high, a total of 101,000 sq. ft. Or, should we omit the possibly superfluous fourth story, 88,000 sq. ft.—which omission would reduce the outside wall space 7,500 sq. ft. or to 36,700 sq. ft. — There would be 6,600 lineal feet of foundation.

The truss roof of 80 × 150′ in plan No. 2, while not of heavy construction, would involve a great deal of material and a construction, which I understand, is expensive.

Plan No. 2 contains nearly 50% more lineal ft. of foundation and nearly 100% more excavation. It contains 90% as much wall surface (I have figured no openings). I can't see how the lighter construction throughout, which plan No. 2 permits, can possibly be the means of a very important saving over plan No. 1.

Point No. 2.   This point has, I believe, been suggested by outsiders. No outsider can possibly see things from our point of view. None could possibly have the courage to undertake the many things we have undertaken, without our view point.

Why should we not erect a building for our office which is not economically adapted to other purposes as well as a Power House unadapted to other purposes. A Pottery Plant ditto. In a few months we will have on our hands a pile of brick erected a few years ago for a chimney at considerable cost. No one considers that an unwise investment. There is no reason for not erecting a home for the heart of our business commensurate with the rest of the plant.

If plan No. 1 is too large — and I have always said it was — we can remedy it by omitting the fourth story, in which case, Plan No. 2 is less than 10% smaller.

If we build plan No. 2 factory construction so that it could be converted into a factory building — which we never would need for a factory building if we didn't need it for an office building — the cost of constructing it with eight-story foundations and walls would be greater than the cost of plan No. 1.

Plan No. 2 could not be enlarged for office purposes except by adding a story to the quadrangle creating a room less desirable than a story in plan No. 1, because the interrupting court would be walled in.

In plan No. 2 we would sacrifice the opportunity we have of protecting our building against our neighbors on either side. It has been your policy to obviate, if possible, even remote contingencies. This contingency is remote, but if it confronted us, it would be serious. We would at once sacrifice the advantage of moving 30′ out of the shade of ''H'', and would also at once sacrifice the valuable advantage of a single entrance from both streets, putting the whole question of entrance and exit in the control of one usher. The cost of governing two street entrances might equal the cost of ushering and elevator service in plan No. 1.

Mr. Heath has raised point No. 3. He is logical in considering a one floor office preferable to one divided on two floors, when interrupted by a court. The question of dividing the work on two floors is itself not of great importance, it is even, a question of which plan would bring all departments closer — a large 30,000 ft. floor, or half the space on one floor, the other half immediately overhead. From any given desk, with convenient stairs provided in plan No. 1, I would, personally, prefer to undertake reaching any given department, than to travel thereto from a given point on one 30,000 ft. floor.

The Office Message Carrier has been considered a factor in this question. I think it is over-estimated. It has done in the past very satisfactory work on perpendicular lines, and what has been done can be done again. Nevertheless, per-

pendicular lines can be eliminated from No. 1, substituting instead, inclined lines in the court; or, if no court, then in openings provided. Because our office is nearly all on one floor it is natural to oppose a different arrangement. We had an experience, however, in the division on three floors in old building A, and even with such poor accommodations, we did not find it impracticable. I believe the office can be on two or more floors with perfect satisfaction to all.

Mr. Heath has said that plan No. 2 would make possible the accommodation of 1,000 clerks in one room. This does not seem to me correct for the following reasons:

The first floor of old A contained with the vault — excluding the rear storeroom and express room — 4,000 sq. ft. of floor. We had therein approximately 125 clerks, which means that a clerk to every 32 sq. ft. gives the worst possible conditions. We could not have packed them in more solidly than we did. 50 sq. ft. per clerk, therefore, is a minimum to figure on even recognizing the advantage that 12,000 sq. ft. of the ground floor of plan No. 2 would be free from posts. This would mean a maximum of 600 clerks on that floor. If we concede that the spaces set aside on the floor plan of floor No. 1 for President, Directors, Secretary, Cashier and Printing Supplies (omitting the entire Advertising Department — putting it all in the basement, whereas we planned to give them some 2,500 sq. ft. in plan No. 1) takes 5,000 sq. ft. away from general office purposes, leaving 25,000 sq. ft. of space for a maximum of 500 clerks.

Plan No. 2 requires that all lockers and closets go in the basement — if we allot to them the space given them in plan No. 1 12,000 sq. ft. would be required.

Plan No. 2 requires the whole Adv. Dept. to go into the basement. It should have 7,000 sq. ft.; City Sales 3 M; Engineering Dept. was allotted 1500 ft; sample room should have 1500 ft. Bicycles and Automobiles 2,000 ft. — a total of 27,000 sq. ft. leaving but 3 M ft. surplus.

Mr. Heath raises a natural question when he points out that in plan No. 1 were located on the unbroken ground floor the departments which could more conveniently distribute themselves around the court on an upper floor, and, contrariwise, distributes around the upper floors the general office work which has claims on the unbroken ground floor. He recognizes that the departments we have allotted to the ground floor are quite the natural ones assigned that position. I have thought of this point too, but it seemed to me imperative that the heavy work of the Adv. Dept. be in the basement, desirable that the remainder of the advertising work be as near to it as possible. Desirable, to have Mr. Esty and the Inq. Dept. be near me and near City Sales' display of Premiums. We want your office, and mine, and the Gen'l Bookkeeper's together. I want Van Duzee near me.

It would not be impossible to give the ground floor and second floor in plan No. 1 to the general office and move the departments which we have designed to go on the ground floor to the third floor.

If you visit the executive offices of a Life Ins. Co. in its twenty story building you are likely to find them on any one of the twenty floors. Ditto, a General R.R. Office. The upper stories are pleasanter than the lower ones. The strongest reason for adhering to the original idea of location would be the probable easier handling of visitors and holding together of the departments which desire to be near the basement departments.

The object of this note is not to delay the building. I am very anxious to see progress made, but to enable you to consider the alternative plan from all view points, and perhaps agree with me that we will make better progress by adhering to the line already laid out.

D.D.M.

[Note added in 1933 to Darwin R. Martin]

11/2/33

Darwin:

Office begun in 1903 was 5 stories and basement. Advertising, except Copy Dept. left in factory. Wright's planning prevailed.

D.D.M.

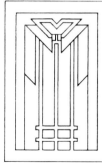

"The Inscriptions on the Court of the Administration Building"

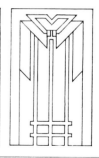

On the magnesite panels between the capitals surmounting the columns that form the central skylighted court in our new Administration Building, inscribed in gold letters, are two quotations from the Sermon on the Mount, and forty-two words. The passages from the Bible are on the large panels at the ends of the court; the words on the smaller panels at the sides.

On one end-panel is the Golden Rule as it is written in the seventh chapter of St. Matthew,

"All things whatsoever ye
would that men should do
to you do ye even so to them"

On the other panel is the seventh verse of the same chapter,

"Ask and it shall be given you
seek and ye shall find knock
and it shall be opened unto you"

The Golden Rule is there because to us it is the simplest, the wisest, the greatest rule of conduct, man to man, employee to employer, employer to employee, company to customer, customer to company, in all the world. Obedience to it is the essence of co-operation for which we stand. It is the epitome of our business ideal; it is what we *want* to do. It is what those who work in our great buildings, offices and factories, *want* to do.

The other passage has been inscribed, because by its se-

From *The Larkin Idea*, 7, May 1907, pp. 1–2.

rene assurance it fosters self-reliance, because it is demonstrable truth.

On each of the panels at the side of the court are three words, sequential in meaning. Simple words were inscribed rather than great quotations because they permit independence of thought and individuality of interpretation. A great thought once in words, however aptly put, is like a carved image; it is accepted as complete by all but the closest reasoners. A simple word is suggestive; it is a text for the exercise of reason or of imagination. And so these simple words, the great words of the English language, rather than quotations:

"Generosity, Altruism, Sacrifice;
"Cheerfulness, Patience, Contentment;
"Integrity, Loyalty, Fidelity;
"Faith, Hope, Charity;
"Liberty, Equality, Fraternity;
"Prudence, Learning, Wisdom;
"Simplicity, Tenacity, Stability;
"Sincerity, Humility, Courage;
"Imagination, Judgment, Initiative;
"Intelligence, Enthusiasm, Control;
"Co-operation, Economy, Industry;
"Thought, Feeling, Action;
"Aspiration, Truth, Nobility;
"Adversity, Refinement, Sympathy."

The letters of these words are wonderfully decorative. In form, they are in harmony with the design of the building. They are done in gold. Viewed from the floors below they and the accompanying decorative arrangements of rectangles catch and reflect the gleam from the skylight, giving against the monotone of the magnesite work a novel, though strikingly beautiful effect.

"Besides the wonderful display of human ingenuity applied to the fulfillment of a thousand ends, . . . I see with delight another great proof of the immense impulse towards better human relations which is a real working religion.

"That is the central point—that the stewardship of so much power is so faithful and true."—A recent comment on our new office.

FROM FACTORY TO FAMILY

Manufacturers create value; middlemen add cost. Most manufactured goods are sold to the consumer at from two to four times the cost of production. This is because the goods pass through many hands; from the factory to the sales agent, from the sales agent to the wholesaler, from the wholesaler to the retailer, from the retailer to the consumer. Each "middleman" adds his expenses, his losses, his profits, etc.; all this is piled up in the retail price, and must be paid by you! The *Larkin* Idea: Save all cost which adds no value.

Chronological List of Writings on the Larkin Administration Building

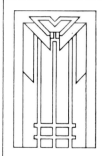
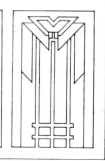

Frank R. Jewett, "The Finished Task" (a poem celebrating the completion of the Larkin Building), *The Larkin Idea*, 6, November 1906, p. 1.

Frank Lloyd Wright, "The New Larkin Administration Building," *The Larkin Idea*, 6, November 1906, pp. 2–9.

William R. Heath, "The Office Building and What It Will Bring to the Office Force," *The Larkin Idea*, 6, November 1906, pp. 10–14.

Anonymous, untitled editorial introducing the Administration Building, *The Larkin Idea*, 6, November 1906, pp. 16–17.

Rogers Dickinson, "A Great American Success," *The Larkin Idea*, 6, February 1907, pp. 1–6.

Anonymous, "Our New Office Scores Again," a brief review of the Administration Building reprinted from *Lux*, a Westinghouse Electric Company staff publication, in *Ourselves*, 4, March 1907, p. 2.

George E. Twitmyer, "A Model Administration Building," *Business Man's Magazine*, 19, April 1907, pp. 43–49; reprinted in an abridged form in *The Larkin Idea*, 7, August 1907, pp. 1–8.

Anonymous, "The Inscriptions on the Court of the Administration Building," *The Larkin Idea*, 7, May 1907, pp. 1–2.

Anonymous, "Beauty Wrought by Gardener and Architect," *The Larkin Idea*, 7, July 1907, pp. 2–3.

Charles E. Illsley, "The Larkin Administration Building, Buffalo," *Inland Architect and News Record*, 50, July 1907, p. 4.

Anonymous, "Current Periodicals: A Review of the Recent American and Foreign Architectural Publications," *The Architectural Review* (Boston), 14, July 1907, p. 184 (illus., p. 183).

Wright, long caption under two photographs of the Larkin Administration Building exterior, *The Architectural Record*, 23, March 1908, pp. 166–67.

Russell Sturgis, "The Larkin Building in Buffalo," *The Architectural Record*, 23, April 1908, pp. 311–21.

Wright, "Reply to Mr. Sturgis's Criticism," published under the title *In the Cause of Architecture* by the Larkin Company (Buffalo, April 1909).

Wright, a long caption in *Ausgeführte Bauten und Entwürfe von Frank Lloyd Wright* (Berlin, 1910), pl. 33.

Twenty photographs of the Larkin Administration Building in *Frank Lloyd Wright: Ausgeführte Bauten* (Berlin, 1911).

Marion Harland, *My Trip Thru the Larkin Factories*, published by the Larkin Company (Buffalo, 1913), pp. 13–22.

Anonymous, *Your Trip Thru the Larkin Factories*, published by the Larkin Company (Buffalo, ca.1920).

ADDITIONAL PUBLICATION OF THE LARKIN ADMINISTRATION BUILDING BY WRIGHT

Exterior elevation of the Larkin Administration Building in "In the Cause of Architecture: The Meaning of Materials —The Kiln," *The Architectural Record*, June 1928.

Wright, *An Autobiography* (New York, 1932), pp. 150–52.

Architectural Forum, 68, January 1938, p. 88. The entire issue was devoted to Wright's work.

Wright, *The Natural House* (New York, 1954), pp. 27, 30, 220.

Wright, *A Testament* (New York, 1957), pp. 48, 131.

Wright, *Genius and the Mobocracy*, 2d ed., (New York, 1949), p. 159.

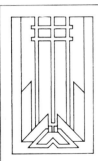

APPENDIX G

Frank Lloyd Wright, "The New Larkin Administration Building"

How it was planned to fill the needs of a great business family—the search for the best in appliances and materials—how each obstacle was overcome—wherein the building pays.

The architect has been asked to tell the *"Larkin* Family" why the big pile of brick across the street from the *Larkin* factories is an economical head-piece to house the intellectuals of a great industry.

Before the office building was begun the physical side of the plant was well developed in the extensive fire-proof buildings devoted to manufacture; but the brains and nervous system to make its corporeal bulk count for something hadn't developed the proper "forehead" with the sort of working-room behind it that would make its nervous energy and intelligence effective to the utmost and, what is good also, to let the light of the Ideal outwardly shine in the countenance of an institution that has in reality become "a great business of the people."

What the *"Larkin* Family" ought to know, I am told, is wherein all this expenditure of thousands upon mere brains and countenance, *pays,* particularly as some of the money has been spent to reach the heart, too.

Has the *Larkin* Company in this instance been true to its traditions and "saved all cost which adds no value?" Perhaps not, if all values are to be reckoned in money. Real values are subjective and more difficult to estimate than the more obvious ones of the balance-sheet.

From *The Larkin Idea,* 6, November 1906, pp. 2–9.

And yet, if, over-and-above the mere house-room required by 1800 workers; clean, pure, properly-tempered air for them to breathe whatever the season or weather or however enervating the environment may be is worth "money" to young lungs and old ones, we have that,—the best in the world.

If ideal sanitary conditions and toilet facilities are worth "money" we have those,—perfect.

If the positive security insured by the use of permanent fireproof materials throughout an isolated building and its fittings and furnishing is valuable,—we have that.

If a restful, harmonious environment, with none of the restless, distracting discords common to the eye and ear in the usual commercial environment, promoting the efficiency of the 1000 or more young lives whose business home the building now is can be counted an asset, why we have that too, together with total immunity from conditions outside the building which are entirely the reverse. If the frame of mind of the worker reacts on his work we have paved the way for a favorable reaction by providing in detail and in ensemble a harmonious unity as complete as it is rare.

If law and order put into close touch with all the facilities for instantaneous inter-communication and easy systematic operation that clever people have yet invented saves time therefore money,—we have that.

In short, if the incentive that results from the family-gathering under conditions ideal for body and mind counts for lessened errors, cheerful alacrity and quickened and sustained intelligence in duties to be performed, we have created some very real values.

There are other things beside, calculated to make this family home helpful and uplifting still more difficult to estimate in money but the men who shape the destiny and determine the character of the work to be done by this family believe in them.

By the shrewd heads of many commercial enterprises these other things are considered to "*pay*" and are ceaselessly exploited as material for advertising, but I think the belief in them in this case lies deeper than that, for I have felt the spirit of the men behind this work and I know that they believe they pay, as the sunshine and the trees, and as the flowers and a clear conscience pay: their love of their work and their pride in it would permit them to do no less.

Let us see whether the means chosen for the purpose of attaining all these things were economical and true or not as there are many unusual features in the construction of the building not easily comprehended without some study. To begin with, the site, for an office building, necessarily was unattractive. Smoke, noise and dirt of railroads were round about, which made it seem wise to depend upon pleasantness within, shutting out the environment completely so far as requirements of light and air would permit. The design of the building derives its outward character from this circumstance perhaps more than from any other. So the structure is hermetically sealed with double glass at all window openings. By mechanical means the fresh air is taken in at the roof levels, drawn to the basement, washed by passing through a sheet of water sprays (which in summer reduces its temperature two or three degrees) heated (in winter) circulated and finally exhausted from beneath the great skylight where the winter's snow will melt as it falls.

Outside the building is an enormous pile of impervious brick with splendid deep reveals. The stair chambers, air intakes and exhausts with their necessary machinery, pipe shafts and plumbing are grouped at all the outer corners of the main rectangle where light is least obstructed from the interior. The resultant walls of solid masonry at the corners where wall surfaces usually are slight give a noble clifflike mass to the structure. Moreover this insulates the stairways where they serve as practical fire escapes so that all the 1800 occupants of the entire building could safely and comfortably escape to the outside grounds in something like three minutes, if such a need in such a building can be supposed. These chambers also establish a ready means of continuous communication between stories at four points on each floor.

By this means the main building is systematically quartered in arrangement and is wired, heated and ventilated in quadruple insuring easy distribution and positive operation throughout the appurtenance systems with easy inter-communications between floors. Then the superimposed stories necessary to accommodate the required number of clerks are all aired, lighted and unified by a long, open, skylighted central court preserving in the occupation of the interior the character of the family-gathering, making the interior as a whole light, airy and beautiful altogether.

The floor areas surrounding this court have all been kept intact for business; the toilet accommodations, entrance and exit features being clustered in the four storied convenience annex which is reached directly from Seneca or Swan Sts., at the ends. This entrance annex has been semi-attached to the side of the main structure so as to obstruct the light from it as little as possible.

The top floor of the annex and of the main building with its mezzanine and outlying roof surfaces are the family recreation grounds where the clerks and their guests may be fed and entertained. Here are completely appointed kitchen, bakery and commodious dining rooms, lecture rooms and library, class rooms, rest rooms and roof gardens, and conservatories that will furnish a gay note to the interior summer and winter.

It can honestly be said that there are no flimsy makeshifts outside or inside the building. Simplicity, straightforwardness, good materials and dignified proportion of the various parts are all that give it architectural effect; the sole ornaments of the exterior are the stone groups surmounting the piers advertising and accenting the terminals of the longitudinal central aisle of the interior court, together with the stone bas-reliefs over the water-basins flanking and accenting the entrances.

The exterior is dark in color and durable. The interior light in color and no less durable. The interior walls are lined with a semi-vitreous, hard cream-colored brick. The floors and the interior trimmings of this brick lining have been worked out in magnesite, a new building material consistently used for the first time in this structure. Stairs, floors, doors, window sills, coping, capitals, partitions, desk tops, plumbing slabs, all are of this material and are worked "in situ" without seams or joints with sanitary curves at all wall surfaces, finishing hard and durable as iron, as light in color as the brick work and, not the least valuable of its properties, light in weight also. The solid concrete floors are cushioned with this magnesite and wood fibre permeated and made fireproof with magnesite, deafening the floors throughout the building and rendering them less cold and hard to the foot than masonry would be. They are then finished with a hard, durable surfacing of the magnesite.

The interior represents a full score of old building-problems in a new phase. Many experiments have been made in order that all the various appurtenance systems, filing systems and furnishings might make a time-saving, consistent, cleanly and easily-cleanable whole. To this end also a vacuum cleaning system has been installed with pneumatic motors to do the sweeping and scrubbing; and everything, where possible, has been designed free of the floor. The water-closets and their enclosures are all swung free of the floor with few horizontal joints anywhere in which dirt may lodge and instead of the usual dusty, banging doors, cleanable sliding screens are used. The metal lockers likewise and the metal desks are all designed with metal bases that at intervals only, touch the floor. The seats themselves are swung free of the floor onto the desk legs, never to scrape noisily about or be lifted by the janitor for cleaning purposes; think of the labor that would be required each night to pile 1800 chairs on top of 1800 desks and then to pile them down again! The desk tops are adjustable to various heights and the cabinets beneath them are interchangeable so that typewriter- and graphophone-desks may be introduced in the rows anywhere at will. The desk tops are of the same material as the floors, as are all the panels in the sides of the desks. The general scheme of arrangement of the desks and filing system is as orderly and systematically complete as a well disciplined army drawn up for review might be and all is threaded together with a system of electric wiring so that the mere pressure of a button puts any official of the organization in instant communication with any other member.

In the interior all matters of heating, ventilating, lighting, plumbing, refrigeration, mechanical carriers, pneumatic cleaning and intercommunication and electrical control have been assimilated into the structure and in such a way that a failure in any point may readily be reached and remedied.

Within the circular Information Desk, a prominent feature of the entrance lobby, are located the telephone switchboards, with a capacity of 300 connections, the electrical Master Clock controlling the numerous secondary clocks and register clocks and automatically ringing the signal gongs throughout the building; the switchboard by which the electric time system is operated, and private telegraph wires of both the Western Union and Postal Companies. From the visitors' gallery surrounding the lobby, furnished appropriately with steel chairs and writing tables, the operation of all of these devices is in plain sight. Wires extend from the switchboards to all parts of the building, accessible through metal outlet boxes sunk in the floors, permitting at any desk a direct and invisible connection with telephone, phonograph, light or power, or all of them.

Little disorder and no confusion arose from the inauguration of the building, for the building is its own furnishing —or its furnishings a part of the building. Finished, it is complete and ready for use. I know of no building in the country so complete in this respect. This means that patience and study were required in the work; and effort to eliminate all crudities and conflicting parts in order that the result might be simplicity itself.

It has taken a longer time to build the building than would have been necessary if the market had contained all the materials, ready at hand, as it does for ordinary buildings.

Unfortunately there is no ready-made market wherein to let contracts for architectural work of this nature. Work like this is not a matter of stock patterns or stock methods: Established processes dislike interruption; workmen do not like to think; contractors are afraid of the new thing for which they have no gauge; so in this instance the *Larkin* Company through the medium of an intelligent, experienced contractor, has gone beyond the middleman in many cases. "From Factory-to-Family" was still the rule in the building of the Office Building; in this instance, however, the family in question is the *Larkin Co.* itself.

The stone came from Lake Superior quarries direct to the building and was cut on the ground by days' labor at a cost $20,000.00 less than the work could have been let for by contract in Buffalo.

The magnesite interior trimming throughout the structure was another case of, — from the magnesite mines of Greece direct to the building, — to be manufactured there by days' labor into the various features of the interior, at a cost less than any permanent masonry-material known, and with a lightness and a sanitary and artistic perfection very difficult if not impossible to achieve in either stone or terra cotta.

Extreme care has been exercised in searching what market there was for the special thing, in almost every case, wanted. For instance, the iron fence enclosure was put out for bids in Buffalo and Cleveland and the lowest bids received were approximately $8000.00, many concerns in Chicago were tried with slightly better results until a man was found who had new machinery capable of punching as though it were mere tin, the heavy iron we proposed to use in its construction. This man made the fence for Jackson Park in Chicago and was accustomed to contract for heavy fence by the mile and he was not afraid to undertake to furnish our fence for $4100.00.

The glass in the ceiling lights cannot be bought again for double the price paid, — another case of finding the right thing after long search. The inside brick will never be sold again at the price the *Larkin* Company paid for it. The reinforced concrete floor-construction was finally let for half the Buffalo bids and it was found impossible to sublet the plain concrete work of the building for the price which the *Larkin* Company paid for it. A sub-contract was twice let for the interior trim in magnesite but each concern got into trouble before the time came to "make good" and then the architect and the contractor had to stump the country for means to carry out the work; many men and firms were consulted, in Chicago, in Buffalo, in Dayton, in Pittsburgh and finally in New York they found the man whose experience and ingenuity has aided the contractor in overcoming obstacles which seemed at the outset almost insurmountable. And I might recite in detail most structural items of the features going to make up the construction. All the

items — and their name it seems to me is legion — have been threshed out to the limit of endurance, with, in almost every case, a gratifying result.

Besides, this building is a better building in many respects than the one we began to build, for the best in appliances and materials were considered to be economical and some search was necessary to uncover the cheapest and best; moreover, the scope of the building broadened as it progressed; in fact the business grew so fast that new requirements had constantly to be met. The one question the directors were determined to have satisfactorily answered when matters of betterment were under consideration was whether the betterments to be made were real and if they were the answer was always "yes."

But perhaps the final proof, on account of the balance sheet at least, of the care and ingenuity exercised in behalf of the structure is the fact that this thoroughbred, fireproof building, by no means impoverished architecturally, including possibly the most complete heating and ventilating system in the country, with much plumbing and elaborate systems of electric wiring, together with its impressive and extensive fence-enclosure, was erected for approximately 17 cents per cubic foot whereas fireproof buildings by no means superior usually run from 23 cents to 30 cents per cubic foot.

The fact remains, for what it is worth, that in this case the *Larkin* Company has not fattened the middleman nor paid the high price attached usually to high specialties but comes into possession of a sound, modern, wholesome building scientifically adapted to facilitate the transaction of its business and insure the permanence of its records and continuity of its service to its customers as well as to promote the health and cheerfulness of its official family at comparatively a very low cost.

The ease with which the interior may be cared for, the relatively low cost of janitors' service and of repairs for many years to come will contribute toward a profitable operation.

Finally — it seems to me — that the American flag is the only flag that would look well on or in this building; the only flag with its simple stars and bars that wouldn't look incongruous and out of place with the simple rectangular masses of the exterior and the straightforward rectilinear treatment of the interior. I think our building is wholly American in its directness and freshness of treatment. It wears no badge of servitude to foreign "styles" yet it avails itself gratefully of the treasures and the wisdom bequeathed to it by its ancestors.

There may be some to question whether it is beautiful or not; there always will be the usual two opinions about that, for it has *"character"* and when character is pronounced in buildings or in people there is always a "for" and an "against,"—even when one's artistic instincts have not been perverted as ours have been by too much borrowed architectural finery. But in-so-far as it is simple and true it will live, a blessing to its occupants, fulfilling in a measure on behalf of the men who planted it there their two great reciprocal duties, duty to the Past and duty to the Future — duties self imposed upon all right thinking men.

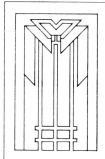

William R. Heath, "The Office Building and What It Will Bring to the Office Force"

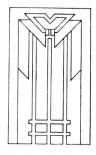

A talk to the office employees of Larkin Co., wherein is set forth some of the things the new building should do for them physically and spiritually.

The site for the Office Building was secured in the fall of 1902, after much careful planning and negotiating. No matter for what purpose land may be required, it is not possible for one company or individual to secure a number of small adjacent parcels at a reasonable price without the greatest care and effort. However, the land was secured and the truck yard, blacksmith shop, store-house, cottages and tumble-down shanties have given place to the splendid brick, stone, steel and magnesite Office Building.

This building did not grow of itself. There is not a brick in it that was not preceded by a thought. There is not a corner of its interior that does not contain the gray matter of many of the best men that work and think, and if the whole building does not contain and yield consciously to its inmates the spirit of the men who made it, it will fall far short of its purpose. So here is the building containing the best of the hands the heads and hearts of its makers turned over to its users; and what will it bring to us?

Let it be understood at the beginning that the large investment represented can never be returned to its owners in dollars, neither can the expenditure be justified in the hope of commercial dividends and, furthermore, its use will continually bring its daily burden of expense. We may know, therefore, that the dedication of this building by its makers

From *The Larkin Idea*, 6, November 1906, pp. 10–14.

to its users is with no sordid hope of material gain.

What will it bring to us? Surely no more than we are able to receive! As we pass along the pathway of life gathering of its abundance here and there, it must have occurred to each of us that the world yields to the individual only what he is capable of receiving; he can take no more than he is able to carry and if he burdens himself with tares and thistles, by so much less can he receive fruits and flowers. I care not how puffed up a man may be or how large he may look, when he steps upon the scales his disguise is discovered. We are what we *are*, no matter what we or others may think.

What will it bring to us? Much or little, of this sort or that, depending upon our capacity and desire.

The building and my subject are dedicated to "The Office Force" and what is that?

What is "The Office"? "The Office" is that branch of the *Larkin* business which merchandises its products.

What is "Force"? "Force" is *power in action*. Power is the ability to perform work and work is the overcoming of resistance.

Therefore, "The Office Force" is that power in action which overcomes the resistance of merchandising.

To tell what the New Building will bring to "The Office Force" requires a brief analysis of the Power back of the Force. The work we have to perform requires physical power, first, because much of our work, perhaps more than we are accustomed to think, is performed by muscular effort — such as messenger service, typewriter operating, filing and the operation of the many modern mechanical contrivances here in use; second, and far more important, because we require a physical being through which other powers may become forces. So "The Office Force" requires a strong, healthy body.

The chief resistance we must overcome, however, is accomplished by mental power. We want to buy goods; but the price, the quality and the quantity resist us. We want to ship goods; but complicated orders, cost of carriage, and damage incident to long hands and frequent handling resist us. We want to please our customers; but physical conditions, misunderstandings and sometimes ignorance resist us. Surely "The Office Force" requires a strong, healthy mind.

But "a sound mind in a sound body" will not overcome all resistance, and unless we have grasped more than this we are not in possession of the whole of the "*Larkin* Idea".

Perhaps this other power is more subjective than objective, yet it is essential to enable us to overcome the resistance from without as well as from within. We want to have courage but cowardice resists us. We want to be generous but selfishness resists us. We want to be honest but false standards resist us. We want to be just but unrighteousness resists us.

It is said that a corporation has no soul, the more reason then why those who serve it should. "The Office Force" must possess a healthy soul.

As the creators of the Office Building have brought to "The Office Force" the best of their hands and heads and hearts, so "The Office Force" must bring into the building a constant energy born of a strong body, mind and soul. It is this constant energy, this united, aggressive, positive effort that is irresistible. Everything short of this is either naught or a minus quantity. The Power of the office is made up of its positive or plus qualities and its weakness, of its negative or minus qualities, and its true value as a force is determined by the sum of all its positive qualities diminished by the sum of all its negative qualities.

Perhaps from this point the value of the building to us can best be considered by eliminating all of "The Office Force" but that contributed by the single individual. What the building will bring to you will depend upon your power as a positive force. What are you worth in the *Larkin* Office in units of force? One may possess power and not use it. The lake on the hilltop possesses static energy; it has power, but it is in reserve. Liberate the water and it flows down the hillside, under control, to turn the wheels of commerce; or, without control, to devastate the valley. The locomotive on the track under a hundred pounds of steam fairly trembles with reserve power which, if kept under control, will expand itself in moving the train, or if uncontrolled will burst forth causing destruction and death. What are you worth in the *Larkin* Office? That is, what power have you and when it is expended in force what percent aids in merchandising the *Larkin* Products and what percent is used up in friction, fuss and feathers?

In making a fair estimate of your work suppose you examine yourself with the aid of the following outline. Remember that if a man's power is one hundred percent and his dissipation one hundred percent, his force is naught.

OUTLINE FOR TAKING STOCK AT INVENTORY TIME.

A. BODY

A. Strength.
  1. Plus qualities:
    i. Power
    ii. Vigor
    iii. Force
  2. Minus qualities:
    i. Weakness
    ii. Languor
    iii. Fragility

B. Activity.
  1. Plus qualities:
    i. Speed
    ii. Promptness
    iii. Readiness
  2. Minus qualities:
    i. Delay
    ii. Tardiness
    iii. Indolence

C. Endurance
  1. Plus qualities:
    i. Courage
    ii. Tenacity
    iii. Pluck
  2. Minus qualities:
    i. Cowardice
    ii. Weakness
    iii. Timidity

B. MIND

A. Intelligence
  1. Plus qualities:
    i. Knowledge
    ii. Concentration
    iii. Judgment
    iv. Tact

  2. Minus qualities:
    i. Ignorance
    ii. Dissipation
    iii. Speculation
    iv. Indiscretion

B. Emotion
  1. Plus qualities:
    i. Loyalty
    ii. Fidelity
    iii. Forgiveness

  2. Minus qualities:
    i. Disloyalty
    ii. Infidelity
    iii. Revenge

C. Will
  1. Plus qualities:
    i. Purpose
    ii. Initiative
    iii. Control
    iv. Industry

  2. Minus qualities:
    i. Indecision
    ii. Inertness
    iii. Rashness
    iv. Laziness

C. SOUL

A. Faith.
  1. Plus qualities:
    i. Courage
    ii. Fortitude
    iii. Constancy

  2. Minus qualities:
    i. Cowardice
    ii. Instability
    iii. Inconstancy

B. Love.
  1. Plus qualities:
    i. Purity
    ii. Generosity
    iii. Sympathy
    iv. Honesty

  2. Minus qualities:
    i. Lust
    ii. Narrowness
    iii. Selfishness
    iv. Dishonesty

C. Reverence.
  1. Plus qualities:
    i. Sincerity
    ii. Humility
    iii. Justice

  2. Minus qualities:
    i. Insincerity
    ii. Conceit
    iii. Injustice

What will the Office Building bring to you? It will aid you in your effort to attain to and possess the positive qualities of your nature by which only you may hope to achieve.

It will supply your body with an abundance of pure air at the right temperature without drafts. It will supply you with an abundance of natural and artificial light, thus avoiding nervous tension. It will surround you with conveniences for refreshment, stimulant and repose and furnish you with an atmosphere of quiet that will contribute in every way to bodily strength, activity and endurance.

To the thinking mind this building will inspire intelligent effort. Every detail shows unstinted thought and evident purpose. Every complex problem of construction and its solution are modestly hidden back of plain surfaces. It has a strength and boldness easily discovered yet not boasted. It possesses beauty without a sacrifice to weakness. Its ornamentation is of its essence. Its unassumed simplicity is to be found only in the great in men and art.

A study of this building cannot fail to stimulate intelligence, inspire the highest emotions and give new purpose for greater achievements.

What will the building bring to you? If you have faith, it will add to your faith, virtue, and give you Courage, Fortitude and Constancy, for there is not a sham nor a "make believe" in it. To your better self it will speak of help and hope.

Turn your attention to its provisions for cleanliness. Small chance for dirt to enter, no place for dirt to hide away and none for dirt to stay. No silence could speak more significantly of purity of life.

In its plain simplicity it could be no more complete. Expense has prevented no needful provision or comfort. The most careful study has been made to provide for the practical and the artistic natures of its occupants. A like generosity displayed in your life and work will contribute largely to your own satisfaction and your efficient service.

The simple lines, harmonious appointments and soft, graceful coloring put your surroundings in sympathy with you, and you in sympathy with your work.

Things as well as people display an integrity or a lack of it. The materials of which this building is made are plain honest brick, stone, steel and magnesite, honestly put together.

The lines are right lines, the angles are right angles. The columns stand free, straight and true. The makers of the building have written "Honesty" on every wall and "Truth" on every pillar. With this example always before you it must be a constant inspiration to your integrity of life and honesty of purpose.

Stand beneath the great central court and look up and you cannot think a mean thought. Stand here for a moment and listen if perchance you cannot hear the words SINCERITY, HUMILITY, JUSTICE. Listen again for the words FELLOWSHIP, HONOR, EXCELLENCE, the three cardinals of the *Larkin* Business.

What will the Office Building bring to you?

If you will, it will bring to you "Life more abundantly."

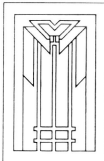

George Twitmyer, "A Model Administration Building"

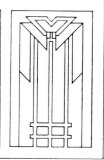

How system and appointment make the handling of over one thousand employes as easily as directing the work of one person. The Larkin Company, Buffalo.

Admirably meeting the intentions of its owners to facilitate the transaction of business, to insure permanence of records and continuity of service to customers and to provide for an official family numbering over a thousand, an environment healthful for body and mind, the new, absolutely fireproof Administration Building recently occupied by Larkin Co., of Buffalo, N.Y., stands a magnificent monument to fidelity to a business ideal. About 30 years ago, equipped with a two-story building, 40 × 60 feet, the Larkin Co. had its beginning. Today its factories and warehouses occupy 50 acres of floors and its executive work is conducted in the most striking private office building in the world.

This building is complete in every detail of construction and unique in nearly every feature of its arrangement and equipment. In its planning and building, adaptability to the peculiar character of the work to be carried on within its walls was the paramount consideration. From this and from the nature of the site, in the heart of a noisy, smoky, manufacturing district that it occupies, the building derives its general character.

The structure is of steel, Lake Superior sandstone and brick. It consists of a main building 100 feet wide and 200 feet long, and an annex 50 feet wide and 100 feet long. The

From *Business Man's Magazine,* 19, April 1907, pp. 43–49.

main building has seven floors: the annex four. In general form and all prominent points the building is rectangular, massive cliff-like walls, relieved by splendid, deep reveals, terminating at the corners in imposing square towers.

THE VENTILATING SYSTEM.

These towers afford room for the machinery of the ventilating system, for pipe-shafts and plumbing and for stairways, so that all floor areas are left wholly free for business purposes. A brick and stone wall surmounted by an iron fence to the height of 17 feet, all of a design in keeping with the building, and so constructed as to be apparently part of it, incloses the building. From the entrance gate a view through the glass main entrance doors, which are in line with it, into the inviting interior is possible.

The inside of the building is finished in a light cream-colored brick, with trimmings of magnesite, practically a new building material in this country.

The superimposed floor areas are arranged around a central, skylighted court, 24 feet wide and 112 feet long. It is 74 feet from the main floor to the pressed plate prism ceiling of the court. Over the glass ceiling is a hipped copper skylight. The space between is used as an exhaust chamber for the ventilating system. The warm exhaust air, in turn, melts the snow as it falls on the skylight in winter.

There are no partitions in the main building and no private offices barring those of the president of the company, formed at the extreme south end of the main floor by semi-partitions of brick, magnesite and glass. On the main floor, between the supporting columns of the central court, are rows of cabinets, about three and one-half feet high, surmounted by a coping of magnesite. This forms an aisle.

ARRANGEMENT OF DESKS.

In this aisle are located the desks of the executive heads, the office manager at the south end with his department meeting that of the secretary, who is at the north end of the aisle, about in the middle of the court.

On the floor area to the east of the aisle are the departments of the auditor and cashier, a wide approach from the entrance lobby and the department of railway claims. To the east are the advertising and printing departments. The mailing department, with its noisy folding and addressing machines, is housed in one of the factory buildings across the street. Although there is a clear view diagonally across this expansive floor, the architect by skillful designing has relieved all hall-like effect.

The second, third and fourth floors, except for half of the second occupied by the typewriters and a smaller part of the third occupied by the mail department, are given over to the accommodation of the routine work of office. An insight into the character of the work conducted here helps one to appreciate the economy of the arrangement on these floors.

The territory contributory to the Larkin business, and this embraces the whole of the United States, is divided into what are termed state groups. In these groups the work of caring for all normal orders is completed—packers' slips and shipping tags are made out, the routing is done, the records are entered, all correspondence incident to the orders is carried on and they are filed. Each group is a complete business unit and by arrangement on the floor areas about the central court is practically isolated from the others, although in easy communication with them.

On the fifth floor are the dining room, bakery and kitchen, with a complete modern hotel equipment large enough to prepare a full dinner for 2,000 people. Nearly a thousand employes are served luncheon here at noon each working day. Cost prices are charged and one is able to get a satisfying lunch for 10 or 12 cents. A table d'hote lunch, consisting of a soup, a meat, vegetables, dessert and coffee, tea or milk, is served for 20 cents, and one a little more elaborate for a quarter. Tables are also provided for the use of those who wish to bring their lunches or part of them from home, as many do.

THE CONSERVATORY FLOOR.

The sixth floor is somewhat broken up. On it, at each end of the court, in plain view from the main floor 74 feet below, is a conservatory. Here are grown palms and other plants of suitable nature. There are also basins, a score or so feet long and of well proportioned width, for aquatic plants. To the east and west at the sides of the central court the sixth floor is without cover, providing a roof garden and promenade for use of the employes during pleasant weather.

The entrance lobby includes all of the first floor of the annex. The rest of this part of the structure is given over to provisions for the convenience and comfort of the employes. On the second floor are locker rooms and lavatories; on the next, quiet, secluded rest rooms and an infirmary and dispensary, where those in need of it may receive the care of a graduate nurse. The fourth floor of this annex accommodates the headquarters of the Young Woman's Christian Association, a library and a schoolroom, from which new employes are sent to the department in which they are to work, fairly familiar with what they were employed to do.

As to magnesite: In the two large vestibules, and in the lobby, we meet most striking examples of what can be done with this material. In the lobby, on the left, are two large, square brick piers, surmounted by capstones and large vases made of magnesite in the unique design that the architect has so well preserved throughout the entire building. These piers form the abutments for a half-circular magnesite counter, 12 feet in diameter made without a joint, back of which is the master clock. The case of this clock is about eight feet high and is a combination of magnesite in its most intricate uses. In the lobby may also be seen columns, balcony railings, doors and even sashes made of this new building material.

Brick piers capped with magnesite, magnesite columns and frames holding plate glass form the protecting fronts about the shafts of two passenger elevators. To the left of these elevators is the cashier's department, exhibiting in its counters, doors and framework other uses made of magnesite. Two safes are constructed of this most excellent fireproof material, the ordinary steel safe doors being set into it as the vaults were built up.

MAGNESITE WORK EVERYWHERE.

In the construction of the three private offices of the president and of the capitals surmounting the piers of court are more splendid examples of magnesite work. Besides these, it is applied to all the interior window sills and lintels, caps and bases, girder covers, ventilating aperture frames and to the floors, of which there is nearly 75,000 square feet. The steps of the stairways, the partitions in the toilet rooms and the wash-basin slabs are also made of magnesite.

While this material in various forms of mixture has been used for floor finish for the past 30 years in Europe, this is the first case where it has been used for entire interior trimmings.

Double glass windows that ordinarily are never opened, and close-fitting doors practically hermetically seal the building. A steam blast system of ventilation keeps the temperature in all parts of the building at from 70° to 72° Fahrenheit throughout the year. There is a constant supply of 112,000 cubic feet of pure, washed and tempered air a minute. The exhaust is 100,000 cubic feet a minute. Thus, the building fairly breathes. The entire air volume of the building, something like 2,000,000 cubic feet, is completely changed every 20 minutes, and without creating drafts.

FRESH AIR SCHEME.

Fresh air is taken into the building at the roof-line and passed to the basement through large brick flues, one for each of the four blast heating units located in the basement, one at each corner of the building. Tempering coils at the base of each flue raise the temperature of the incoming air in freezing weather to above the freezing point; then it passes through water sprays, produced by centrifugal pumps forcing the water through piping and spray nozzles into spray chambers.

The fresh air now passes through eliminaters to the blast fan suction chambers; these eliminaters remove the excess humidity in the atmosphere. From these chambers the blowers deliver the fresh, pure air into plenum chambers, each of the four chambers being divided, the upper space provided with re-heating coils from which the hot air is taken, the lower chamber containing tempered air.

From the plenum chambers the air is forced through concealed galvanized iron distributing ducts to all parts of the building. These pipes connect with both hot and tempered air chambers and are provided with mixing dampers controlled by thermostats located in the part of the building each supplies. These thermostats control the mixing dampers automatically as the temperature changes, so the right mixture of hot and tempered air is admitted to the ducts to maintain the desired temperature. Four exhaust blowers are employed to remove the foul air.

In cold weather the warm air is admitted near the floors and exhausted from near the ceilings. In hot weather the order is reversed. For use in hot weather there is provided with each blast apparatus a mechanical cooling device. Refrigerating pipes are located in the four spray chambers. The temperature of the fresh air coming in contact with these pipes is lowered sufficiently to make the building comfortable during the hottest weather.

NO ARTIFICIAL LIGHT NEEDED.

The windows at the sides and ends of the building and the skylight over the court so illuminate all floor areas that very little artificial light is needed, on clear days practically none. Provision for artificial lighting the building has, however, been carefully worked out, and the massive bronze light fixtures, strong though simple in design, are unusually effective ornamentally. Except in the central aisle, the lighting is from the ceiling. One hundred and fifty candle power Nernst glowers in ribbed glass globes, about 12 feet above the desk tops, give a generous illumination so diffused that it is not noticeably more trying to the eye than daylight. In the main aisle the same effect is secured by a cluster of four 100 candle power glowers and globes like those used in the ceiling lights. The fixtures supporting these clusters stand upon the floor; they are of bronze and consistent in design with those at the ceiling.

To those familiar with how a complete equipment of desks and cabinets and the economic arrangement of them can facilitate the progress of the work in a great office of this kind, the desks and cabinets in this building, at first glance, present themselves as most admirable. Desks and cabinets are of steel; the lockers in the cloak rooms are also of steel and have combination locks. Twelve carloads of desks and 18 of cabinets make up the equipment.

All desks are flat-top and built in simple, straightforward lines without elaborate ornamentation of any kind. The tops are of a fireproof composition very much like wood in the characteristics noticeable to the users. The steel work is richly enameled in harmony with the color scheme of the interior.

These desks are of three distinct types. The regular clerk's desk, of which there are now a thousand in use in the building, is most ingeniously devised. They are built in pairs, one facing another. This unit is so arranged that it may be joined to others like it, forming a row of desks the correct length to accommodate the clerks of a given department. The tops of the desks are adjustable and may be lowered when used for typewriters; for the use of correspondents, graphophones, and with the aid of this instrument from three to four thousand letters, dictated in the Larkin offices each day, are set in them.

ATTACHED STEEL CHAIRS.

The chairs, which are of steel, leather cushioned, are supported from one of the desk legs and so are swung free of the floor. This arrangement is patented and is here used for the first time. At the close of the day the chairs are folded up, by dropping the back onto the seat, by the clerks, and pushed under the desks. The tops also are cleared of all work, papers going into one of the desk drawers, books and cards filed into the cabinets provided for them. In less than two minutes from the sounding of the time-gong every clerk's desk in the building may be absolutely cleared, leaving not so much as a scrap of paper in sight. Under such conditions the janitor with a vacuum cleaning apparatus makes short work of the day's accumulation of dust.

The chief clerk's desks are very much like the ordinary double pedestal flat-top desk, except that they are of steel with decorative panels of magnesite. The chairs for these desks are attached like those on the regular clerks' desks.

The desk outfit in the central aisle of the main floor consists of the two individual desks for the office manager and the secretary, one at each end of the aisle and of seven large desks, 5 × 14 feet, and eight desk-like tables, 4 × 11 feet. Desks and tables are arranged alternately. The desks accommodate four executives and two clerks, the executives facing each other at the ends, the clerks in the middle. Each executive has quarter of the table back of him, where an individual graphophone, always ready for use, is provided for him. Desk and table are so placed that by merely turning in his swivel chair the executive is brought into a working position at either; both desks and tables are amply supplied with drawers. The chairs used here are the first steel, arm, swivel chairs ever built.

SHEET STEEL CABINETS.

The filing cabinets are of enameled sheet steel and are built into the walls. They are the first sectional steel cabinets ever placed in use. Arranged on a unit system, an easy interchange of sections is possible. No matter what changes may be made in the size of forms to be filed in the future, the cabinets may be easily adapted to accommodate them. The vertical system of filing is used throughout. The cabinets in the central aisle and those backing them are provided with locks, a single lock controlling all drawers in a section.

A volume could be written upon the electrical adjustments employed in the building. The wires are all concealed, the wire conduits running in the floor under the magnesite surface. There are 400 outlet boxes for the wires, so that it is possible to convey a telephone or power current wire invisibly to any desk on any floor. For the operation of the graphophones a special current of 20 volts is provided, and has been found far better than the 110-volt current, cut down with a lamp in series, generally used. This is the only special office graphophone current in use in the world. From the outlet boxes both direct and alternating currents are available, so that any of the electrically operated business machines may almost instantly be installed at any desk.

The master clock, located within the circular desk in the reception lobby, automatically operates the clocks and timegongs throughout the building. Here also is the switchboard for something over 300 telephone connections.

COMFORT OF EMPLOYES.

Throughout the whole structure and its appointments there is a keenly evident forethought for the bodily comfort of the men and women whose daily business home it is as for the most economical and convenient business arrangement.

Indeed, no outlay was spared to make the lighting, ventilating, plumbing and every feature that means comfort for the daily worker, the best in the world. At the many lavatories individual towels are provided at the expense of the company, to be used once and then laundered. It is safe to say that every appointment of the building is as far in advance of what is usually seen as this individual towel is in advance of the old office towel that hangs from a roller on the wall.

In the near future a uniform in the shape of a smock or apron is to be provided and laundered by the company for the young women. This will be intended to protect their gowns and to preserve the color scheme, for at present the ensemble of blacks, reds, whites and greens, individually becoming, most assuredly, is undeniably at variance with the color scheme of the interior.

From a spot on the sixth floor of this magnificent building, called by an employe "inspiration point," there is stretched before one a scene unlike any other in the world. Directly in front are the dignified capitals surmounting the columns of the central court. On the floor areas below and in the main court hundreds of people busily transacting the affairs of this great institution are in plain view. One is reminded of nothing so much as of a mammoth watch. There are the departments; each steadily, quietly rotating about its own axis, yet in perfect co-ordination with the rest, and each so delicately meshed to its neighbor that one helps the other and in no way interrupts its progress. It is enterprise, American enterprise, that drives the wheels; carefully organized systems and methods are the jewel bearings; good will, the lubricant.

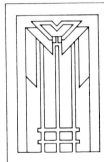

Marion Harland,
"The Administration Building"

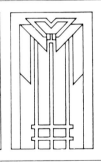

On alighting in front of the great rows of factories, the Administration Building is before you. It combines strength with dignity. Its lines are plain and its construction is arranged to utilize daylight to the fullest extent. Altho it has been visited by hundreds of thousands of people, who admired its beauty, strength and utility, and altho people from distant lands overseas came here and carried away details of the building to use at home, this 20th century structure is unknown to millions of our own people.

If I were describing a large hotel I should refer to foyer, reception rooms, rugs, bronzes, flowers and other attractions. But in dealing with this plant I purpose going to the heart of things, rather than describing in detail the exceptional appointments of what a delighted visitor christened the "Temple of Labor."

The building was erected in 1906, on a separate tract on the north of Seneca Street, extending thru to Swan Street. It is five stories in height. Were it like many office buildings in great cities, I should not dwell upon its construction. But as it is conceded to be one of the world's finest buildings, it deserves more than passing mention, because of its original features, which always excite visitors' wonder. The building is fireproof. On entering its Seneca Street portal they see a tablet reading: "Honest labor needs no master, Simple justice needs no slave." Directly beneath is a sheet of pure running water, typical of the activities within the edifice, and the purity of everything made in the adjacent factories.

From *My Trip Thru the Larkin Factories* (Buffalo, New York, 1913), pp. 13–22.

On the left of the Swan Street portal at the rear, I read a tablet on which is inscribed: "Freedom to every man and commerce with all the world." The Company's export business, and importations of raw materials, reflect this sentiment.

This is what a foreigner, Mr. H.P. Berlage, the eminent architect in Amsterdam, Holland, wrote about it in a foreign architectural magazine, under the title, "Newer American Architecture": "The Administration Building of the Larkin Factories, in Buffalo, N.Y., U.S.A., is excellently lighted, despite the enormous wall masses. Whatever conception of the commercial building we may have here in Europe, nothing exists of such power as this American Building. . . . I went away with the conviction that I had seen a genuinely modern work, and filled with esteem for the master who had the power to create a building which seeks in vain its equal in Europe!"

The officials and about 1,200 clerks are very comfortably housed herein. I learned that in its adjacent factories, 1,100 men and 500 women are employed. The Company's Pottery near here employs 300 workers, so that in Buffalo alone there are about 3,100 employees. In the Branch Offices, Warehouses and Showrooms in New York, Boston, Philadelphia, Cleveland, Chicago and Peoria, 700 men and women are employed. There are also several hundred employees in the Company's Mill and Chair Factory in Memphis, Tenn., and 270 workmen in its Bottle Factory at Greensburg, Pa. This makes a total of nearly 4,500 employees on its payrolls.

I was told that the popularity of Larkin goods is so great

that strong overtures had been made to have Branches opened in every section of the country. But experience has proved that, aided by the Company's Buffalo factories, and those controlled by it in other places, the present Branches are well able to serve customers acceptably.

The basement is equipped with separate lockers for men and women. A pure-drinking-water-system, and modern sanitary arrangements, show the Company's care. Here is the Repair Shop, where hundreds of typewriters, billing, adding, and other machines are kept in good condition. Numerous devices for turning out forms and various kinds of letters required by the Home Office and Branches, are in service all day and often at night. This busy hive houses the Exchange which handles the pouches used in the pneumatic system with which this building and the factories are equipped. It also contains the Outgoing Mail Department.

The great Central Court, extending from the main floor to the roof, has an attractive skylight, which, with the large single-pane glass windows, admits a flood of daylight. The building is immaculate and looks as if it had recently been completed.

At the south end of the main floor are the offices of the President, the Vice-Presidents, the Treasurer, and his assistants. The officials do not seclude themselves, and it is always possible to interview them on legitimate business. Here are the cashiers and pay clerks. The Statistical Department is nearby and is the depository of costs that are constantly consulted. Across the lobby is the Employees' Sales Department. It deserves mention that very large quantities of Products, Premium Merchandise, and Groceries are needed to fill orders from thousands on the Company's payrolls, who buy everything possible here. As one said, "We believe in using Larkin goods."

Elsewhere on this floor are located the Accounting, Auditing, and Invoice Checking Departments. Everything received must pass thru them, so that any mistake may be detected before the articles go into consumption or are shipped. The Advertising Department, whose duties are indicated by its title, is situated on the west side, near the Secretary's office, in the north end. The Secretary oversees transactions of buyers and their assistants. Between his office and the south end of the Court are various Buyers'

Offices, the Editorial Offices of "The Larkin Idea," and the Company's other publications; also the Office Manager's Department.

One of the many unusual features which place this building in a class by itself is its furniture. All desks are made of steel, with fire-proof composition tops. The metal chairs have leather seats and backs, and swing from the desks. They can be folded and swung under the desks, allowing the floor to be cleaned without handling them. This feature saves the labor and expense which would follow if hundreds of chairs had to be piled on top of hundreds of desks and replaced after sweeping. As a systematic housekeeper who believes that time and toil saved are time and toil gained, this method of economizing both met with my unqualified approval and led me to wonder if some practical woman's brain had not been consulted when the office furniture was selected.

On the second floor are some of the Sales-Accounting Departments, which are divided into various States and Countries, each handling all details connected with orders turned over to it for attention. (Others are on the third and fourth floors.) Thousands of orders arrive daily, are here checked, entered and distributed for prompt attention among various departments and in the factories.

Here are transcribers — young women supplied with wax phonograph-cylinders — whose duty is to reproduce on typewriting machines all matter that was spoken when the records were made in other departments. These records are made as operatic airs and speeches are made for reproducing by talking machines. There is accommodation for 150 operators, each of whom is supplied with an electrically operated phonograph outfit and tubes for carrying sound to the ears.

When a transcriber needs more work, an interesting device signals. The distributing clerk observes a red rod above the desk, and hands the disengaged operator additional records, whereupon the rod is lowered out of sight. The use of the phonograph greatly simplifies business. It would be more difficult and take longer to handle the great volume of correspondence but for its aid.

On the second floor, at both ends of the Court, are located the Stenographers' Departments, in which writing machines only are used. The stenographers handle all clerical work for which the phonographs are not adapted. Here is the Annex to the second floor. It has a Dispensary, with a nurse in attendance, who is supplied with everything required for first aid, or temporary treatment of disabilities. In connection with it are three rooms equipped with five hospital beds.

The Rest Room nearby has ample space, good light and attractive furniture. A player-piano adds variety and pleasure during the luncheon hour. Some of the young women come here to read; others prefer dozing, and some desire music. All are rested by their stay.

In addition to the Sales-Accounting Departments on the third floor, Inward and Registered Mails are handled. Thousands of letters arrive during the day, are skilfully sorted, classified and quickly distributed. It is amazing to see the rapidity with which mails are handled. This is necessary so that prompt shipments may be made.

Here is the Library, whose shelves contain several hundred volumes furnished by the Company. The room is attractively furnished and well lighted. The Buffalo Public Library maintains a branch here, with about 400 volumes, which are frequently exchanged. Any employee has access to the latest magazines, and may take current issues home. There is also what is known as the "suit-case aid." Clerks make a list of books wanted, and the desired books are brought here from the main Public Library during the day. Applicants take the books home at night and save time and carfares. The third floor Annex also contains the rooms of the Young Women's Christian Association, where helpful counsel may at all times be had from the Secretary and her assistants. Nearby is the Lecture Room in which — when not used for lectures — class instruction is given. Pupils gain a better understanding of the more important work and are qualified for advancement. The rudiments of the business are taught in a beginners' class. In the south corridor of the third floor is a grand piano, with a portable player, for the workers' use.

On the third floor Annex a School of Instruction is maintained, which qualifies clerks for more effective work. Students receive pay while being taught. The Company seeks efficiency in everything and spares neither effort nor money in its quest. When possible, high school graduates

are engaged for clerical work. They consider it an honor to belong to the Larkin forces. On the fourth floor, in addition to two other Sales-Accounting Departments, is the Inquiry Department, which gives customers timely information. Business from any part of the world goes direct to its department by an overhead carrier system, which conveys carriers from desk to desk, floor to floor, and to and from the factories. Electricity is used for propulsion. Carriers travel to and fro continuously, rapidly and silently. Even smallest orders must go thru a regular course, and are filled as carefully as large ones. Everything is systematically done.

As this business serves over two million customers, it must have safeguards to reduce errors to the lowest point. The system is simplified as much as possible, and a definite routine is followed, to avert mistakes and delays. This requires clerks, correspondents, recorders, routers, billers and inspectors. The inspectors come last and review everything done, going carefully over the routing and billing, to insure accuracy before the shipment leaves the factory.

The fifth floor is devoted to the Restaurant and Kitchens. Interesting as were all the departments of the business, I confess that I inspected this section with peculiarly close attention and enjoyment. My experiences in housekeeping on a small scale led me to study closely the same kind of work when it is done more by wholesale than is possible in the ordinary home. So I kept my eyes open for all impressive details and I found a number to compel my admiration. The Kitchen in the north end is in charge of a competent chef, and burns only natural gas. From it all hot meats, vegetables and soups are served. The Bakery, at the south end, supplies bread, rolls and desserts. The Restaurant accommodates 600 persons at one sitting, altho only a small part can be shown in the picture on page 15. This room, which is very attractive, is fitted in mission style with solid tables, and chairs with leather seats. The tables have swinging tops which can be tilted and used as seat-backs, when additional seating accommodation is required for larger gatherings. Hanging on the walls are worthy paintings of value. The Restaurant is conducted for the Company's clerks, and deserves high praise. I enjoyed the meals I ate there. All food is supplied at cost — sometimes below cost. To directors and distinguished guests is served the same food as the youngest clerk may order. Prices range from 1c. to 15c. a dish. The menu always shows from 65 to 80 articles. Soup costs only 3c.; roast beef and mashed potatoes 15c.; coffee with cream 3c.; ice cream 3c. Tables are reserved for visitors who have gone thru the factories. On returning from the inspection, guests, the number of whom was telephoned ahead, find awaiting them a collation of crackers, peanut butter, coffee and ice cream. The menu is changed with the season. The visitors' corner is a pleasant resting place.

At the north end of the Court the Golden Rule stands out in attractive letters on a panel. On the east and west sides and at the south end, other sentiments are inscribed, which fill those who use the building with lofty ideals and noble purposes. Beautiful conservatories flourish at the north and south ends of the two spacious tiled roof gardens. In pleasant weather these gardens are used for recreation. On clear days an extensive view in all directions awaits visitors.

At the south end is "Inspiration Point," a name given by visitors, which has clung to it for years. From this coign of vantage I looked down on a part of three floors and the main floor, and saw hundreds of busy people at work. The outlook was inspiring. These alert men and women take a real interest in customers' orders.

An Employees' Savings Department encourages thrift among the workers. The Company receives their deposits as a demand loan only. Interest is compounded and credited at the rate of 5% per annum on the first of every January, April, July and October, even on the smallest balance. The Company will repay the loan on demand, in amounts of not less than $1, with accrued interest. This Savings Department exists solely for the accommodation and benefit of Larkin employees. It speaks well for them that on the day I was at the Department there was on deposit over $238,000 to their credit.

Wires of both telegraph systems lead direct to this floor, and the Company is always in communication with all parts of the world.

During recent years hundreds of thousands of people have come here. It would require several volumes merely to publish the names of men prominent in financial, manufacturing, commercial, professional, and other circles who went thru the plant. I need not publish a full list of all distinguished foreigners who included its inspection in their American visit. Among the names registered here are these:

Baron Elichu Shibawaska. President First Bank, Tokio, Japan;

Nakano Buei, President Tokio Chamber of Commerce;

Baron and Baroness Kanda Naiba (he is a famous Japanese Educator);

Nimami Washitaro, Doctor of Agriculture, Japan;

Iwayo Sueo, the Japanese author;

Doi Mishio, President Chamber of Commerce, Osaka, Japan;

Matsura Toshia, Assistant Mayor of Osaka;

Nishi Mura Jiber, President Kioto Chamber of Commerce;

Otani Kaher, President Yokohama Chamber of Commerce;

Hara Rynta, Chief Engineer Yokohama Water Works.

In a party of visiting German scientists and educators who inspected the factories were:

Dr. Ing. Okkar von Miller, member of the House of Lords of Bavaria, Germany;

Count von Podewils-Durniz, former Secretary of State of Bavaria;

Prof. Dr. W. von Dyck, Rector Emeritus of the Technical University, Munich;

Dr. Wilhelm von Borscht, Lord Mayor of Munich;

Herr Ph. Gelius, Architect of the Museum of Munich;

Herr Alex Shirmann, Director of the Library of the Munich Museum;

Dr. Fuchs, Professor of Physics and Mathematics;

Herr Ingenieur Trautwein, Civil Engineer;

Herr Ingenieur Orth, Mining Engineer, and

Dr. Colin Ross, Secretary of the Commission.

Many foreign delegates to the International Congress for Testing Materials also went thru the factories. Among them were:

Prince Andrew and Princess Sophia Gagarin,

Prince Serge Gagarin, Prince Levin, these four being from Russia;

Alfred Deinlein, Chief Engineer of Ministry of Commerce, Vienna;

Peter Christophe, Chief Engineer Bureau of Roads and Bridges, Belgium;

H.J. Rabozee, Commandant of the Reserve Corps of Engineers, Brussels, Belgium;

E. Rung, Lieutenant of the Royal Corps, Denmark;

M. Malaval, Engineer of the Naval Artillery of France;

Col. J. Leon Gages. Director of Construction at Bourges;

Privy Councilor Monch, of the Imperial Marine Department of Germany;

Navy Councilor Schulz. of Germany;

Privy Councilor Jaeger. of Prussia;

Prof. Shoehe Tanaka, Doctor of Philosophy in Japan;

Dr. Fritz Carns, First Secretary of the Chamber of Commerce and Industry, Reichenberg, Austria;

Dr. Robert Mayer, Secretary of the Chamber of Commerce, Brunn, Austria.

The Governors of several States also inspected the Larkin factories. Among the more recent visitors were Governors Folk, of Missouri; Norris, of Montana; Burke, of North Dakota; West, of Oregon, and Carey, of Wyoming.

Dr. Grenfell, Medical Missionary to Labrador, visited the factories last year, delivered an address, and ordered $458 worth of Products and Groceries to be sent to meet his vessel, the "George B. Cluett," in Boston. On January 16, 1912, my friend, Dr. Harvey W. Wiley, formerly Chief of the Bureau of Chemistry of the U.S. Department of Agriculture in Washington, D.C., lectured before the workers on his views of the Pure Food question. I was told that on going thru the factories he had only highest praise for everything he saw. Visitors from home or abroad always receive a hearty welcome.

Upon my asking the reasons for the great activity I saw, the management said, "It is the splendid loyalty and good will of our friends, more than anything else, which keeps this business at the top." The Company seems to regard itself as a trustee administering a large estate for the benefit of those interested. Its chief concern appears to be how it can best serve customers.

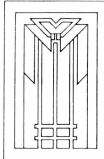

APPENDIX K
Russell Sturgis,
"The Larkin Building in Buffalo"

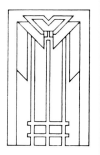

This business building, the architectural creation of Mr. Frank Lloyd Wright of Chicago, is reproduced in many excellent photographs, some of which will be shown in this article and others in the March number of the Architectural Record. From among them I select Fig. 1 as the most capable of giving a general idea of the design. The plan given in Fig. 8 shows the purpose of each member of the building, and the scale can be estimated as to the heights, on the basis afforded by the steps of the entrance doorways, checked by the height of the doorway (seen in Fig. 1) themselves, and by comparison with the plan. It is not safe to utilize the courses of brick in this way, because their height is uncertain; the bricks may be of unusual dimension or laid with unusually wide joints. The nearest towerlike mass in Fig. 1—that against which the telegraph pole is seen relieved—is about 90 feet high. The broader mass behind it would be, then, about 110 feet high, and this appears to be the highest level of the walls. A perspective draughtsman can easily determine the relative proportions, as width compared to height, etc., but this front may be taken, in the absence of any figure dimensions on the plan, roughly as 90 to 95 feet in width, not, of course, including the north wing seen in Fig. 2.

That front shown in Fig. 1 is called in this paper the east front. The longer side, showing in the same picture seven windowed bays divided by square buttress-piers, is called here the south flank.

It is possible to gain some knowledge of the character of the building by means of photos of the interior. Twenty excellent interior views are found in the collection above mentioned, and Fig. 3 shows how the building has a nave

From *Architectural Record*, 23, April 1908, pp. 310–21.

and aisles—the nave shown in the illustrations having windows at the ends, and a skylight overhead; each aisle is divided up into four lofts or stories of 16 to 17 feet each, in the clear. The broad end windows, seen in Fig. 3 at the end of the great hall, are the same windows that show in Figs. 1 and 2 between the buttresses, and they correspond with the arrangement of the south front, as in Fig. 1—note the four stories of broad windows flanked by narrower ones, which are seen within and without alike. One relation between exterior and interior is seen in this—the square brick piers which divided what we here call the nave from the galleries at each side—a long double row of them are on the same axes as the buttress-like piers crowned by globes and human sculpture, in Figs. 1 and 2.

In Fig. 3 there are partly seen the large galleries at the left and at the right hand of the central skylighted nave. These halls are of only moderate height—one story of windows to each, as seen in Fig. 4, which gives the interior of the fourth story, south side. Each one, as well as the floor of the high nave, is filled rather closely with desk-tables at which are seen seated clerks fully occupied in their employ. In this view, we are looking eastward, the window on the left and in face of us are those seen from outdoors in Fig. 1, and the central nave is north of us, on our right.

The western end of the building is very closely like the east front; but the northern side as shown in Fig. 2 is masked by projecting masses of building which include a great vestibule with entrance doorways to east and west. In the northeast detail view, Fig. 5, the doorway at the head of the steps where a young man is standing is one of those two entrances; it has the firm name on the large fan-light, and is probably the working entrance. The plan shows a similar doorway at the west of this one, and opposite to it. The houses of the town and a church crowd the site rather closely on the northern side.

The square towers at either end and flanking the entrance in Fig. 5 are about 18 feet in horizontal dimension. That one seen in Fig. 5 has the overplus of water very skilfully treated as a cascade with a sculptural setting. The two outer towers, seen in Fig. 1, have small doorways, with steps of approach. These are ventilator and stairway towers, and that with the fountain contains also a staircase.

In tracing the analysis of this building through all this pile of photographs, and in setting down, as above, its scheme, we have also partly prepared ourselves to judge of it as a work of architecture. The lover of architecture who looks, perhaps for the first time, at a building so entirely removed as this one from the traditional styles and schools feels a shock of surprise, and this a surprise which is the reverse of pleasant. Few persons who have seen the great monuments of the past, or adequate photographs of them; who have loved them and have tried to surprise their secret of artistic charm, will fail to pronounce this monument, as seen in Fig. 1, an extremely ugly building. It is, in fact, a monster of awkwardness, if we look at its lines and masses alone. It is only capable of interesting that student who is quite aware that the architects of the modern world during fifty years of struggle have failed to make anything of the old system — the system of following the ancient styles with the avowed purpose of developing some one of them and going on to other things.

For such a task, the as yet unperformed duty of making comely a hard working and economical building, the designer might feel that Roman colonnading was out of the question, as extravagant in cost and waste of space, and the frankly arcuated styles of the Middle Ages unavailable for similar or equally cogent reasons. He might find his only available suggestion from old times in the seventeenth century Italian, and the eighteenth century French palaces — in styles which depended upon fenestration. And then he might well say that he was tired of seeing imitations of those monuments; that the popular and successful architects of the time have filled our cities with such an array of feeble school studies, based upon plans good in themselves but powerless to suggest an architectural treatment of the whole, that he will have none of that pseudo style.

Admitting, then, that the chase of the Neo-Classic, of the Gothic, of the French Romanesque, has come to nothing, that we are as far as we were in 1850 from a living style of architecture, and even from anything which is worthy to be called architecture at all, when a large mass of the work of a period is taken together, we shall find that the building we are considering puts on a new aspect.

Do we find in this building none of those familiar motives — those accepted details which are architecture for us? It is because the designer of this building was determined to furnish nothing which his practical requirements did not call for. Is there no visible proof? It is because a flat roof is just as easy to make tight and durable, with modern appliances of building, and because a swarm of skylights and other utilitarian openings are better and more easily accommodated in and upon a flat roof. As there are no chimneys, giving an opportunity for an agreeable breaking of the masonry into the sky and the sky into the masonry? It is because there are no separate fires, each fire requiring its own flue, and that flue carried well above all obstructions. There is probably one fire, and one only, in the building; moreover, that one fire is driven by a forced draught and requires no tall chimney shaft to make it burn. Is there no system of fenestration — the windows, and therewith the doors, showing in pretty groups or in long-drawn sequence carefully balancing one another? That is because the building consists of five equal stories, used for similar purposes; divided generally into long, unbroken halls — lofts, in short; and because it seems a feeble thing to do — to break up the arrangement of windows *merely* for the sake of pretty proportions. Are the grouped rooms and closets of utility arranged, even at the expense of the building, by thrusting forward their crude masses to mask and distort, what might have been the effect of the main structure, all as seen in Fig. 2? That is because this is to be an economical, working building, and offices of a great business house, and because it was thought well to be resolute in the chosen way and not to pretend to build a monument of architecture when a working structure was desired.

It is, indeed, quite certain that in New York the newly erected business building at the corner of Wall Street and Broadway, shown in Fig. 7, is more nearly like what a business building ought to be than the elaborated and delicately detailed skyscrapers around. It is certain that nothing is gained to architecture by trying to make a business building architectural in the good old sense. The fine arts have nothing to do with the hustle and bustle of daily bread-winning operations. Those are hostile influences, as Ruskin pointed out much more than half a century ago; or it might be urged with still greater force that fine art and active mercantile pursuits are mutually exclusive. If you are to enjoy a work of art you must have leisure and a quiet mind; if you are to produce a work of art you must have peace and a single mind. In neither case will it do to have hanging over you the peremptory calls of the money-making organization — not one paymaster, who might perhaps forget his utilitarian requirements in the light of design and the joy of creation; but the commercial enterprise which can have no enthusiasm and no care for finer things than commerce.

We are left, then, with our sympathies enlisted in Mr. Wright's behalf, to consider what else might have been done, had the architect felt that he could not bear to turn out a building so ungainly, so awkward in grouping, so clumsy in its parts and in its main mass. Rejecting all that older styles have to offer us in the way of construction and in the way of detail, we may still ask, How did the designers work when men knew how to design? What, apart at least from the unconscious following of the style accepted during this period was their main object? They sought for light and shade. The interesting treatment of light and shade, the production of graceful and simple combinations of light and shade was their chief aim. A thought in architecture is generally a thought in light and shade.

When the great buildings of the world were designed everything else which was capable of design received it; and all design in pure form, as in sculpture, in relief modeling, in grouping and massing, is design in light and shade. The simple requirements of every-day life were met by the maker of vessels and utensils with as free and as successful a method of designing as the requirements of state and of religion; and he worked in form principally, that is, in light and shade. Earthen vessels and metal utensils were gracefully designed. And all this not because the maker cared greatly to produce a decorative object, for he also was dimly conscious of the fact that it was hardly worth while to waste

design on a working tool, but because it was inevitable that a man who did fine things on a Monday would still do comely things on a Tuesday. How can you make a clumsy and an awkward thing if you have made graceful ones for forty-eight hours on end? It is a blessed trait of our nature that good habits as well as bad habits may be formed and will stick. And so the designs of a good time for architectural art are sure to be good designs, that is, to have such forms that the light and shade upon them would be lovely. The design before us could not have been made by any able man at a time when there prevailed a worthy style of design in the world around him.

One may try, comparing these seven or eight views of the exterior — one may try the experiment of familiarity to see whether with longer acquaintance the building is less ugly than it seems at the first look. Ruskin tells the story of his having been led astray by the theory of Use and Wont — by the notion that our liking for certain forms and colors is the result of familiarity, and nothing else, and he says that he kept a skull on his mantelpiece for months, but found it just as ugly when the months had passed. And so it is in all probability with this exterior. If we are to consider it as a piece of abstract form, as a thing which is itself ugly or the reverse, the opinion will remain fixed that nothing uglier could exist among objects that were found perfect in condition, cared for, and showing the signs of human thought and purpose. We should see in a moment that where such qualities as those are found to exist, the building cannot be wholly contemptible. That it is wholly repellant as a work of human artisanship which might have been a work of art and is not — so much is probably the verdict of most persons who care for the fine art of architecture.

Light and shade have been mentioned above as the chief elements in our art, and one of the ways in which light and shade are used continually in architectural design is in the way of moldings. What is a molding? What are moldings? It is, they are, a modulation of the surface following continuous lines, straight and curved. Moldings are an abandonment of plane and uniform surface for a broken and generally rounded surface, as along an edge, and a group of moldings consists of an alternation of projecting and retreating forms, mainly of curved surface and of small dimension, although these are broken, interspersed here and there by narrow strips of flat and uniform surface, which we call fillets. Moldings do not weaken the wall where the window jamb, the door jamb, the horizontal cornice or sill course is modified by their interposition. Suppose, for instance, that one who lived opposite this Larkin Building were to have his way for a month, and were to utilize his time in making the building less clumsy in his eyes—would he not begin by molding those square corners which are thrust upon us so sharply in all the exterior views, working those corners into upright beads and coves, developing, perhaps, in an angle shaft with capital and base? This, of course, is not an essential feature. To insert it would be to give, perhaps, too nearly mediaeval a look to the design. Suppose that the corners of one of those towerlike masses were molded to such an extent that eight inches on each side of the arris, everywhere, were to be reduced to a series of soft surfaces, concave and convex, parallel one to another, and carried up from a little above the base to a little below the coping? They may be cast in brick, two or three separate patterns of molded brick sufficing for the whole composition. These moldings must either stop or return; and there are very interesting ways of arranging for either. They may stop against the stone coping or belt course itself; or they may have a piece of cast brick or of terracotta or of cut stone, in the mass of which the stop of the groups of moldings may be against a splay or a concave or a convex curved surface.

Moldings are important and valuable, and the designer who rejects them altogether handicaps himself—and yet there are even better things than moldings. The horizontal bands in a building like this would be interesting if they were molded; and yet they would be more interesting still if they were carried out in some greater projection in the face of the building and supported on corbels or on a little arcade. But it is evident that the first principle laid down by the designer for his own guidance was this—to avoid everything that would look like a merely architectural adornment, to add nothing to the building for the sake of architectural effect. He would repel the idea of a projecting cornice as readily as he would the full classical entablature for the top of one of these square towers, which would be no better working elements of the building if they were so adorned. Either you must add to a building something which is unnecessary, and which nothing but existing tradition even suggests to you, or you must have a bare, sharp-edged pile of blocks—a group of parallelopipedons like this. The designer seems to have said that even the rounding off of the coping shall be eschewed. He has determined that the square corner, the right angle, the straight edge, the sharp arris, the firm vertical and horizontal lines, unbroken, unmodified, uncompromising in their geometrical precision—that these and these only shall be the features of his building. But as that characteristic of the building prevents it from having any delicate light and shade, therefore it stands condemned in the eyes of any person who looks at the building asking for beauty of effect.

There is, however, mass. There is the possibility of proportion, the proportion of the smaller to the greater, and the possibility of fitting one to another firmly and with grace. There is the proportion obtainable by the horizontal distribution, the alternating of curtain walls with towers, of projecting and receding masses; and there is the possibility of vertically succeeding masses, the parts which serve for a kind of basement at either end, and those towers and buttresses which rise above them. There is even a possibility of contrast between walls filled with windows and the massive blank space of the wall which rests upon the piers between the windows.

If, now, we seek to take up a sympathetic position, to consider the building as perhaps the architect himself considered it, there are to notice the care given to the plan and disposition of the halls and rooms, the care which has evidently resulted in a successful utilitarian building. Construction which is the simplest and most obvious, and which cannot go astray because everything is reduced to the post and lintel; workmanship which is faultless, simple and straightforward brickwork; piers and walls fairly and smoothly built; slabs and beams of stone which have been planed and dressed in the mill and left with sharp arrises; a view down the central hall as seen in Fig. 3, which is impressive because of the straightforwardness and simplicity of everything, and because of the clear daylight which fills all parts of the hall; the evidences which the pictures multiply of a minute prevision in the way of office furniture, safes and cupboards for filing papers, tables and chairs of metal and solid wood, all of the simplest conceivable forms; the electric bulbs set in racks at a convenient height above tables and counters, which racks, though of inconceivable ugliness, have yet the character of simple utility — all these things unite to make a building which no one can fail to accept. The iron railing which encloses the site comes nearer to being really a design than the larger details, generally; for in this a true economy and a sagacious utility take the place of a sense of form. Our standard is lower, when we consider some hundreds of running feet of fencing.

And so in the exterior it is allowable to the student to feel that a square brick shaft is as fit to contain a winding staircase or an elevator as a round or octagonal cut stone shaft costing five times the money; that windows are not absolutely necessary when there can be a skylight; and that where there are no windows, and no breaking up for windows without necessity, the result is inevitable — the result that there will be no pierced parapet nor any modifying of the uppermost story to replace in a way the cornice which, of course, such a building does not require. Here is a well-thought-out design, every detail of construction and all the appliances have been studied with care. Here is an excellent arrangement of large windows, raised high toward the ceiling, broad and low and shaped as they ought to be for utilitarian results. It is clear that there is nothing to burn about the building; it is as fireproof as such a building can be made. And while everything has been carried out with a view to practical utility, there has been also some attempt to adorn, to beautify. But we have already seen reason to think that this attempt has failed. See for the attempt and for the failure, in Fig. 8, that curious base arranged beneath the brick piers on the right; it is the Attic base reduced to its simplest form, the familiar old Attic base, with its rounded moldings turned back into the square-edged bands which those moldings were in their origin. And those square moldings are put in, the larger below and the smaller above, with the evident purpose of serving as ornament. Accepting this, let the eye now take in the curious square block decoration of the same pier in its upper part, higher than the door and between the great doorway of the entrance where the firm name is painted on the glass, and the small staircase doorway on the right. Is this a serious attempt to create a new system of design? May we assume that the inevitable squareness of the brickbuilt pier, all molded and specially

cast brick being rejected, satisfies the designer so well that he gladly makes everything else, his sculptured ornaments and his bronze fittings, as square as the masses of brickwork? Look, then, at the system of metal frames in which the electric globes are suspended. From this picture go back to Fig. 3 and study those straight-edged and sharp-cornered groups of ornament at the tops of the great piers, and directly below the skylight see those square ornaments which are clearly nothing but ornaments. Fig. 4 shows two groups of those extraordinary connections — those terminals of the great supporting piers at the end of the high nave opposite the one shown in Fig. 3. It is unnecessary to describe the design of these strange masses of square-edged patterning; no human designer could make anything graceful or even anything effective out of such elements as those. Taking all this accumulation of strange, sharp-edged solids, offering no modulation of surface — nothing but sharp contrast and checkered black and white — and the wonder will grow upon you more and more, how such a costly, careful, thoughtful, well-planned building should be made up of such incongruous parts, leading to such a hopeless result.

One cannot help liking broad surfaces of fair brickwork, and yet those very masses of brickwork may be so much more interesting; they may be invested with color. There is the third chance for the designer! After light and shade have escaped him, or have been rejected, deliberately, and when the artistic use of mass and proportion are out of the question, he has still at his disposal the interest and charm of color, and this exterior calls for it loudly. The careful brickwork, even as it is, has a certain momentary pleasure to offer those of us who feel dissatisfied with the flimsy character and the inappropriate ornament of the buildings around. Such a pleasure lasts but an instant, however. You turn from the florid façade to the plain brick gable wall or rear with a sense of relief, but it is merely an instantaneous pleasure which you feel in escaping from something painful. If we are to look at the building a second time, and that with renewed pleasure, we must have something else; and, where delicate play of light and shade is denied us, as here, variety of color pattern would be an admirable expedient. It is not necessary to expatiate on this view of the case, for any one who has ever made patterns in mosaic or has enjoyed the patterns that others have made for him will see what a pleasure this building might have been to the designer and to the student, had its grimness of aspect been modified by color patterns. Even the simplest stripes found in the wall of that New York apartment house which faces on Fourth Avenue and East Sixty-eighth Street, three horizontal courses of dark brown brick, one of scarlet brick, and so on, in alternation, even that is beautiful. More elaborate, more effective combinations might be made where colored bonds pass through — cut across — groups of moldings.

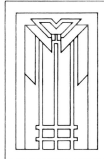

Frank Lloyd Wright, "Reply to Mr. Sturgis's Criticism"

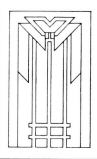

It is quite clear that Mr. Sturgis would prefer the Larkin Building, as the lady thought she would the noble savage, —"more dressed."

To see an eminent architectural critic picking over, bit by bit, his architectural rag-bag for architectural finery wherewith to clothe the nakedness of the young giant whose very muscularity offends as it confronts him is pathetic.

"Admitting that the chase of the Neo-Classic, of the Gothic, and of the French Romanesque has come to nothing," I submit that we are further away from a living style of architecture than ever, chiefly because of the conception rooted in the mind of architect and critic alike that architecture consists, or ever did consist, in manufacturing with ornamental moldings and chamfered edges a fabric flickering with light and shade, to be applied to a structure as a porous plaster might be applied to an aching back, or worn as a dickey in the time of our grandfathers — *for effect.*

Nor may we surprise the secret of the artistic charm of the beloved monuments marking our spiritual greatness in the past by trifling too intimately with their mere aspect. To accept Tradition thus will bring us to them as the camera brings the photographer to Nature. No real inspiration is to be derived from them so, for some day, somewhere, somehow, owing to changed conditions, should we fail to find the familiar motives, "those accepted details which are architecture for us," we shall be futile. Is it not pitiable that a great art should thus become to us a matter of certain accepted details or *be not at all?* This is the degradation of the parasite, the stultification of the connoisseur, the culture of

From *In the Cause of Architecture* (Buffalo, New York, April 1909).

the pseudo and the neophyte. With it the artist has nothing to do.

Bread-winning operations are not hostile to art! Mr. Ruskin's influence *was* hostile to art, and now a half-century old it has retarded our development by, at least, half that period of time; for he falsified the nature of our æsthetic problem, and left in his wake a train of reactionaries not yet disposed of; reactionaries content to ignore the opportunities made for us by the new conditions and new tools inevitably ours; willing to see and even to urge us, to accept as standard and wear in the market place finery borrowed (when it is not stolen) for the occasion from wholly alien sources.

"When the great buildings of the world were designed" they were legitimate expressions of the industrial order and social ideal underlying them; and in the measure that they were eloquent of those conditions and ideals, and we understand why they were so eloquent, will they educate us. If, at any one time in history, the familiar details of previous architecture were Architecture, whence came so many forms utterly opposed in character? How was the Gothic born, — the only organic architecture of which we know?

We have in this country industrial conditions totally different in cause and effect from anything which determined previous forms, and a polyglot tangle of racial traditions which inevitably corrupts when it does not destroy the style of any architectural detail on record. We may shake up these details in a hat and draw one with as much logic as to have Smith calling for Romanesque, Brown for Gothic, Hammerstein for Rococo, or Sturgis for Italian Renaissance! So we have woven the artistic expression of our civilization into a tissue of lies, a Nessus shirt. But this is no excuse for further bastardizing our standards, or ground for relegating beauty to the archives. A common sense of poetic justice still lives among us, and we still feel and think more than ever we did. There is a common chord in all this that will be heard; and it is not a plea for ugliness. It is a plea for first principles, — for less heat and parasitism, and more light and pragmatic integrity; for less architecture in quotation marks and more engineering. I feel that the sceptre of his art has all but passed from the hands of the architect to the hands of the engineer, and if it is ever to be the architect's again he must take it from the engineer by force of superior virtue.

Counseling return to first principles, I make no plea for ugliness, nor is ugliness necessary, — although I think the buildings Mr. Sturgis, in an unguarded moment permitted himself to build, are very ugly. But I recognize what Mr. Sturgis evidently does not recognize, and that is that ugliness exists in the eye of the beholder rather than inheres in the thing beholden. As to just what constitutes ugliness all men differ, — as they should. For me, meretricious ornament, devoid of significance, and manufactured for its own sake is ugly, honesty seldom is. Ugliness is a matter of the false and of discord. Awkwardness may be only undigested greatness. That the cry for integrity can gain ground in common æsthetics, our present artistic standards will deny, but our future development will affirm. Meanwhile, to say that a building is ugly is no more criticism than to say a man is a fool! To base either statement upon photographs would be merely tentative, were it not pernicious. Nor will the attempt to fix an arbitrary standard based upon "the details that make architecture for us" do more than make the load that creative effort has to lift, more difficult, more thankless and foster ad nauseam, ad libitum the stupidity and the cowardice with which contemporary society has for centuries tumbled her bravest and most faithful servants into unmarked, paupers' graves.

The Larkin Building is not pretty; it was not intended to be. But it is not discordant and it is not false. It must stand or fall by its merits, good or ill. Its designer was "determined to furnish nothing that his practical requirements did not call for," and he is proud of "the visible proof" of the fact, — but not in the spirit laid down for him by his critic. He is proud because with a single-mindedness, absolute

from the purely æsthetic viewpoint, he realized that his artistic opportunity consisted in the simplest and truest expression of those requirements possible to him in bricks and mortar.

Concerning its superficial aspects presented by the photographs upon which Mr. Sturgis has worked, photographs 1 and 2 are taken with a wide-angle lens from the third story window of the factory opposite, — not a normal point of view. Yet from this point of view, which depresses the skyline, he deplores lack of variety, when by consulting the views on page 173 of the "Record" for March a truer idea of the real skyline presented to the observer of the actual structure may be obtained. I think Mr. Sturgis, himself *on the ground,* would agree that it is sufficiently varied to satisfy his desire for the picturesque.

As with the skyline, so with the mass; it becomes significant enough when you know its qualifications, and those you may know only when you know the building *on the ground.* Fig. 2 and Fig. 6 are undoubtedly murderous, wide-angle slanders. I protested against their use by Mr. Sturgis for any purpose whatever. Fig. 1, although foolishly taken from an abnormal viewpoint, I find not so bad, the play of light and shade of the columnar fenestration to the left contrasting agreeably with the plain wall surfaces of the upright shafts with proportions of unmistakable dignity and power. The taller shafts seen here are in reality "chimneys," except that the currents of air within them are drawn down instead of up. Also the outer expression of the central aisle in this view, the rhythm of the greater sculptured piers with their smaller companions opposed and related as they are to the bold piers which the stair chambers become, I find æsthetically rather fine, even "comely," — cliff of paving brick though it is.

Of course, there are no fires in the building; the fire is in the power house across the street. But there are aggregations of powerful ventilating machinery at the base of the shafts which Mr. Sturgis says mask the main structure. I prefer to take the view, equally consistent I believe, that they emphasize it and at the same time advertise the nature of the whole arrangement which, although extraordinary, with its purpose in view is organically sound. It is not the awkward grouping of masses that troubles Mr. Sturgis, but simply that they are not modified by the means of grace he must have if "Architecture" is a consideration, because the structural masses may remain as they are and be trimmed à la Gothic, Romanesque, or even Italian Renaissance, and please him well—as I can demonstrate to him, by illustration.

As for the light and shade of molded brick, or the absence of variegated color, the footnotes at the bottom of page 166 and 167 of the March "Record" will explain their utter futility,—granting their desirability æsthetically, which I do not. They would only emasculate the surfaces. I have found that the chief function of ornamentation of surfaces or of moldings is to modify or mortify emphatic members of emphatic surfaces by frittering them away in light and shade, and this in arranging and qualifying masses may serve to assist articulation of parts. It was not employed in this composition precisely because from an economic and æsthetic standpoint it was not needed.

I would in turn remind the student of architecture that a molding is only a means of articulating the elements of structure, and is tolerable in composition only when saying something pertinent eloquently. Moldings could have said nothing in this structure that is not better said without them or by the plain stone courses which say all that is artistically necessary.

There is also the important question of scale to be considered in the treatment of any theme, and it matters little whether the scale be coarse or fine, ornate or otherwise, so long as the values are consistently maintained. They are consistently maintained in the Larkin Building.

In the interior view, Fig. 3, does Mr. Sturgis fail to notice how the fourth story gallery front is dropped behind the piers, associated in like materials with the capitals, in effect freeing the shafts above the third floor, broadening the court at the crucial point, and enriching the whole as it composes with skylight, capitals, and the ceiling beams which sweep over them to the outer walls on either side? Does he not notice how this simple expedient gives rhythm to the arrangement when otherwise it would have lacked it? Is he insensible to the manner in which the forms are all held together in scale and character with a unity rare in this day and generation? He may not like the forms, prefer repoussé to retroussé, yet intelligently acknowledge the virtue of the one while preferring the other.

It is necessary to say that the "strange ornaments purely as such beneath the skylight" are electric light fixtures fixed upon the capitals—four sides alike?

(The work has been criticised from photographs.)

The base he refers to was as simple as it is because I preferred it so, which was fortunate for the materials of which it was built and the process of magnesite casting that made it, made it impossible to fashion it otherwise. So with the industrial bases of the other angular forms contributing to this perplexing result.

Concerning the æsthetics of the bare, square forms which Mr. Sturgis finds so impossible, the designer of the Larkin Building wishes here to record in type what he has already recorded in buildings, that he prefers to think in terms of clean, pure, unadulterated forms. A clean cut, square post could not be improved for him by chamfering the edges. There is a certain æsthetic joy in letting the thing alone which has for centuries been tortured, distorted, and dickered with in the name of Art, letting its native dignity show forth once more. I confess to a love for a clean arris; the cube I find comforting, the sphere inspiring. In the opposition of the circle and the square I find motives for architectural themes with all the sentiment of Shakespeare's "Romeo and Juliet": combining these with the octagon I find sufficient materials for symphonic development. I can marry these forms in various ways without adulterating them, but I love them pure, strong, and undefiled. The ellipse I despise; and so do I despise all perverted, equivocal versions of these pure forms. There is quite room enough within these limitations for one artist to work I am sure, and to accord well with the instinct for first principles.

Enough of this begging faults of design and proportion by this academic habit of working up a sort of ornamental froth, calculated to obscure the real issue and befuddle the sensibilities of the plain man. When forms are modified the modification should mean something. Unless you know what the modification means let the form alone. It will never disgrace you in the eyes of posterity. If we will not bastardize our standards we need not bastardize our forms!

After all there is a deeper phase of this problem than any aspect touched upon by Mr. Sturgis, which is the true æsthetics of the proposition. In this structure these matters are all questions of *constitution*, and of greater importance than as to whether it should mince in its gait or even the angle at which it carries its fan.

We may dismiss the Larkin Building from this discussion, however, with the remark from the man who made it that while he has seen no photographs which carry a sense of its quality it has seemed to him that even in those which he has seen the clearly defined, honest, blocklike masses, the clean angles and squared forms are particularly appropriate to the purpose, to which the building is devoted — the housing of an industry. It is more strictly a utilitarian building than the fantastic compromise shown by Mr. Sturgis in Fig. 7, and is located in a factory district.

The forms of the various "features," ordered as they are, are all working harmoniously in their several functions altogether in the interest of the purpose they were intended to serve. True, this might be also said of any engineering work, except that to be wholly truthful, this must be added, —that in all this there is a definite, consistent quality of *style*, directly the result of determining the grammar of every form in its make-up, and holding them all well together from a purely æsthetic view-point. A bold assertion surely, and inconsistent with the assertions of Mr. Sturgis. But to perceive this is denied to those who assert that certain accepted details have fixed architecture for us, and who hold with him that these details are prescribed by fashion.

By the purely æsthetic view-point I mean the point of view of the man who sees in the thing that which is its soul, its simple truth, and sees it in such terms of form, line, sound or color as to reveal its life, and so that the revelation is in itself a harmonious organic entity. It follows then that this revelation must always lie well within and be true to the means used to produce it. Studied from the ground on this basis a criticism of the Larkin Building would shed some light and be helpful. Such criticism creative work of this nature needs, and in time will have, but not until its life and purpose are better understood. Meanwhile, the superficial observer obsessed by the *letter* of tradition says it is ugly. The man in whom the *spirit* of tradition still lives, the man who looks deeper and into the future, has said it is inspiring. Well! it was built for the man who for the sake of the future gets underneath, and not for the man who, startled, clutches his lifeless traditions closer to his would-be-conservative breast and shrieks, "It is ugly!" It may be ugly, certainly it must so appear to some; but it is noble. It may lack playful light and shade, but it has strength and dignity and power. It may not be "Architecture," but it has integrity, and its high character is a prophecy. The building is, frankly, "a group of bare, square edged, parallelopipedons, uncompromising in their geometrical precision, without delicate light and shade," but fitted to one another organically and with æsthetic intent, and with utter contempt for the fetish so long worshiped that architecture consists in whittling their edges or in loading their surfaces with irrelevant sensualities or in frittering away their substance in behalf of the parasitic imagination of the slave of "styles." It is a bold buccaneer, swaggering somewhat doubtless, yet acknowledging a native god in a native land with an ideal seemingly lost to modern life — conscious of the fact that because beauty is in itself the highest and finest kind of morality so in its essence must it be true.

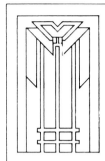

Notes

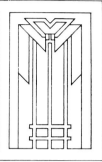

CHAPTER ONE

1 Wright designed more than fifty buildings between 1893 and 1902, of which about forty were residences; the rest were apartment buildings, stables, boat houses, a school, a library, a religious center, and a clubhouse. Around 1900 he also designed a tall building project in Chicago, the Abraham Lincoln Center for his uncle, Rev. Jenkin Lloyd-Jones.

2 Major building commissions in Buffalo usually went to local firms, such as Green & Wicks, R.J. Reidpath, or George Cary. Occasionally such commissions were awarded to such distinguished outsiders as Adler & Sullivan, Daniel Burnham, H.H. Richardson, and Cyrus L.W. Eidlitz. The best source on the architecture of Buffalo is Reyner Banham et al., *Buffalo Architecture: A Guide* (Cambridge, Mass., 1981).

3 The importance of Chicago to the Larkin executives is reflected in a letter/report of March 20, 1903, from Darwin D. Martin to John D. Larkin where every building cited by Martin as a model for some aspect of the Larkin Administration Building (the Chicago National Bank, Marshall Field, the Real Estate Exchange, the Board of Trade Building, and the Bell Telephone Building) is located in Chicago.

4 Frank Lloyd Wright, *An Autobiography,* rev. ed. (New York, 1943), pp. 89–111.

5 Ibid., p. 107.

6 Ibid., p. 123.

7 Grant C. Manson, *Frank Lloyd Wright to 1910: The First Golden Age* (New York, 1958). Chapter Two of the book *The Buffalo Venture,* represents the most extensive treatment yet attempted of Wright's work in Buffalo.

8 Ibid., p. 147.

9 Among the Grant C. Manson Papers in the Oak Park, Illinois, Public Library is a letter dated September 11, 1957, from Manson to Jean Duffy of the Reinhold Publishing Company. In it Manson describes reprimanding Wright for altering a drawing he had made of the Luxfer Prism Building of 1895. Manson also relates that he corrected Wright's recollection that the Heurtley house was the first in which he employed a raised basement (the Husser house was the first).

10 Martin maintained a variety of diaries and records of his correspondence throughout his life. Of particular value to this study is a 1903 business diary in which Martin recorded important events and conversations that occurred in the Larkin Company. In addition, he maintained a personal diary of the events in his life and that of his wife, Isabelle. Late in life Martin attempted to write an autobiography based on this material and on additional diaries that are now lost. The autobiography for the years 1865 to 1897 exists in manuscript form. All of these documents are among the Darwin D. Martin Papers, Archives of the State University of New York, Buffalo (hereinafter called the Martin Papers).

11 Martin personal diary, September 13, 1902, Martin Papers: "With Will visited Oak Park, Ill." In a letter to the author, September 4, 1981, Everett Martin, son of William Martin, reported that according to his

sister, Bernice Davis, William and Darwin Martin encountered Wright's studio during a drive through Oak Park and Buffalo. A similar version of the story appears in Leonard K. Eaton, *Two Chicago Architects and Their Clients: Frank Lloyd Wright and Howard Van Doren Shaw* (Cambridge, Mass., 1968).

12 That the Martin brothers did not meet Wright on this occasion is clear in a letter written by Darwin Martin to Elbert Hubbard, his friend and former supervisor at the Larkin Company, on September 19, 1902. An undated letter in the collection of Edgar Tafel describes what seems to be the same visit to Wright's studio described by Martin. The letter probably dates from the 1940s and was written by Marion Mahoney, who worked with Wright and later married Walter Burley Griffin, also an assistant to Wright. It is addressed to "William" (probably William Purcell): "One day only Walt [Griffin] was in the office when he saw that a car had stopped in front. He went out and invited them in. In the talk following they spoke of the factory they were intending to build—the Larkin Building."

13 Letter, Darwin D. Martin to Elbert Hubbard, September 19, 1902.

14 Letter, William E. Martin to Darwin D. Martin, ca. October 20, 1902. The letter is dated "Oct. 1902" and makes reference to Darwin's approaching birthday, which was on October 25.

15 Darwin Martin's mother died in Bouckville, New York, in 1871, when he was six years old. His father left Darwin's two oldest brothers and his sister Delta in the east and took the two youngest boys to Iowa. At the age of twelve Darwin joined his brother Frank selling soap in Newark, New Jersey; Brooklyn, New York; and Boston, Massachusetts, for the Larkin Company. The next year he was sent to Buffalo, where he lived alone in a boarding house. His diaries during this period express a longing to be reunited with his family. Darwin found his most rewarding familial relationship with William, who was the only other member of the family to achieve any measure of financial success (in the stove-polish business).

16 Letter, Darwin D. Martin to William E. Martin, October 29, 1902.

17 Martin personal diary, November 18, 1902, Martin Papers.

18 Appendix A, an unsigned, typewritten document among Darwin Martin's papers, appears to be a tentative list of the office building requirements probably developed by Martin in the month following Wright's initial visit to Buffalo in November 1902.

19 Martin business diary, January 15, 1903, Martin Papers.

20 Martin business diary, January 16, 1903, Martin Papers.

21 Ibid., January 26, 1903.

22 Ibid., February 2, 1903.

23 Ibid., March 6, 1903.

24 Letter, Darwin D. Martin to John D. Larkin, March 12, 1903.

25 Martin's use of the term "intoxicated" carried a special significance because he was a Christian Scientist and a teetotaler.

26 Letter/report, Darwin D. Martin to John D. Larkin, March 20, 1903.

27 Wright, *An Autobiography*, p. 110.

28 "Poor health" must be a euphemism for Sullivan's alcoholism, but it is not clear whether it is Martin's or Wright's euphemism.

29 Letter/report, Darwin D. Martin to John D. Larkin, March 20, 1903.

30 Martin business diary, April 13–15, 1903, Martin Papers.

31 Ibid., May 9, 1903.

32 Ibid., May 11, 14, 1903.

33 Ibid., May 25, 26, June 30, 1903.

34 Ibid., June 30, 1903.

35 Ibid., October 10, 1903.

36 Ibid., November 6, 1903.

37 Ibid., November 23, 1903.

38 An entry in Martin's business diary, September 11, 1903, Martin Papers, supports the contention that there was a division between the factories and the office: Heath said to Martin "that Mr. L——has indicated by a couple of gentle rebuffs that he thought office stood together against factory, though he never saw any indication of the kind."

39 An entry in Martin's business diary, February 7, 1903, Martin Papers, expresses the tension between Coss

and Martin: "When Bown went to WHC [Coss] for information on chimney at 5 PM today Mr. C remarked 'I see you are getting the fever.' Mr. Bown says 'What do you mean by that?' I related it to Mr. Heath saying I would bear this sort of thing long as I c'd but there was a limit and finally the matter would have to be tried out." With regard to Martin's relationship with John D. Larkin, Jr., there is this entry for February 11: "At luncheon: J.D.L. Jr., to WHC: 'The chimney is just going up in lumps.' WHC to J.D.L. Jr., 'Yes, sir, they'll shove it up about twenty feet a day now.' Said to annoy me."

40 Wright, *An Autobiography*, p. 151.

CHAPTER TWO

1 According to Carl H. Scheele, *A Short History of the Mail Service* (Washington, D.C., 1970), pp. 91–114, Congress established a uniform letter rate of three cents per half-ounce for first-class mail in 1863; postage was reduced to two cents per half-ounce in 1883 and to two cents per ounce in 1885. Rural free delivery went into effect in 1896.

2 Relevant to the study of the development of mail-order businesses is Harry L. Hansen, "Premium Merchandising to the Ultimate Consumer" (Ph.D. diss., Harvard University School of Business Administration, 1938).

3 This account of Larkin's early career is drawn from: "One of Buffalo's Most Successful Manufacturers," *Buffalo Courier*, May 29, 1904; "John Durrant Larkin," in *The Memorial and Family History of Erie County, New York* (Buffalo, N.Y.) Vol. I, 1906–8, pp. 79–81; *Ourselves*, 18, February 15, 1926 (John D. Larkin memorial issue); Mary Heath, *The Elbert Hubbard I Knew* (East Aurora, N.Y., 1929; reprinted with a new introduction by Clark W. Heath, Stoughton, Mass., 1981), pp. 144, 147; Horton H. Heath, "Elbert Hubbard—Salesman," *Printer's Ink Monthly*, 23, October 1931, pp. 51ff; Larkin family genealogy, prepared by Harry Larkin, Jr.; partnership agreement between Justus Weller and John D. Larkin of April 1865, collection of Daniel I. Larkin; and numerous conversations with Daniel I. Larkin between 1981 and 1985.

4 Letter, John D. Larkin to William R. Heath, February 17, 1899, Collection of Dr. Clark W. Heath.

5 Dr. Silas and Mrs. Julianna Frances Hubbard had six children: Charles, b. 1850, Hannah Frances, b. 1853, Elbert, b. 1856, Anna Mirenda, b. 1861, Mary, b. 1864, and Honor, b. 1868.

6 This according to letters written by John D. Larkin in 1875, Collection of Daniel I. Larkin.

7 According to the Articles of Partnership, April 1, 1878, Collection of Harry Larkin, Jr., Larkin and Hubbard began with $18,000 capitalization, $12,000 from Larkin, $6,000 from Hubbard. Profits and losses were to be divided, two-thirds to Larkin, one-third to Hubbard. A second partnership agreement was drawn up on January 1, 1884 and a third on June 17, 1885, the latter representing a capitalization of $77,000, $47,000 of which belonged to Larkin and $30,000 to Hubbard, but an equal division of profits was agreed on.

8 According to Daniel I. Larkin, who has read and made notes on the currently inaccessible books of the Larkin Company in preparation for a history of the company, the firm was recapitalized in 1920, at which time its stock value was increased from $1 million to $30 million. Total sales in 1920 amounted to $31 million.

9 For accounts of Larkin's approach to business, see: Horton Heath, "Elbert Hubbard—Salesman," p. 54; *Ourselves*, 18, February 15, 1926; and Jack Quinan, "John Durrant Larkin," *The Frank Lloyd Wright Newsletter*, 5, 1982, pp. 1–3.

10 For biographies of Elbert Hubbard, see: Felix Shay, *Elbert Hubbard of East Aurora* (East Aurora, N.Y., 1926); Mary Heath, *The Elbert Hubbard I Knew* (East Aurora, N.Y., 1929); Freeman Champney, *Art and Glory: The Story of Elbert Hubbard* (New York, 1968); and Charles F. Hamilton, *As Bees in Honey Drown* (Cranberry, N.J., 1973).

11 Horton Heath, "Elbert Hubbard—Salesman," pp. 74–75.

12 Information concerning the nature of the work performed by Larkin, Hubbard, Martin, and the Coss brothers and their relationships between 1875 and the early 1880s is derived from a typescript based on the diaries of Darwin D. Martin, Martin Papers, Archives

of the State University of New York at Buffalo.

13 Darwin D. Martin, *The First to Make a Card Ledger*
(Buffalo, N.Y., 1932), unpaged pamphlet.

14 Horton Heath attributes the idea for the three-cake,
ten-cent box of soap to his uncle, Elbert Hubbard
("Elbert Hubbard—Salesman," p. 56); Darwin D.
Martin attributes it to his brother, Frank Martin (*The
First to Make a Card Ledger*).

15 Discussions of the principal innovations in the history
of the Larkin Company are found in: *The Larkin Idea*,
May–November 1901 ("The Story of the Larkin
Idea," pp. 51–63, has the by-line "Darwin D. Martin"); John D. Larkin, Jr., "Our Pioneers," *Ourselves*,
13, May 1921, pp. 1–2; Letter, Darwin D. Martin to
Crate Larkin, November 3, 1924, in which Martin explains the history of the "product and premium
policy"; Mildred B. Schlei, "The Larkin Company—
A History," Master's thesis, University of Buffalo,
N.Y., 1932), pp. 5–25; and Martin, *The First to Make a
Card Ledger*. These sources generally agree on the
sequence of events but disagree slightly on the
attribution of innovations and the dates of events.
The Schlei thesis is the most comprehensive attempt
at a history, but it is untrustworthy insofar as the
author relied substantially on interviews with
members of the Larkin Company active from 1930 to
1932, none of whom was active in the 1880s and 1890s.

16 Martin, "The Story of the Larkin Idea," p. 52.

17 Martin, *The First to Make a Card Ledger;* and Schlei,
"The Larkin Company," pp. 22–25.

18 Schlei, "The Larkin Company," p. 13.

19 Ibid., p. 14.

20 John D. Larkin, Jr., "Our President, John D. Larkin,"
The Larkin Idea, 9, March 1913, p. 1.

21 Schlei, "The Larkin Company," pp. 22–25.

22 Ibid.

23 The following concerning Martin's early years in the
Larkin Company and his efforts to educate himself
was gleaned from: Martin diaries typescript, Martin
Papers; and Martin, *The First to Make a Card Ledger*.

24 Martin, *The First to Make a Card Ledger*.

25 Minute books of the Larkin Soap Manufacturing
Company, Collection of the Buffalo and Erie County
Historical Society.

26 Martin diaries typescript, December 14, 1891, Martin
Papers: "Mr. Hubbard says J.D.L. & Co. will be
turned into a corporation next year. Double entry
books will be kept and a new bookkeeper required. I
replied, 'I am he!' (Told only of my personal books
for practice.)." Martin had been keeping double-entry
books for a sachet-powder business he secretly ran
with his older brother, Frank Martin.

27 According to Horton Heath, "Elbert Hubbard—
Salesman," p. 75:

> The spice and savor had gone out of the soap
> business for Elbert Hubbard. He even made an
> abortive attempt to dispose of his stock in the
> business to soap purchasers as a new type of
> "premium." In Mr. Larkin's mind it was an increas-
> ing conviction that his brother-in-law was not a safe
> sort of person. The year 1892 marked the beginning
> of a severe business depression, comparable with
> that of 1930, the sales curve at the factory flattened
> and sagged disappointingly, and Hubbard more
> than once entertained doubts as to the future of the
> business. Mr. Larkin, never led astray by his
> imagination, was unperturbed. There was an amica-
> ble meeting of the minds, and in January, 1893,
> Hubbard departed with his freedom and $65,000 in
> cash and notes, subsequently paid in full by Mr.
> Larkin.

A different version of the story was told to me by
Daniel I. Larkin, who has seen correspondence
between Elbert Hubbard and John D. Larkin during
this period. According to him, Hubbard threatened to
sue Larkin for his share of the business, and although
he was dissuaded from doing so, their relationship was
severely strained as a result.

28 Schlei, "The Larkin Company," appendix 1.

29 Letter, Darwin D. Martin to Elbert Hubbard,
September 19, 1902.

30 Martin diaries typescript, March 14, 1893 and 1896, p.
184 (day and month not specified), Martin Papers.
Regarding Martin's raise from $10,000 to $25,000 in
1899, see Martin personal diary, September 1899,
Martin Papers.

31 Schlei, "The Larkin Company," appendix 1.

32 The first of Larkin's eight letters to Heath is dated January 2, 1899; the last, March 15, 1899, Collection of Dr. Clark W. Heath.

33 Letter, John D. Larkin to William R. Heath, January 7, 1899, Collection of Dr. Clark W. Heath.

34 Martin diaries typescript, 1897, p. 186, Martin Papers.

35 John D. Larkin to William R. Heath, op. cit.

36 These composite sketches of Martin and Heath were developed from their diaries and correspondence, from photographs, and from the author's interviews and correspondence with their children and with former Larkin Company employees.

37 See Chapter One.

38 The profile of Larkin is based on the sources cited in notes 1 and 6 and on interviews with his nephew, Dr. Clark W. Heath; his grandsons Harry Larkin, Jr., Daniel I. Larkin, and Harold Esty, Jr.; and his granddaughter, Elizabeth (Robb) Duane, who lived with Larkin from the time of his wife's death in 1922 until his death in 1926.

39 In an interview with the author on September 16, 1981, Harry Larkin, Jr., recalled that his grandfather would no sooner complete a new livestock barn at his farm in Queenston, Ontario, than he would begin plans for another. Additional evidence of this special enthusiasm for building exists in the form of "Larkland," a compound of five Neo-Colonial Larkin family houses constructed between 1910 and 1920 on Lincoln Parkway and Windsor Avenue in Buffalo.

40 On the Larkin industrial complex, see: Reyner Banham, "Buffalo Archaeological," *Architectural Review* (London), 167, February 1980, pp. 88–92; and Banham, "Buffalo Industrial," *Little Journal* (Journal of the Society of Architectural Historians of Western New York), 3, February 1979, pp. 2–19.

41 *Ourselves*, 2, May 16, 1904, p. 3; *Ourselves*, 3, October 1, 1906, p. 1.

42 *Ourselves*, 1, July 1, 1903, p. 2: "Mail received—The number of letters now received daily is about 5,000."

CHAPTER THREE

1 The Sullivan-derived pier-and-spandrel structural system with which Wright began was retained and is visible in photographs of the light court (see Fig. 29) and the north elevation (see Fig. 67).

2 Wright's Helen Husser house of 1899 has Sullivan-esque decoration in its terra-cotta frieze and its arcaded windows, but the first Prairie houses of 1900 and 1901 (the *Ladies Home Journal* houses, the Harley Bradley, Warren Hickox, and Ward Willits houses) have none.

3 Larkin's interest in Louis Sullivan is revealed in a letter from Martin to John D. Larkin, March 20, 1903, Martin Papers. Grant C. Manson in *Frank Lloyd Wright to 1910: The First Golden Age* (New York, 1958), was unaware of Larkin's interest in Sullivan and wrote: "As always, the Sullivan tradition in public architecture was so compelling that Wright's vision, even in 1904, automatically surrendered to it at first. But swiftly his design was transformed in all its details into something personal to himself, and Sullivan was forgotten" (p. 150).

4 Manson, *Frank Lloyd Wright to 1910*, pp. 156–58. The similarities were pointed out to me by Paul Sprague.

5 The smaller preliminary drawings are in sepia ink on tracing paper and measure 11 × 9 inches (first set) and 13 × 12 inches (second set). The master working drawings are mounted on linen and measure 37 × 25 inches. Bruce Brooks Pfeiffer of the Frank Lloyd Wright Memorial Foundation points out that the six plans measuring 36 × 25 inches must predate the master working drawings because they are similar in size (they are much larger than the first two sets of drawings) and because they contain tentative versions of plans and elevations that are more thoroughly worked out in the master working drawings. The remaining drawings vary considerably in medium, technique, size, and subject matter. Some may have been done in preparation for the Wasmuth portfolio published in Berlin in 1910. A group of highly stylized silhouette views of the building was done by Henry Klumb in 1929, according to Donald Hoffmann, *Frank Lloyd Wright's Robie House: The Illustrated Story of An Architectural Masterpiece* (New York, 1984), pp. 25–27.

6 Letter, Darwin D. Martin to John D. Larkin, March 20, 1903.

7 Manson, *Frank Lloyd Wright to 1910*, p. 147. Manson published four early preliminary drawings from the

first set. His Fig. 96A, "A Preliminary Sketch for the
Larkin Building, Buffalo, as seen from Seneca
Street," is drawing 0403.011 in the Archives of the
Frank Lloyd Wright Memorial Foundation. Of the
images in Manson's Fig. 96B—a longitudinal section,
a Seneca Street elevation, and a plan—the first two
no longer exist in the Wright archives. The plan
Manson published is a redrawn version of the Wright
archives' drawing 0403.012.

8 The two missing drawings from the first set of
preliminary drawings (see note 7) have counterparts
in the second set. This indicates that there were,
almost certainly, twelve sheets in each of the original
groups of preliminary drawings.

9 Letter, Darwin D. Martin to John D. Larkin, March
20, 1903.

10 Manson, *Frank Lloyd Wright to 1910*, p. 150.

11 "Skeleton Specifications," accompanying the first set
of preliminary drawings of the Larkin Administration
Building Archives of the Frank Lloyd Wright
Memorial Foundation.

12 Frank Lloyd Wright, *An Autobiography*, rev. ed. (New
York, 1943), p. 151.

13 It cannot be said with absolute certainty that Wright
made these marks, or when they were made, although
there is a strong likelihood that he made them as he
rethought the configuration of the towers.

14 Darwin D. Martin to John D. Larkin, March 20, 1903.

15 Martin business diary, May 14, 1903, Martin Papers.

16 Ibid., June 30, 1903.

17 Frank Lloyd Wright, *An Autobiography*, p. 151.

18 Letter, Darwin D. Martin to William E. Martin, April
4, 1904.

19 Frank Lloyd Wright, "The Destruction of the Box,"
an address to the Junior Chapter of the American
Institute of Architects, New York City, 1952; reproduced in Edgar Kaufmann and Ben Raeburn, eds.,
Frank Lloyd Wright: Writings and Buildings (New York,
1960), p. 284.

20 Martin business diary, 11, May 14, 1903.

21 Frank Lloyd Wright, *Genius and the Mobocracy*, 2d ed.,
(New York, 1971), p. 70: "But later I discovered his
secret respect, leaning a little toward envy (I was

ashamed to suspect), for H.H. Richardson." Regarding Wright's derivative early houses, Wright, *An
Autobiography*, pp. 110, 129.

22 Wright, *An Autobiography*, p. 151.

23 Ibid., pp. 13–14, 194.

24 Frank Lloyd Wright, "The New Larkin Administration Building," *The Larkin Idea*, 6, November 1906,
pp. 2–9.

25 The light court in the Bradbury Building has both
staircases and elevators.

26 See William H. Jordy, *American Buildings and Their
Architects: Progressive and Academic Ideals at the Turn of
the Twentieth Century* (New York, 1972), pp. 321–23.

27 Martin did so and reported back to John D. Larkin in
a letter of March 20, 1903: "The problem of open
court is no problem at all. There is no question of
draughts, of heating or of lack of heat involved.
There are two open courts each about 50 × 75′ in
Marshall Field & Co., one in an eight story and the
other in a twelve story building. The departments in
the court on the ground floor are the pleasantest in
the buildings." Martin's figures are slightly inaccurate,
as Burnham designed a nine-story building on the
corner of Wabash and Washington streets in 1892 and
a twelve-story building on the corner of East Ran-
dolph and State streets in 1902, both with light courts.

28 Manson, *Frank Lloyd Wright to 1910*, p. 147.

29 D.H. Burnham's Ellicott Square Building (1895–96);
O'Rourke, Aiken & Knox's Old Post Office (1894–
1901); and the Sweeney Store (architect and date
unknown).

30 Martin's and Heath's desks are located in the very
center of the light court in a main-floor plan repro-
duced in H. Th. Wijdeveld, ed., *The Life-Work of the
American Architect Frank Lloyd Wright* (Santpoort,
Holland, 1925), p. 4. But according to former Larkin
Company employees and descendants of Martin and
Heath, the men occupied desks at opposite ends of
the light court, not at the center.

31 See Chapter Two.

32 On the impact of the Froebel method on Wright, see:
Richard C. MacCormac, "The Anatomy of Wright's
Aesthetic," *Architectural Review* (London), 143,

February 1968, pp. 143–46; Stuart Wilson, "The 'Gifts' of Froebel," *Journal of the Society of Architectural Historians,* 26, December 1967, pp. 238–41; Jordy, *American Buildings,* pp. 190–94; and Manson, *Frank Lloyd Wright to 1910,* pp. 5–10; Edgar Kaufmann, jr., " 'Form Became Feeling,' a New View of Froebal and Wright," *Journal of the Society of Architectural Historians,* 30, May 1981, pp. 130–37.

33 According to Darwin D. Martin's business and personal diaries, Martin Papers, Archives of the State University of New York at Buffalo, Frank Lloyd Wright visited Buffalo on the following dates: November 18–20, 1902; April 13–15, 1903; April 25, 1903; May 8–11, 1903; May 25, 1903; June 30–July 1, 1903; September 10–11, 1903; October 9–11, 1903; November 23–25, 1903; March 19–21, 1904; April 4, 1904; April 15–16, 1904; May 8–10, 1904; August 30, 1904; September 20, 1904; November 10, 1904; November 25, 1904; January 10–12, 1905; February 11, 1905; May 20–22, 1905; June 11–13, 1905; July 10–12, 1905; July 28, 1905; August 17, 1905; September 3, 1905; September 30–October 3, 1905; October 28, 1905; November 8–9, 1905; March 16, 1906; May 10, 1906; July 25, 1906; October 23, 1906; November 17, 1906; and May 29–30, 1907. Darwin D. Martin visited Wright's studio in Oak Park on the following dates: September 11–13, 1902; March 12–19, 1903; September 27, 1903; January 29–31, 1904; November 11, 1904; and December 31, 1904.

34 Reyner Banham, "Buffalo Industrial," *Little Journal* (Journal of the Society of Architectural Historians of Western New York), 3, February 1979, p. 5; and Vincent J. Scully, *American Architecture and Urbanism* (New York, 1969), p. 123.

35 Frank Lloyd Wright, "The Art and Craft of the Machine," an address given to the Chicago Arts and Crafts Society at Hull House, March 6, 1901; reprinted in Kaufmann and Raeburn, eds., *Frank Lloyd Wright: Writings and Buildings,* pp. 55–73.

36 Walter Gropius, "Die Entwicklung Moderner Industriebaukunst," *Jarbuch des Deutschen Werkbundes,* 1913; Le Corbusier, *Vers une Architecture* (Paris, 1923); and Eric Mendelsohn, *Amerika: Bilderbuch eines Architekten* (Berlin, 1926).

37 Oskar Beyer, ed., and Geoffrey Strachan, trans., *Eric Mendelsohn: Letters of an Architect* (London, 1967), p. 69.

38 Le Corbusier, *Towards a New Architecture* (New York, 1960), p. 33.

39 Wright voices his feelings about Le Corbusier's work in his review, "Towards a New Architecture," *World Unity,* 2, September, 1928, pp. 393–95.

CHAPTER FOUR

1 In the Larkin Company's personnel magazine, *Ourselves,* which was published six times a month beginning in April 1903, the office staff was offered self-improvement articles, inspirational messages, company news, and a running account of changes in the premium catalogue. Among the activities and benefits listed in *Ourselves* were a glee club, a bowling club, music concerts, YWCA membership, an annual field day, rewards for useful suggestions for improving office productivity, tuition refunds to employees who attended public classes of instruction and received grades of 75 percent or higher, and loans to employees who wanted to build a house and had a minimum of $500 in savings.

2 Interview with Mary Burke, a secretary in the Larkin Administration Building from 1917 until 1923, conducted on May 25, 1978.

3 *Ourselves,* 1, July 1, 1903, p. 2: "Mail Received—The number of letters now received daily is about 5,000: 6:30 AM—2550; 7:30 AM—600; 845 AM—200; 10:30 AM —1110; 2:45 PM—550."

4 One of several pictures (see Fig. 6) that accompanied "A Notable Buffalo Exhibit," an article on the Larkin Company in the Buffalo Courier, October 6, 1901, shows aspects of an organizational system much like the one that was established later in Wright's building.

5 "Arrangement of Groups and Divisions," *Ourselves,* 3, December 1, 1906, p. 2.

6 Wright explains his organic approach to architecture in *An Autobiography* (New York, 1943) pp. 146–49; see also William Jordy, *American Buildings and Their Architects: Progressive and Academic Ideals at the Turn of*

the Twentieth Century (New York, 1972), pp. 195, 207.

7 The vertical movement patterns of the Larkin and Guggenheim buildings and the horizontal movement options provided in the bi-nuclear plans for Wright's Studio, the Larkin Building, Unity Temple, the S.C. Johnson and Son Administrative Center, and the Guggenheim Museum represent Wright's design to provide a sense of boundless space rather than the confinement of the closed box.

8 According to Daniel I. Larkin, the location of John D. Larkin and Justus Weller's soap-manufacturing business, on Halstead Street in Chicago, was about two blocks from the edge of the fire. He further reports that each of the five Neo-Colonial Larkin mansions on Lincoln Parkway and Windsor Avenue in Buffalo are framed in reinforced concrete so as to make them more fireproof than houses utilizing wood construction.

9 George E. Twitmyer describes the magnesite in "A Model Administration Building," *Business Man's Magazine*, 19, April 1907, p. 46 (see Appendix 1).

10 There are two slightly different accounts as to how the magnesite was used. Richard Bock, Wright's collaborator on the sculpture in the Larkin Building, described it on page 12 of his unpublished autobiography, a copy of which is held in the Oak Park, Illinois, Public Library: "One novel building material was being used in the interior—this was magnesite—for both floors and walls—an absolute fire and sound proof material. This was a plastic form of material which was spread to a depth of about an inch over a 'cushion' of hard plaster and excelsior. This formed a cellular construction containing innumerable locked air spaces. The whole resulted in a perfect construction element." The second account appears in an anonymously written tour script for the Larkin complex (December 1, 1925), made available to me by Daniel I. Larkin: "Our office is absolutely fireproof, being constructed of fireproof brick and steel. The cement used is magnasite [*sic*] which besides its fireproof quality is soundproof. In construction this cement is applied to a framework of felt over steel which absorbs the usual office noises and eliminates echoes."

11 This according to Harry Larkin, Jr., who worked in the Larkin Company from 1931 to 1940.

12 David A. Hanks, *The Decorative Designs of Frank Lloyd Wright* (New York, 1979), pp. 83–88.

13 The four-legged, freestanding metal office chair weighs 67 pounds.

14 I am grateful to Harry Larkin, Jr., for this information. This insurrection may explain why some of the wooden dining room chairs appear on the main floor of the light court in photographs from the 1920s (see Fig. 51).

15 Letter/report, Darwin D. Martin to John D. Larkin, March 20, 1903.

16 H. Allen Brooks, ed., *Writings on Wright* (Cambridge, Mass., 1981), p. 143. The configuration of the stairs, landings, and slotted windows of Unity Temple in Oak Park, Illinois, 1906, is similar to that of the Larkin stair towers.

17 Twitmyer, "A Model Administration Building," p. 147.

18 From "Opportunity," an unpaged booklet for prospective Larkin employees produced by the Office Employment Department of the Larkin Company in 1921.

19 Russell Sturgis, "The Larkin Building in Buffalo," *The Architectural Record*, 23, April 1908, pp. 311–21.

20 The system is entitled "Heating and Ventilation" both in Wright's "Skeleton Specifications" of early 1903 and in the master specifications from later in 1903 (both are in the Archives of the Frank Lloyd Wright Memorial Foundation). Wright makes only a passing reference to the "ventilating system" in the first edition of *An Autobiography* (New York, 1932), p. 151.

21 Frank Lloyd Wright, *An Autobiography*, rev. ed. (New York, 1943), p. 150.

22 Reyner Banham, *The Architecture of the Well-Tempered Environment* (Chicago, 1969), p. 92: "In the basement it [the air] was cleaned and heated, or after the installation of the Kroeschell refrigerating plant in 1909, cooled—but never humidity-controlled, and hence Wright's judicious quotation marks around the words 'air-conditioned' (in the town where Carrier was perfecting humidity control he had better be careful!)." As any careful reader of Wright's autobiography knows, he took outrageous liberties with language

and wildly overused quotation marks. See p. 33 of Wright's *An Autobiography* (1943 edition), for instance. It is difficult to believe that quotation marks could represent caution on Wright's part, as Banham suggests; Wright seems to have put "air-conditioned" in quotation marks for the same reason he did so with other newly coined twentieth-century words, like "skyline," "motel," or "streamline."

23 "Larkin Company Administration Building Specifications—Frank Lloyd Wright, Architect, 1903," Item 91, Archives of the Frank Lloyd Wright Memorial Foundation.

24 Ibid., Item 91.

25 Ibid., Item 92.

26 Ibid., Item 102.

27 Ibid., Item 103.

28 According to Margaret Ingels, *Willis Carrier, Father of Air Conditioning* (Garden City, N.Y., 1952), p. 17: "Air conditioning is the control of humidity of air by either increasing or decreasing its moisture content. Added to the control of humidity are the control of temperature by either heating or cooling the air, the purification of the air by washing or filtering the air, and the control of air motion and ventilation."

29 Banham, in *Well-Tempered Environment*, p. 275, cites the Huguet Silk Mills installation as the "turning point" in the history of the development of environmental-control systems on the grounds that Carrier was able to offer the following guarantees:

> We guarantee the apparatus we propose to furnish you to be capable of heating your mill to a temperature of 70°F when outside temperature is not lower than 10°F below zero.
> We also guarantee you that by means of an adjustable automatic control it will enable you to vary the humidity with varying temperatures and enable you to get any humidity up to 85% with 70°F in the mill in winter.
> In summer-time we guarantee that you will be able to obtain 75% humidity in the mill without increasing the temperature above the outside temperature. Or that you may be able to get 85% in the mill with an increase in temperature of approximately 5°F above outside temperature.

30 The date appears in a chronology of major developments in the history of air conditioning in Ingels, *Willis Carrier,* (Garden City, N.Y., 1952). Ingels's chronology is not wholly reliable, as several of the entries, including that for the Larkin Building, are not supported by documentation. According to her files, which have been retained by the Carrier Corporation, she telephoned Arnold Goelz, former Chairman of the Board of the Kroeschell Engineering Company, in June 1952 to inquire about the role of the Kroeschell Ice Machine Company in the history of the development of refrigeration and air conditioning. Goelz told her that the Larkin unit was installed in 1908, but in his follow-up letter of June 26 he changed the date as follows: "In about 1909, Kroeschell furnished the refrigeration system used in connection with an air cooling installation, at the Larkin Company's office building in Buffalo, N.Y., Frank Lloyd Wright was the architect. The CO_2 coils were sprayed with water." In the same letter Goelz discussed the dates of four other significant early Kroeschell installations; he began each description with "In about . . ." or "As near as I can recall . . ." The trustworthiness of Goelz's recollection, made forty-five years after the fact, is questionable.

31 Ingels, *Willis Carrier,* p. 17.

32 Twitmyer, "A Model Administration Building," p. 47.

33 Banham, *Well-Tempered Environment*, p. 92.

34 Wright's air-conditioning system shows some awareness of Carrier's work, but it also draws on similar developments in Chicago, something that has not been given adequate attention by historians of environmental-control systems. Wright used Jenney & Mundie's Chicago National Bank of 1900–1901, for example, as a model for the heating and ventilation system of the Larkin Building. William LeBaron Jenney's description of his system in "Ventilating and Heating the Chicago National Bank," *The Engineering Record*, 44, 1901, p. 503, is very similar to Wright's specifications for the Larkin Building system :

> The air is admitted into the building through louvred openings several feet above the roof level. . . . At the basement the fresh air shaft opens into a chamber from which the air passes in

turn through tempering coils, the air-washing apparatus, the blower, heating coils, and then into the various ducts. . . . The mixing chambers are located immediately beyond the heater. The tempering coils have the double office of maintaining only a relatively low temperature in the cold portion of the air mixed, so that drafts are less liable to occur with sudden closure of mixing dampers against hot air, and of preventing freezing in that air washing apparatus. There are four tempering coils, of the Waters' base pattern. . . . Next in the path of the in-coming fresh air, as indicated in the accompanying drawings, is the air-washing device, which consists of top and bottom lines of spray pipes of 1¼-inch brass pipe having brass tees with ¾-inch outlets spaced 2 inches apart. . . . Three feet beyond the brass screen is an Acme water eliminator, which is an arrangement of baffle plates built of 16-ounce copper, installed under a guarantee to give 98 per cent extraction with an average humidity of 75 to 85 per cent between the eliminator and heating coils beyond, the purpose being to establish an average of 65 to 70 per cent humidity in the ducts and building.

35 Marion Harland, *My Trip Thru the Larkin Factories* (Buffalo, N.Y., 1913), p. 18.

CHAPTER FIVE

1 Numerous examples of bird's-eye views of nineteenth-century industrial architecture can be seen in Edmund V. Gillon's *Early Illustrations and Views of American Architecture* (New York, 1971), pl. 683ff.

2 Even the extruded panel in the center of the building's façade at the fifth- and sixth-floor levels, which assumes the appearance of another tower in oblique views (see Frontispiece), has a functional purpose: It is the result of the outward expansion of the kitchen and conservatory spaces, which is, in turn, a response to the setback of the fifth-floor balcony fronts from the light court.

3 Russell Sturgis, "The Larkin Building in Buffalo," *Architectural Record*, 23, April 1908, pp. 311–21 (see Appendix κ).

4 On Richard Bock, see: Donald Hallmark, "Richard W. Bock, Sculptor; Part I: The Early Work," *Prairie School Review*, 8, no. 1, 1971, pp. 5–29; and Bock's unpublished autobiography, a copy of which is held in the Oak Park, Illinois, Public Library.

5 One example of this can be seen in the use of globes in the exterior sculpture: the global motif was justified by the fact that although the Larkin mail-order business was confined to North America, raw materials for perfumes, sachet powders, and foodstuffs were obtained worldwide. (This was pointed out to me by Daniel I. Larkin.)

6 The figures behind the globes were only partially carved since they were not visible from the street.

7 Wright's treatment of the Larkin signs is consistent with his subtle treatment of decorative elements throughout his oeuvre. As with the richly decorative terra-cotta friezes tucked into the shadows under the eaves of the Heller, Winslow, and Dana houses, the "message" of the Larkin scrolls is apparent only after the building has been given careful scrutiny. Also, the surrounding Larkin factories and warehouses carried very conspicuous signs that eliminated the need for obvious identification on Wright's building. These signs were described in *Ourselves*, 3, June 1, 1906:

> One of the great features of Buffalo to people coming or going out on trains is the unique and impressive electric sign on display of the Larkin Co. hundreds of feet long, on the tops of their buildings. When out in California last Winter I met people who had passed through Buffalo, and the thing that impressed them most, that they instantly spoke of, was this lettering in light of the Larkin Co.

One also suspects that Wright was confident that the distinctiveness of his building would provide sufficient identification, which proved to be the case.

8 Most of Wright's decorative patterns derive from plants, but he avoided the literalness and the sensuality that characterized the lush plant motifs used by Tiffany, Sullivan, and the European Art Nouveau designers. Instead, Wright favored sumac, butternut,

ferns, and other flora as models because of the rhythmic patterns of their leaves and the architectonic structure of their stems.

9 Dr. Evelyn Jacobsen informed me in an interview of January 18, 1979 that her father, William Heath, composed the inscriptions for the Larkin Administration Building. This is corroborated in a letter written by Wright on February 25, 1951 (Archives of the Frank Lloyd Wright Memorial Foundation) in answer to a letter in which one Doane Eaton had asked who authored the fountain inscriptions: "The quotation was written by William T. [sic] Heath, a secretary [sic] of the Larkin Company whose house I built in Buffalo. He wrote it: Honest labor needs no master, Simple justice no slaves. I put in the second 'needs' with his consent when it was carved in the red sandstone."

10 Bock's sculpture reflected his Beaux-Arts training even more obviously in the years prior to his involvement with Wright. See plates in Hallmark, "Richard W. Bock."

11 No photographs have come to light in which the attributes of the Seneca Street fountain can be seen clearly.

12 The fountains appear to have had even more allusive references. The Larkin Company frequently promoted itself as a "wonder" of the western New York region, second only in importance to Niagara Falls. The miniaturized waterfalls of the fountains provided an association with the famous natural wonder some fifteen miles away. A photograph of six Larkin employees seated in front of one of the entrance fountains appears in *Ourselves*, 9, November 1, 1914, and is captioned: "Misses Haas, O'Laughlin, Willis, Seel, Schmidt, and Shea at our own Niagara."

13 Among the fifteen descendants and former Larkin employees interviewed for this book no one has any recollection of these sculptures.

14 This relief is identified as the "Aurora" panel in the *Buffalo Arts Journal*, 11, no. 7, October 1925, p. 54.

15 Bock's sketch, in the Richard W. Bock Sculpture Collection at Greenville College, Greenville, Illinois, shows a weakly drawn figure to which Wright's

geometrizing lines have not yet been applied. Hallmark has noted, in "Richard W. Bock, Sculptor; Part II," that figures of this cruciform type appear in another Wright-Bock collaboration, the bronze lightoliers in the form of Mercury for the Mason City National Bank, Mason City, Iowa.

16 Wright's ability to put in physical form the ideas of others was pointed out to me by Edgar Kaufmann, jr., in a letter of February 9, 1981.

17 See Daniel T. Rodgers, *The Work Ethic in Industrial America, 1850–1920* (Chicago, 1978), pp. 83, 87–89.

18 The following piece, from *Ourselves*, 7, September 16, 1912, p. 1, is typical:

DIGNITY OF LABOR

All useful work is honorable. The best life is that in which the powers of mind and body are most beneficiently employed. An indolent life, whether passed in poverty or wealth, is a degraded life. No man can serve God by any other means than by serving his fellow-men. We do not disparage the church or worship of God, in public or in private places, but he is the truest and most devout worshipper who goes about the practical duties of life in the right spirit, feeling that he is responsible for the use he makes of his time, talents, strength and opportunities. The man who, according to his ability, does the most to promote the welfare of his fellow-men, be he scavenger or statesman, hod-carrier or preacher of the Gospel, is the best man on earth. The dignity of labor is not dependent on the sphere of one's activities so much as nearness of his approach to his highest possibilities of usefulness. A good cobbler is a more dignified and honorable worker than the man who, having no capacity for intellectual pursuits, scorns to toil for a livelihood and wastes his time and energies in "following a profession."

An example of the Larkin company's efforts to build a positive attitude toward work was a production called "The New Vision: A Masque of Modern Industry," commissioned from Hazel MacKaye by the company and staged by Larkin employees in Delaware Park, Buffalo, on June 29, 1916, for the benefit of five hundred Larkin Club secretaries and their friends and associates. The theme of the masque was described in a pamphlet published by the company at the time of the production: "That when Industry is mastered by Ignorance, and all the qualities that go with Ignorance, like Disorder, Sloth, Greed, Inefficiency, and Strife, Industry becomes useless and unable to serve mankind. When, however, Industry is freed from Ignorance by Imagination, and the spirits which accompany Imagination, like Service, Co-operation, Order, System, and Ambition, then Industry becomes the true servant of mankind and indispensable to its happiness." In a production featuring costumed employees who danced and spoke lines, Industry and its forces fought against Ignorance and its forces. The conflict was solved by Imagination and her spirits, who inspired Industry to build a Golden Kettle from which fine and useful things emerged — soaps, soap bubbles, perfumes, and other products — to "enrich and nourish mankind." I would like to express my appreciation to Daniel I. Larkin for calling my attention to this pageant and its significance and for lending me the publication.

19 Martin's diaries (Martin Papers) indicate that he worked six ten-hour days a week, including frequent evenings and some Sundays, for the Larkin Company throughout his youth. In an interview conducted on November 2, 1979, Lars Potter, who joined the Larkin Company in 1910, stated that Martin spent his "whole life there in the company; he seemed to *live* there."

Both Harry Larkin, Jr., and Daniel I. Larkin recall that their grandfather was wholly dedicated to "the works" (as he called the Larkin Company). It was his practice to arrive early in the morning and to be among the last to leave in the evening.

20 Rodgers, *The Work Ethic,* pp. 79–80.

21 For a candid and engaging view of the early years of the Taliesin Fellowship, see Edgar Tafel, *Apprentice to Genius* (New York, 1979). In a telephone conversation with the author on December 20, 1983, Tafel related the following insight into Wright's attitude toward

work: During a visit to the Tafel home in New York around 1950, Wright asked Edgar's brother, "What is your aim in life?" To which the young man replied, "Happiness." Wright responded, " 'Happiness is a by-product of work.' "

22 Letter, John D. Larkin to William R. Heath, February 22, 1899, Collection of Dr. Clark W. Heath.

23 Letter, Darwin D. Martin to Frank Lloyd Wright, October 28, 1910.

24 Letter, Frank Lloyd Wright to Darwin D. Martin, October 30, 1910.

25 The sets of three-word groups are as follows:

Adversity	Generosity	Simplicity	Sincerity
Refinement	Altruism	Tenacity	Humility
Sympathy	Sacrifice	Stability	Courage
Aspiration	Cheerfulness	Prudence	Imagination
Truth	Patience	Learning	Judgment
Nobility	Contentment	Wisdom	Initiative
Thought	Integrity	Liberty	Intelligence
Feeling	Loyalty	Equality	Enthusiasm
Action	Fidelity	Fraternity	Control
	Co-operation		Faith
	Economy		Hope
	Industry		Charity

26 "The Inscriptions on the Court of the Administration Building," *The Larkin Idea,* 7, May 1907, pp. 1–2. That Darwin D. Martin, and possibly others in the Larkin Company, had some input into the inscriptions is indicated in a letter from Darwin D. Martin to William R. Heath of July 24, 1906:

I want to suggest that the Company have the courage to let at least one of these quotations be taken from the words of the greatest teacher that ever lived, — Jesus Christ. Perhaps in the year 1906 and maybe in 1916 it will surprise some people to meet such a quotation in a counting room, but the building itself is in advance of the times; the quotation would only be in advance of the times. Grant that it would necessarily establish for the whole business an exceedingly high standard. Grant that in the eyes of some it might look like cant. It

need not be cant. It need not be too high a standard. The Master said nothing that is not of
practical application on every week day in every
business house.

    Should this suggestion meet the approval of the
Directors, then suggestions can be invited from the
office of a selection from the words of Jesus Christ.

27 Quotations from Emerson appear in *Ourselves*, 2, May
    16, 1904, p. 4; *Ourselves*, 7, December 25, 1912, p. 1;
    Ourselves, 2, November 1920 (*Ourselves* became a
    monthly in 1920 and 1921, then reverted to a weekly),
    p. 2; *Ourselves*, 13, February 1921, back cover; and
    Ourselves, 17, May 1, 1925, p. 1.

28 Entries concerning evenings spent at Heath's home
    for the purpose of reading and discussing Emerson
    appear on January 10, 17, and 24, 1908, in a diary and
    scrapbook maintained by Walter V. Davidson, a
    Larkin Company accountant, and his wife, Christiana.
    The diary is now in the possession of their daughter,
    Jean Cross.

29 Ralph Waldo Emerson, *Nature* (East Aurora, N.Y.,
    1905).

30 Letter, Darwin D. Martin to Frank Lloyd Wright,
    October 28, 1910.

31 Raymond H. Geselbracht, "Transcendental Renais-
    sance in the Arts: 1890–1920," *New England Quarterly*,
    48, December 1975, pp. 463–86.

32 Wright, *An Autobiography*, (New York, 1932), p. 15.

33 Some of the plants located in the conservatories are
    identified in "Beauty Wrought by Gardener and
    Architect," *The Larkin Idea*, 7, July 1907, pp. 2–3, as
    follows: Kentias (palms), *Rhapis flabelliformis* (a palm),
    Cibotium scheidei (a fern), *Rhapis humilis* (a rare type of
    palm), and *Phoenix canariensis*. A contemporary
    description of the effect of the gilded mottoes appears
    in the anonymously written article "The Inscriptions
    on the Court of the Administration Building," *The
    Larkin Idea*, 7, May 1907, pp. 1–2 (see Appendix E).

34 Anonymous, "The Inscriptions on the Court of the
    Administration Building," pp. 1–2.

35 Among the master working drawings in the Archives
    of the Frank Lloyd Wright Memorial Foundation is a
    first-floor plan (sheet 9806) showing desks labeled

"Mr. Heath" and "Mr. Martin" together at the
epicenter of the main floor of the light court. This
plan was published in H. Th. Wijdeveld, ed., *The
Life-Work of the American Architect Frank Lloyd Wright*
(Santpoort, Holland, 1925), p. 4. There is another,
apparently later, main-floor drawing (sheet 6872),
dated April 1906, in the Archives of the Frank Lloyd
Wright Memorial Foundation that shows Heath's and
Martin's desks at opposite ends of the main floor of
the light court. It is this working arrangement that
those interviewed for this book remember.

36 Prather, who worked in the administration building
    from 1907 to 1914, was interviewed on November 5, 1982.

37 Mueller began working in the Larkin Company as a
    messenger boy in 1918. He showed an interest and
    ability in art, and the company paid his way to the Al-
    bright Art Academy for several years. He eventually
    joined the Larkin Company Art Department. He was
    interviewed on April 3, 1981.

38 Letter from Mrs. Milton Davidson to her children,
    December 3, 1907, Collection of Jean (Davidson) Cross.

39 Oskar Beyer, ed., and Geoffrey Strachan, trans., *Eric
    Mendelsohn: Letters of an Architect* (London, 1967), p. 68.

40 Evelyn Jacobsen was interviewed on November 20,
    1975, January 18, 1979, September 28, 1981, and
    February 2, 1983. She worked in the Larkin Company
    YWCA for two years.

CHAPTER SIX

1 Frank Lloyd Wright, "The New Larkin Administra-
    tion Building," *The Larkin Idea*, 6, November 1906,
    pp. 2–9. *The Larkin Idea* was printed in editions up to
    500,000 around 1905. This article was reprinted in
    Prairie School Review, 7, no. 1, 1970, pp. 14–19.

2 Ibid., p. 3.

3 Ibid., p. 9.

4 Ibid.

5 William R. Heath, "The Office Building and What It
    Will Bring to the Office Force," *The Larkin Idea*, 6,
    November 1906, pp. 10–14 (see Appendix H); Anony-
    mous, editorial statement, ibid., pp. 16–17. The
    November 1906 issue of *The Larkin Idea* was devoted

entirely to the new administration building. Heath's article and the anonymous editorial accompanied Wright's article (see note 1). The cover and the frontispiece of this issue were adorned with Larkin Company artists' renderings of the new building, and the opening page was devoted to a poem about the building, "The Finished Task," by Frank R. Jewett, an employee.

6 Anonymous (possibly William R. Heath), "The Inscriptions on the Court of the Administration Building," *The Larkin Idea*, 7, May 1907, pp. 1–2 (see Appendix E).

7 Rogers Dickinson, "A Great American Success," *The Larkin Idea*, 6, February 1907, pp. 1–2. The relevant parts of the article are included here:

> I stood in the court of one of the largest private office buildings in the world. It was an amazing sight to see the hundreds of people taking care of the work of this one concern. Here was visible evidence of the results of good facilities of communication by railroad, steamboat, mail and wire, for here was a concern founded on the close direct touch with individuals all over the country.
>
> The great office building of the *Larkin Co.* was built especially to provide a convenient, healthful and pleasant place for the employees and every known device that would expedite the work has been provided. In this impressive building, where even the desks are fire-proof, and the very air one breathes is purified, the *Larkin* family of over 1,000 workers is kept constantly employed communicating with the greater Larkin family of customers. Family is the only word to use in connection with this business, for its success is due to the personal relations the company has with its customers through correspondence and direct dealing.

8 George E. Twitmyer, "A Model Administration Building," *Business Man's Magazine*, 19, April 1907, pp. 43–49; reprinted in *The Larkin Idea*, 7, August 1907, pp. 1–8, in an abridged form.

9 Marion Harland, *My Trip Thru the Larkin Factories*

(Buffalo, N.Y., 1913). "Marion Harland," the pen name of Mary Virginia Terhune, was in her eighties when she wrote this booklet for the Larkin Company. She had previously written *Some Colonial Homesteads, More Colonial Homesteads,* and *Where Ghosts Walk,* as well as articles for *Harper's Weekly* and *Cosmopolitan.* Around 1920 the Larkin Company published a similar booklet entitled "Your Trip Thru the Larkin Factories," by an anonymous author. It was obviously influenced by the Harland booklet, but it is shorter (forty-eight pages) and describes new office equipment that did not exist in 1913.

10 Twitmyer, "A Model Administration Building," p. 43.

11 Wright, "The New Larkin Administration Building," p. 4.

12 H.P. Berlage, "Neuere Amerikanische Architektur," *Schweizerische Bauzeitung*, 60, September 1912, pp. 148–50.

13 The following is a typical Twitmyer passage from "A Model Administration Building": "Except in the central aisle, the lighting is from the ceiling. One hundred and fifty candle power Nernst glowers in ribbed glass globes, about 12 feet above the desk tops, give a generous illumination so diffused that it is not noticeably more trying to the eye than daylight" (p. 47).

14 The following descriptions of the lounge space on the third floor of the annex demonstrate the difference between Twitmyer's and Harland's approaches:

> On the second floor are locker rooms and lavatories; on the next, quiet, secluded rest rooms and an infirmary and dispensary, where those in need of it may receive the care of a graduate nurse. (Twitmyer, p. 46)
> Here is the annex to the second floor. It has a Dispensary, with a nurse in attendance, who is supplied with everything required for first aid, or temporary treatment of disabilities. In connection with it are three rooms equipped with five hospital beds. The Rest Room nearby has ample space, good light and attractive furniture. A player-piano adds variety and pleasure during the luncheon hour. Some of the young women come here to read;

others prefer dozing, and some desire music. All are rested by their stay. (Harland, p. 17)

15 Twitmyer, 43; Harland, 13.

16 David Hanks, in *The Decorative Designs of Frank Lloyd Wright* (New York, 1979), p. 84, indicates that despite Wright's claim that the furniture he designed for the Larkin Building was the first metal office furniture ever produced, such furniture was being made by the A.H. Andrews Company of Chicago around 1900.

17 Charles Illsley, "The Larkin Administration Building, Buffalo," *The Inland Architect and News Record,* 50, July 1907, p. 4.

18 Ibid.

19 Daniel I. Larkin, Rev. Thomas Heath, and others interviewed by the author remarked that when they entered the light court, their focus was drawn upward by the magnetism of the skylight.

20 Vincent J. Scully perpetuated this line of thinking when he wrote in *American Architecture and Urbanism* (New York, 1969), p. 23: "Furness, grain elevators, American factories by the hundreds, Sullivan, all are recalled, no less than the medieval cathedrals— naved, bayed, and harmonically massed—whose pictures Wright's mother had hung in his rooms."

21 Anonymous, "Current Periodicals," *The Architectural Review* (Boston), 14, July 1907, p. 184.

22 Frank Lloyd Wright, "In the Cause of Architecture," *The Architectural Record,* 23, March 1908, pp. 155–221; and Russell Sturgis, "The Larkin Building in Buffalo," *The Architectural Record,* 23, April 1908, pp. 311–21.

23 Wright, "In the Cause of Architecture," p. 167.

24 Sturgis, "The Larkin Building in Buffalo," p. 312.

25 Ibid.

26 Ibid., p. 313.

27 Ibid., p. 319.

28 Ibid., p. 317.

29 Ibid., pp. 311–12. After several references to the photographs in his opening paragraphs, Sturgis writes: "In tracing the analysis of the building down through all this pile of photographs, and in setting down, as above, its scheme, we have also partly prepared ourselves to judge of it as a work of architecture."

30 Wright's "Reply to Mr. Sturgis's Criticism" was published under the title *In the Cause of Architecture* in April 1909 (see Appendix L). A copy of Wright's typescript is in the Darwin D. Martin Papers in the Archives of the State University of New York, Buffalo. The only extant copy of the publication is inscribed "W. R. Heath" and is in the possession of Harry Larkin, Jr. Wright's article was reprinted as: Jack Quinan, "Frank Lloyd Wright's Reply to Russell Sturgis," *Journal of the Society of Architectural Historians,* 41, October 1982, pp. 238–44.

31 Quinan, "Frank Lloyd Wright's Reply," pp. 238–44.

32 Ibid.

33 Ibid.

34 Ibid.

35 Although Sturgis refers to the main façades facing Seneca and Swan streets as the east and west façades, the building is aligned with its long axis oriented about 25 degrees east of true north. Thus the Seneca Street façade is more accurately the *south* elevation. Sturgis compounds the error when he labels his Fig. 1 "Larkin Office Building—Rear," and Fig. 2 "Larkin Office Building—Front." These are actually two views of the same façade, the south façade, photographed from viewpoints that are 45 degrees apart.

36 Wright, "Reply to Mr. Sturgis's Criticism." When Wright referred to the fourth story gallery front he actually meant the fifth story level. He apparently ignored the main or first floor and counted the first balcony (the second floor) as the first story.

37 *Architektonische Rundschau,* no. 3, supplement 2, 1908. This information was published by Arnold Lewis in "Hinckeldeyn, Vogel, and American Architecture," *Journal of the Society of Architectural Historians,* 31, December 1972, p. 277, n. 3. My thanks to Lewis for calling it to my attention.

38 Frank Lloyd Wright, *Ausgeführte Bauten und Entwürfe von Frank Lloyd Wright* (Berlin, 1910); and *Frank Lloyd Wright, Ausgeführte Bauten* (Berlin, 1911).

39 Berlage, "Neuere Amerikanische Architektur." This translation is from H. Allen Brooks, ed., *Writings on Wright* (Cambridge, Mass., 1981), p. 133.

40 Peter Blake, "A Conversation with Mies," in *Four Great Makers of Modern Architecture: Gropius, Le Corbusier, Mies van der Rohe, Wright* (New York, 1970), p. 101.

41 Jan Wils, "Frank Lloyd Wright," *Elsevier's Geïllustreerd Maandschrift,* 61, no. 4, 1921, pp. 217–27. This translation, by Elsa Scharbach, is from Brooks, ed., *Writings on Wright,* pp. 142–44.

42 Brooks, *Writings on Wright,* pp. 142–44.

43 Oskar Beyer, ed., and Geoffrey Strachan, trans., *Eric Mendelsohn: Letters of an Architect* (London, 1967), pp. 68–69.

44 The following publications represent some of the interest in Wright between 1911 and 1929: J.J.P. Oud, "Architektonische beschouwing bij bijlage VII," *de Stijl,* 1, no. 4, 1918, pp. 38–41 (a short discussion of the Robie house); Bruno Taut, *Modern Architecture* (London, 1929), pp. 68–69; Werner Moser, "Frank Lloyd Wright und Amerikanische Architektur," *Werk,* 5, May 1925, pp. 129–51; C.R. Ashbee, "Frank Lloyd Wright: Eine Studie zu seiner Würdigung," in *Frank Lloyd Wright: Ausgeführte Bauten* (Berlin, 1911); H. de Fries, *Frank Lloyd Wright: Aus dem Lebenswerke eines Architekten* (Berlin, 1926); and H. Th. Wijdeveld, ed., *The Life-Work of the American Architect Frank Lloyd Wright* (Santpoort, Holland, 1925).

45 Sheldon Cheney, *A Primer of Modern Art* (New York, 1924), pp. 326–28; Fiske Kimball, *American Architecture* (New York, 1928), p. 194; Suzanne LaFollette, *Art in America* (New York, 1929), pp. 288–89; and Henry-Russell Hitchcock, *Modern Architecture: Romanticism and Reintegration* (New York, 1929), pp. 104, 114, 116.

46 Some of the principal discussions include: Sheldon Cheney, *The New World Architecture* (New York, 1935), pp. 92–94 (3 illus.); Sigfried Giedion, *Space, Time and Architecture,* 5th ed. (Cambridge, Mass., 1967), pp. 420–22 (5 illus.); Hitchcock, *In the Nature of Materials* (New York, 1942), pp. 29, 39, 49, 50–52ff. (8 illus.); Peter Blake, *Frank Lloyd Wright: Architecture and Space* (Baltimore, 1960), pp. 50, 54–56ff. (2 illus.); Vincent J. Scully, *Modern Architecture* (New York, 1960), pp. 122–23 (4 illus.); Nikolaus Pevsner, *Pioneers of Modern Design,* 2d ed. (New York, 1949), pp. 117–19 (2 illus.); Reyner Banham, *The Architecture of the Well-Tempered Environment* (Chicago, 1969), pp. 86–92 (5 illus.); William Jordy, *American Buildings and Their Architects: The Impact of European Modernism in the Mid-Twentieth Century* (New York, 1976), pp. 11, 116, 152, 215, 279, 297–302ff. (3 illus.); and Kenneth Frampton, *Modern Architecture: A Critical History* (New York, 1980), pp. 60–62 (1 illus.).

47 Frank Lloyd Wright, *An Autobiography* (New York, 1932), p. 151.

48 Grant C. Manson, *Frank Lloyd Wright to 1910: The First Golden Age* (New York, 1958), p. 147.

CHAPTER SEVEN

1 Nikolaus Pevsner, *Pioneers of Modern Design,* rev. ed. (Baltimore, 1974), pp. 191–94; Sigfried Giedion, *Space, Time and Architecture,* 5th ed. (Cambridge, Mass., 1967), pp. 420–22; Henry-Russell Hitchcock, *In the Nature of Materials* (New York, 1942), pp. 50–52.

2 For discussions of the decline of Buffalo's economy, see Richard C. Brown and Bob Watson, *Buffalo: Lake City in Niagara Land* (Woodland Hills, Calif., 1981), pp. 220–23, and Mark Goldman, *High Hopes: The Rise and Decline of Buffalo, New York* (Albany, N.Y., 1983).

3 Mildred B. Schlei, "The Larkin Company — A History" (Master's thesis, University of Buffalo, NY, 1932), pp. 2–3.

4 *Ourselves,* 13, February 1921, p. 29: "Larkin Economy Stores began Jan. 7, 1918 . . . they have expanded until we have 73 in Buffalo and surrounding territory, 23 in Peoria and surrounding territory and 11 in Chicago. Sales started at a very small figure and have increased until during 1920 they were between $4,000,000 and $5,000,000 or approximately ½ of the total business of the company."

5 From an unpublished chronological history of the Larkin Company covering the years 1918 to 1940, prepared by Daniel I. Larkin from the minute books of the Larkin Company and other sources (hereinafter called Larkin Chronology). I am grateful to him for providing access to this chronology and for

numerous conversations that clarified aspects of the following account.

6 Upon hearing of Martin's retirement from the Larkin Company, Maurice Preisch, a New York lumber dealer, wrote him on September 15, 1925: "D.D. Martin and the Larkin Company has always meant practically one and the same thing to me and I am wondering if the recent changes in management of the company will not have an adverse affect in its fortunes, which have been most remarkable up to now." Similarly, F.C. Hitch of the Royal Baking Powder Company wrote on September 9, 1925: "While I was associated with Larkin Company for only a few years, it did not take me long to discover who was the guiding genius in the organization." (Both letters are among the Martin Papers.)

7 In response to Maurice Preisch's letter (see note 6), Martin wrote on September 16, 1925: "No, Larkin Co. will be under the same management and policy without me as it has been for the past ten years, namely, that of J.D.L. Jr. I expect no adverse effect from my retirement. Any such would be disastrous to me."

8 *Ourselves*, 16, June 6, 1924, p. 1, contains a statement announcing Heath's retirement, signed "John D. Larkin."

9 Martin's retirement is announced in *Ourselves*, 17, September 4, 1925, p. 1. That Martin's retirement followed an argument with John D. Larkin, Jr., was related to me by Daniel I. Larkin.

10 These were George Barton, Darwin D. Martin's brother-in-law; Frank Jewett; and George Kirby, a boyhood friend of Darwin D. Martin from Mount Ayr, Iowa, whose sister was married to William E. Martin. Announcement of Jewett's retirement appears in *Ourselves*, 17, September 18, 1925, p. 1; Barton's retirement in *Ourselves*, 17, September 30, 1925, p. 3; Kirby's retirement in *Ourselves*, 18, March 31, 1926, p. 1. These departures represent a removal of the Martin forces from the Larkin Company.

11 *Ourselves*, 17, September 18, 1925, p. 1.

12 *Ourselves*, 18, February 15, 1926, is a commemorative issue devoted entirely to John D. Larkin. John D. Larkin, Jr., brought his sons. Crate and John III, into the company in 1923 and 1926, respectively.

13 *Ourselves*, 18, January 13, 1926, p. 1.

14 This according to Daniel I. Larkin, conversation with the author, July 1982.

15 Larkin Chronology.

16 Schlei, "The Larkin Company," p. 41.

17 Walter F. Winters, "The Larkin Co. Inc., 1941–45," an unpublished report prepared for the Board of Directors of the Larkin Company in 1945 and now in the possession of Daniel I. Larkin.

18 Larkin Chronology.

19 *Buffalo Courier Express* (hereinafter *Courier*), October 5, 1939, p. 10.

20 Larkin Chronology.

21 *Buffalo Evening News* (hereinafter *B.E.N.*), May 24, 1943, p. 1.

22 *Courier*, October 2, 1948, p. 15.

23 *B.E.N.*, November 1, 1946, p. 25 (second edition).

24 Ibid.; also *Courier*, November 2, 1946, p. 22.

25 *Courier*, November 20, 1946, p. 6; and *Proceedings of the Council of the City of Buffalo*, November 26, 1946, pp. 2511–12, item 63.

26 *Courier*, November 2, 1946, p. 22; and *B.E.N.*, November 1, 1946, p. 25 (second edition).

27 *Courier*, March 15, 1947, p. 15.

28 *Courier*, October 9, 1949, p. 8–B.

29 *B.E.N.*, October 15, 1947, p. 22; also *B.E.N.*, May 16, 1950, p. 27.

30 *Proceedings of the Council of the City of Buffalo*, April 29, 1947, p. 1051, item 20; and *Courier*, May 7, 1947, p. 1.

31 *Courier*, October 2, 1948, p. 15.

32 *Courier*, June 2, 1948, p. 15, and June 22, 1948, p. 13.

33 *Courier*, April 17, 1949, p. 16–c.

34 Ibid.

35 *B.E.N.*, May 24, 1951, p. 51.

36 *Courier*, October 9, 1949, p. 8–B.

37 *New York Times*, January 27, 1950, p. 41.

38 *New York Herald Tribune*, October 27, 1949, p. 22.

39 *B.E.N.*, November 16, 1949, p. 27.

40 *B.E.N.*, May 16, 1950, p. 27 (third edition).

41 Sharon Lefauvre, interview with Nelson Reimann on November 30, 1977, for a term paper on the destruction of the Larkin Administration Building (author's possession).

42 Nelson Reimann, telephone conversation with the author, June 1982.

43 *B.E.N.,* May 24, 1951, p. 51.

44 This according to Bruce Brooks Pfeiffer, an associate of Wright and his wife, Olgivanna, since 1947; conversation with the author, October 1981.

45 Howard Massing, telephone conversation with the author.

46 Frank Lloyd Wright, *An Autobiography,* rev. ed. (New York, 1943), p. 152.

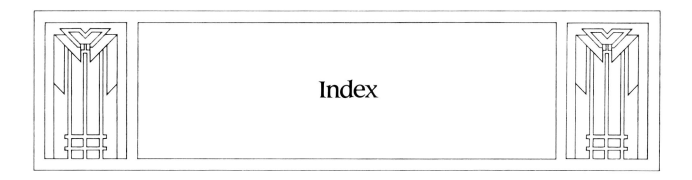

Index

Figure numbers are given in italics after page numbers